# Melancholic Joy

ALSO AVAILABLE FROM BLOOMSBURY

*How to be a Failure and Still Live Well: A Philosophy,* Beverley Clack

*The Meaning of Life and Death: Ten Classics Thinkers on the Ultimate Question,* Michael Hauskeller

*The Existentialist's Guide to Death, the Universe and Nothingness,* Gary Cox

# Melancholic Joy

## On Life Worth Living

**Brian Treanor**

BLOOMSBURY ACADEMIC
LONDON • NEW YORK • OXFORD • NEW DELHI • SYDNEY

BLOOMSBURY ACADEMIC
Bloomsbury Publishing Plc
50 Bedford Square, London, WC1B 3DP, UK
1385 Broadway, New York, NY 10018, USA

BLOOMSBURY, BLOOMSBURY ACADEMIC and the Diana logo are trademarks of Bloomsbury Publishing Plc

First published in Great Britain 2021



Cover design by Charlotte Daniels
Cover image © Inigo Cia / Getty Images



A catalogue record for this book is available from the British Library.

A catalog record for this book is available from the Library of Congress.

ISBN: HB: 978-1-3501-7773-4
PB: 978-1-3501-7774-1
ePDF: 978-1-3501-7775-8
eBook: 978-1-3501-7776-5

Typeset by RefineCatch Limited, Bungay, Suffolk

For **Darya and Ciara**,

who make the good days twice as good,

and the bad days only half as bad.

# Contents

Acknowledgments viii

**1** Sadness Will Last Forever 1

**2** Joy and the Myopia of Finitude 23

**3** From Mortality to Vitality 47

**4** A Twilight Hope 73

**5** Amor Mundi 95

**6** Melancholic Joy 117

Notes 143

Index 203

# Acknowledgments

I am thankful to many people who have supported me in various ways during the writing of this book.

I have been lucky enough to teach at Loyola Marymount University for the past eighteen years, where the Bellarmine College of Liberal Arts and the Charles S. Casassa, S.J. Chair have given me the time and resources to pursue my writing.

In the wider intellectual community, the Pacific Association for the Continental Tradition provided a singularly rich environment in which to nurture and develop these ideas. The eclectic membership of that group was unwaveringly encouraging of this project; and I had many fruitful conversations related to topics in the book with Jason Wirth, Gerard Kuperus, Marjolein Oele, Elizabeth Sikes, Tim Freeman, and Josh Hayes.

A number of the "big picture" questions about this project, and many others, were worked out over long walks with Richard Kearney. Jeff Bloechl and Chandler Rogers both offered helpful feedback and encouragement at various points. Zak Cook, another hiking partner, provided learned and intelligent comments from a non-academic perspective.

I am particularly indebted to Dan Bradley, Chris Lauer, Dan Speak, and James Taylor not only for their friendship and for insights and suggestions provided in many memorable conversations, but also for their careful attention to early drafts of the manuscript and their helpful comments. The final product is much improved because of their input.

Because the percolation or gestation of this project was ongoing for some time, thinking, reading, reflecting, writing, and revising took place in a variety of locations. I've long held that concrete, material places are important in constituting our horizons—philosophical and poetic as well as physical. Thus, I feel compelled to express my gratitude to a number of places that informed my own experience of the goodness of being and my gratitude for being alive during the writing process (chapter five will make clear why such appreciation is appropriate): the High Sierra of California, particularly Yosemite Valley, Tuolumne Meadows, the Grand Canyon of the Tuolumne, and the Palisades; the San Juan Islands and Gulf Islands of the Salish Sea; the Lofoten archipelago; Briançon and environs, especially the Ailefroide; and the island of Vis and Croatian Adriatic. My sincere apologies to all the other places, wild or mild, that I've omitted due to the constraints of space; I remember you all appreciatively.

My thanks to the editors and staff at Bloomsbury—especially Liza Thompson, Lisa Goodrum, and Lucy Russell—for their support and patient encouragement. Although the writing of *Melancholic Joy* took place before COVID-19, the publication process got underway very early in 2020; thus, Liza, Lisa, Lucy, and their colleagues were, I'm sure, working under incredibly challenging circumstances as stay-at-home orders impacted life in England and North America. My thanks as well to the anonymous readers who supported the project so forcefully after its initial submission to Bloomsbury.

I am perpetually grateful to my wife, Gitty, with whom I have shared over thirty years of joy, and to my daughters, Darya and Ciara, who have opened my life to new dimensions of love and been my enthusiastic partners on increasingly ambitious adventures. They are, for me, the brightest and most important orienting stars in the night—the tripartite Polaris of my personal *Ursa Major*—without whom my world would be immeasurably darker, more confusing, and more impenetrable.

For permission to reproduce selections of individual works, grateful acknowledgement is made to the following people and organizations. "Last Stand" and "Admissions" by Dennis O'Driscoll (*Dear Life*, 2014) is reprinted here by kind permission of Carcanet Press Limited, Manchester, UK; and, in North America, reprinted with the permission of The Permissions Company, LLC on behalf of Copper Canyon Press, www.coppercanyonpress.org. Jim Moore, excerpt from "It Is Not the Fact That I Will Die That I Mind," from *Underground: New and Selected Poems*. Copyright © 2005 by Jim Moore. Reprinted with the permission of The Permissions Company, LLC on behalf of Graywolf Press, Minneapolis, Minnesota, graywolfpress.org. Ellen Bass, excerpt from "The Thing Is" from *Mules of Love*. Copyright © 2002 by Ellen Bass. Reprinted with the permission of The Permissions Company, LLC on behalf of BOA Editions Ltd., www.boaeditions.org. David Moreau, excerpt from "Borrowed Time" in *Sex, Death, and Baseball* (Portland, ME: Moon Pie Press, 2004). Reprinted with permission from Mr. Moreau and Moon Pie Press. Robinson Jeffers, excerpt from "The Answer" in *The Collected Poems of Robinson Jeffers*, vol. 2 (Stanford, CA: Stanford University Press, 1989). Reprinted with permission from Stanford University Press. "A Brief for the Defense" from *Refusing Heaven* by Jack Gilbert, copyright © 2005 by Jack Gilbert. Used by permission of Alfred A. Knopf, an imprint of the Knopf Doubleday Publishing Group, a division of Penguin Random House LLC. All rights reserved. Parts of chapter two and chapter three appeared as "Joy and the Myopia of Finitude" in *Comparative and Continental Philosophy*, vol. 8, no. 1 (spring 2016) and "Vitality: Carnal, Seraphic Bodies" in *The Journal of French and Francophone Philosophy*, vol. 25. no. 1 (July 2017); they are reproduced here in a revised form.

# Chapter 1
# Sadness Will Last Forever[1]

## 1. We perish, each alone

"We perished. . . each alone."[2] Mr. Ramsey, the melancholic metaphysician of Virginia Woolf's masterpiece, *To the Lighthouse*, repeats these lines from William Cowper's poem *The Castaway* while en route to the novel's eponymous seaside beacon. Moments later he completes the thought with the final lines, "But I beneath the rougher sea / Was whelmed in deeper gulfs than he," both twisting the blade of his own distress and, arguably, wallowing in a kind of self-absorbed pity that is blind to the sufferings and fears of others. It would be easy, and perhaps not inappropriate, to read this as a manifestation of Ramsey's aching need for sympathy, which is highlighted in his interactions with Ms. Ramsey and Lily Briscoe in the preceding pages of the novel. But while we may be justified in cringing at Ramsey's acute neediness—his daughter Cam is "outraged" at his self-absorption—I'm not sure that the sentiment itself is to blame.

We perish, each alone.

This we suspect is the terrifying, fundamental existential reality with which each of us must, eventually, grapple. In the end, night falls absolutely, ushering in an unending nothingness; and each of us must tread the final steps of that path alone—right up until the path itself dissolves beneath our feet, precisely because all possibilities come to an end for us. Of course, rationally we know that all others face this same fate and suffer a similar loss. And emotionally we may well come to view the "ultimate necessity"[3] of nothingness in the lives of others as even more offensive than it is in our own. Gabriel Marcel claimed that the ultimate tragedy is not my own death, but the death of those that I love.[4] However, even if we recognize that every death is a tragic loss and that every other in distress is worth saving, and even if we would voluntarily sacrifice ourselves rather than allow our loved ones to perish, it remains the case that each one of us knows best precisely what will be lost when we die.

As Jim Moore observes, the most disturbing element of death is not the fact that I will die, but rather that, when I die, certain manifestations of love and appreciation will die with me.[5] The point is not that Moore, or I, or you love "better" than anyone else, but rather that the *particularities* of our love will be lost with us: my "secret spots" in the Sierra Nevada, where I rarely encounter other people despite the stellar climbing and good camping, right next to a fine swimming hole; the rain on the window in my favorite carrel at the library; how the alpenglow on interlaced ribbons of rock and ice on the Chamonix Aiguilles reminds me of Hopkins's "dappled things. . . adazzle, dim"[6]; the day the green flash ignited the winter horizon at Zeros as I sat on my surfboard in the cold water; the way my wife curls against my back in the too-small bed from our undergraduate days, which we've never bothered to replace; how my daughters casually nestled together while reading on the couch in the evening, like somnolent bear cubs in a hibernation den. "No one knows that but me, / No one knows how to love the way I do."[7]

Death and nothingness are an offense, in part, because every death is the loss of an entire world—constellations of love and intimacy, imagination and meaning, hopes and dreams. I know my world, my love, more intimately than any other; and I am horrified at the loss of that world and that love as much as by any cessation of my own being or projects.

## 2. The woeful nature of reality

Today we find ourselves faced with all the traditional reasons to despair: loneliness, fallibility, impotence, loss, tragedy, senselessness, death, and the like. For many people, these reasons to despair are exacerbated by either the modern disenchantment of the world, a postmodern suspicion regarding grand narratives, or both. And, piled on top of this, the news of the day seems to sound a relentless drumbeat of woe. In the last decade we have seen countless novel reasons to despair: seemingly endless wars in the Middle East; the rise of the so-called "Islamic State" and the atrocities it committed; the heart-wrenching plight of refugees, and the callous indifference of many governments and people to their plight; diseases both novel and resurgent: the worst outbreak of Ebola on record, as well as the emergence of H5N1 flu, MERS, and COVID-19, the full effects of which are unclear as I write;[8] an alarming increase in antibiotic-resistant pathogens, which could knock medicine a step or two back toward the Middle Ages; resurgent xenophobia, misogyny, racism, anti-Semitism, homophobia, and other forms of hatred in the public sphere; widening economic inequality; accelerating nuclear proliferation; the threat of another global economic downturn; increasing anthropogenic climate chaos; and more. The list, full of dire problems both chronic and acute, seems endless. Today, perhaps more than ever, reality seems to "*counsel* despair"[9] and, consequently, "in the deepest heart of all of us there is a corner in which [we suspect that] the ultimate mystery of things works out sadly."[10]

## 2.1 *J'ai mal*[11]

On reflection, there appears to be little reason for optimism or joy at the individual level. Much of life is taken up with the banal and stifling routine of securing one's daily bread: paying the rent and bills; battling traffic; enduring meaningless work at an office indistinguishable from millions of other offices; grappling with faceless bureaucracies (political or commercial) as we navigate our social belonging; and other similarly unfulfilling drudgeries. Against any fleeting moments of pleasure punctuating the doldrums, we must weigh the fact that every life is also punctuated by moments of fear, experiences of acute loneliness, no small measure of anxiety, the ultimate insignificance of our most cherished projects, countless losses and failures, as well as psychological and physical suffering. And, to put an exclamation point to the issue—or perhaps just an ellipsis, trailing off into nothingness—in the end death has the last word, not only for us but for everyone and everything we love as well. It's true that psychological defense mechanisms like selective memory and attention can help us to accommodate ourselves to such depressing fare; but that does not do away with it or get around its omnipresence. Much of life is boring, all of our lives involve suffering, and everyone dies.[12]

After the "death of God" proclaimed by Nietzsche and others, some philosophers found refuge in the idea of freedom and creativity. However, it turns out our very freedom may be in large part illusory. Our actions and opinions are shaped, often profoundly, by forces outside our conscious control—biology, psychology, cultural precedents and social mores, individual history, and environment—indicating that we are not quite as free as we generally suppose (consider the infamous Stanford Prison Experiment). We do not live, but are rather *lived by* "some murmuring non-entity both shadowy and muddled."[13] Is it any wonder that in order to cope, most of us are, most of the time, hedonistic egoists, whether that hedonism is expressed through indulgence (some quasi-Huxleyan "soma"), in obsession with the trivialities (Ivan Ilyich's obsession with whist), or, more commonly, relentless and conspicuous acquisition in a consumer society.

Such egoism is not innocent; more than being neglectful, it often harms others directly. For those of us in the global north, our everyday egoism is likely to perpetuate obscene economic and environmental injustice. Not only do we shut the door on the widow, orphan, and stranger, our bourgeois pleasures are predicated on their continued alienation and suffering. Our demand for ever cheaper consumer goods is satisfied only because those goods are often produced by people in substandard working conditions in jurisdictions with no environmental oversight.

And despite this self-centered focus on ourselves and our projects, we accomplish nothing that endures; all our efforts are imperfect, incomplete, and impermanent, which leads to regret. We like to pretend we are special, that no one has ever lived, or laughed, or loved as we have. But the truth is, most of us are completely, forgettably ordinary. I'm no Shakespeare, and neither are you. Unlike Plato, no one will be reading my books 2,500 years from now. It's likely that, outside of a tax record or some other random bit of bureaucratic information stored on whatever information system we use in the future, no one will remember me more than a single generation after I die. And, even were that not true, it wouldn't matter. On a long enough time horizon, it's all lost. Michelangelo, Socrates, Buddha, the builders of the pyramids, the anonymous artists of Lascaux—all mere blips on the geological clock. Like the dinosaurs or our common protozoic ancestors, dust we, and all our works, are; and to dust we, and all our works, will return.

Adding insult to injury, before death we suffer. As Oscar Wilde put it: "the secret of life is suffering. It is what is hidden behind everything."[14] As I write this, my own body may harbor the malignancy that will kill me and, even if that's not yet the case, it is inevitable, both for me and, much worse, for everyone I love. Consider as well the viciously interlocking teleologies of different life forms, the parasitism and predation to which all life is subject.[15] Some accounts suggest that over half the forms of life on Earth are engaged in parasitism.[16] Nature, including humanity, consuming and being consumed: a carnivorous, incessantly grinding Mobius loop, like Satan's jaws as they eternally masticate Judas, Brutus, and Cassius in Dante's *Divina Commedia*. Reality "red of tooth and claw" indeed.[17]

## 2.2 The *abattoir* of history

Collectively we're no better off. For while it is true that things can improve, it is also the case that such examples of progress are distributed very unevenly, that progress in some areas is entirely compatible with decline in others, and that the very idea of "progress" misunderstands how culture, science, and evolution itself unfold.

True, there have been remarkable advances—technologically, socially, even morally—over the course of human history. We've decreased poverty, eliminated certain diseases, increased human life expectancy, walked on the moon, peered to the edges of the observable universe, and puzzled out the conditions at the origin of the cosmos. More, we've made strides, uneven to be sure, on moral and ethical issues, improving—although not fully securing—equality for women and peoples of different races. We're beginning to think seriously, if belatedly, about the moral status of non-human animals and more-than-human nature.

But against all that progress, which is real, we have to face our shameful and persistent failures: ongoing racism, misogyny, bigotry, and religious sectarianism; willful ignorance; xenophobia; mechanized and impersonal warfare; genocide; slavery; human trafficking; economic injustices and exploitation; mass displacements; torture, rape, and abuse; and a "doomsday clock" that is positioned all-too-close to midnight. All this and more runs rampant in human history, and persists in myriad contemporary forms. Looking only at the recent past, it's difficult to see the 20th century as anything other than a physical, moral, and spiritual *abattoir*. Estimates vary, but the last century may have seen in excess of 200 million deaths resulting from war and political oppression alone.[18] The two World Wars, including the Shoah and other Nazi murders, the firebombing of Dresden, and the atomic bombs dropped on Hiroshima and Nagasaki; millions of murders under Stalin and Mao; the Killing Fields of Cambodia; the Rwandan genocide by machete; the mass murder, rape, and cannibalism of Pygmy peoples in and around the Democratic Republic of Congo (this even into the 21st century)—even a partial list is enough to overwhelm our capacity to be scandalized or to care. *Two hundred million*. Try to imagine two hundred million of anything. The number exceeds comprehension. And that accounting is the bitter harvest of but a few of the myriad ways in which humans prey on and abuse each other. "When we are born, we cry that we are come to this great stage of fools"; if Lear's account of neonatal squealing is not strictly accurate, perhaps it should be.[19]

True, every generation feels, to some degree, that it is living at the end of the world. One might argue that the sack of Rome by Brennus and the Senones in the 4th century B.C., the Black Death of the 1300s, the European colonization of the Americas, and the Cuban Missile Crisis all felt like the coming of the Apocalypse to those affected and afflicted by them. But solidarity and sympathy with our ancestors is cold comfort. Despite our uneven success at social and moral improvement, many of these sources of anxiety feel all-too-familiar: the threat or presence of violence in many places; life circumscribed under authoritarian rule; the possibility of new pandemics like COVID-19, or worse; ongoing concerns with nuclear proliferation; and more. And, heaped on top of those long-standing causes for despair, we find ourselves confronted with threats that seem genuinely unprecedented, like anthropogenic climate change.[20] Dwelling too long on any one of these topics, to say nothing of considering their collective weight, risks despair not only in those inclined to melancholy, but even in more sanguine natures.

## 2.3 The silent darkness between the stars

Despite our finitude and fallibility, despite our blemished history, we struggle on, working to establish some measure of coherence, for however long we might enjoy it, and to hand on that capital and that order to those who follow us. That struggle—for achievement, for recognition, for status, for wealth, for security—can occupy a person for a time, perhaps for much of her life; but at some point most people have the suspicion that it's futile, just a sham, a thin and fragile veil drawn over a decidedly darker chaos.

> He walked out in the grey light and stood and he saw for a brief moment the absolute truth of the world. The cold relentless circling of the intestate earth. Darkness implacable. The blind dogs of the sun in their running. The crushing black vacuum of the universe. And somewhere two hunted animals trembling like ground-foxes in their cover. Borrowed time and borrowed world and borrowed eyes with which to sorrow it.[21]

Our everyday delusions are a consequence of an all-too-human perspective, and of failing to take seriously the significance of deep time. We distract ourselves by thinking of the quarterly finance report to avoid thinking of a lifetime, much less a generation, century, millennium, or eon. Those longer perspectives haunt us with the realization that no matter what we do, for good or for ill, individually or collectively, it's all just a blip in cosmic time.

> Once upon a time, in some out of the way corner of that universe which is dispersed into numberless twinkling solar systems, there was a star upon which clever beasts invented knowing. That was the most arrogant and mendacious minute of "world history," but nevertheless it was only a minute. After nature had drawn a few breaths, the star cooled and congealed, and the clever beasts had to die.[22]

The Earth is roughly 4.5 billion years old, and our Sun has been around for about 4.6 billion years. However, our Sun is consuming its main sequence hydrogen fuel and headed, in approximately another 5 billion years, toward becoming a red giant, the diameter of which may eventually exceed the orbital distance of the Earth from the Sun. At this point—actually, long before it due to increased luminosity and solar radiation—life on Earth ends, no matter how advanced it is.

But, the optimist says, that's a long, long time away, and technology advances so quickly that perhaps we may be traveling among the stars. Alas, this too may be nothing but a temporary reprieve. Although there are alternative theories, one leading view is that the second law of thermodynamics seems to predict the eventual heat-death of the universe in thermodynamic equilibrium. If you drop a warm rock into a bucket of cold water, the warm rock heats the cold water and the cold water cools the warm rock and soon you have a uniform temperature across everything in the bucket—thermal equilibrium. This model holds true for all closed systems: without being constrained or acted on from the outside, energy, like the warmth of the rock, always dissipates and will never spontaneously re-concentrate itself. The energy will never spontaneously reorganize itself so that the rock is warm and the water is cold. In a closed system, like this hypothetical bucket, entropy—the measure of energy *un*available for work—always increases. Thus, we also describe entropy in terms of disorder which, over time, always increases. The result? Things quite literally fall apart; it is the common doom of all matter.[23] The body dies, the house decomposes, the mountain erodes. The universe is expanding, and at an increasing rate. Eventually matter and energy will become dispersed homogeneously throughout the universe; that homogeneity means no "work" can be done. Nothing happens. On a long enough timeline, it may well be that there are no stars to travel among, no planets to inhabit, nothing but an endless night of evenly distributed, utterly disordered, subatomic particles.[24]

Earth as we know it is a beautiful, local reversal of entropy—life emerges from inorganic material and evolutionary pressures make it more complex, more ordered, over time. However, this order and stability are both illusory and temporary, an artifact of the fact that the Earth is not a closed system; it continually receives new energy from the Sun. But this will come to an end, for our Sun as for every other star in the universe, with, to be sure, a number of "bangs" along the way, but ultimately as a long, drawn-out whimper. Observing the clever creativity of our species of hairless apes, "the cosmos yawns and takes another spin."[25] That is, until the universe too expires, and there is no more yawning, no more spinning, just. . . no more. We all perish, each alone; and then, eventually, it all comes to an end, without remainder. The *musica universalis* is, it seems, played in a minor key.

## 3. Contemplating the end of the world

Perhaps then it is no surprise that there are so many depictions of reality as fundamentally disappointing in contemporary philosophy, literature, and art. Of course, humans have always been concerned with finitude and death. Some of our earliest written documents record our struggle to discover or create meaning in a seemingly indifferent, meaningless, and brutal world, during lives that can feel frustratingly brief, fallible, impotent, and incomplete: the Akkadian/Sumerian *Epic of Gilgamesh* (which rails against finitude), the Babylonian *Dialogue of Pessimism* (lamenting the futility of human action), the *Book of Job* in the Hebrew Bible (raging against the injustice of suffering), the Hindu *Bhagavad Gita* (which struggles with finitude, impotence, and insoluable ethical conflict), the Gnostic *Gospel of Philip* (which claims Creation was a mistake), neo-Gnostic traditions (some of which, going further, attribute the creation of the material world to Satan himself), and other, equally distraught accounts hailing from almost every human culture.

Among contemporary forms of philosophy, at least in the West, the so-called continental tradition of philosophy is the field most clearly concerned with questions of meaning, including the "meaning of life." And it seems particularly inclined, in answering that question, to come to melancholic, pessimistic, or even miserabilist conclusions.[26] It expresses this temperament in diverse works grappling with nihilism, despair, melancholy, pessimism, misanthropy, anomie, ennui, resignation, indifference, and so on.

Consider a few signal examples that preceded or flowed from what we think of as continental philosophy: Jean-Jacques Rousseau, who argued that man, born self-sufficient and with a certain sort of virtue in the state of nature, has fallen into ruin by pride (*amour-propre*), acquisitiveness ("This is mine"), and the decadence of civilization; the pessimism of Giacomo Leopardi's massive *Zibaldone*, which depicts nature as a terrifying, blind, indifferent force that creates and destroys with equal fervor, and asserts the triple negation: we know nothing, we are nothing, and there is nothing to hope for; Arthur Schopenhauer, an arch-pessimist who argued that the phenomenal world we experience is a manifestation of a blind, uncontrollable, and malignant "will" or "striving," and consequently the best we can aim for is a quasi-Buddhist resignation; Søren Kierkegaard—a second "melancholic Dane"—who was fixated on dread, anxiety, and despair (the "sickness unto death"); Nietzsche, who famously declared the "death of God" and diagnosed Western civilization as heading toward a crisis of values and nihilism; Sigmund Freud, whose work on unconscious drives, the "uncanny" (*Das Unheimliche*), and the relationship between mourning and melancholy influenced hermeneutics, ethics, and psychoanalysis; Martin Heidegger's early emphasis on "being toward death" (*Sein-zum-Tode*) as the defining characteristic of human existence, and on the associated concepts of *Angst* and *Unheimlichkeit* (the "uncanniness" of feeling not-quite-at-home); Gabriel Marcel's claim that reality "counsels despair"; Jean-Paul Sartre's descriptions of alienation and nausea; Emmanuel Levinas's account of the lurking menace of the *il y a*, the "there is" of naked being; E. M. Cioran's stark nihilism and pessimism, which views birth itself as a horror and tragedy; Peter Wessel Zapffe, a pessimistic antinatalist—"Know yourselves. . . be infertile and let the earth be silent after ye"—whose bleak meditations rival Cioran's and echo Leopardi; philosopher and psychoanalyst Julia Kristeva's work on the "black sun" of depression and on the "abominable real"; Jean-François Lyotard's late concern with "the inhuman"; Eugene Thacker's "cosmic pessimism" in the face of deep time; Ray Brassier, who seeks to push nihilism to its most extreme and logical conclusion, and who excoriates philosophy for being occupied with pathetic and useless attempts to establish grounds for meaning in a meaningless real; and Michel Henry's concern with "practices of barbarism."[27] This is not to say that each of these thinkers is relentlessly despairing, negative, melancholic, or pessimistic—that's far from the case; rather, it is to note that a gloomy preoccupation is evident in continental thinking taken as a whole.

The full list of thinkers fixated on the woeful nature of reality is so long and so diverse that it would require several volumes to trace our saturnine obsessions from their pre-philosophical origins in the mists of myth through to their contemporary manifestations in philosophy, literature, poetry, theater, cinema, and other forms of expression. Given that an exhaustive genetic etiology is not feasible here, let's briefly consider just one of the most representative examples. The average person, operating on hearsay, might erroneously peg Nietzsche as the arch-nihilist. Or, if she were a bit more well-read but equally in error, perhaps Sartre. But painting either of these thinkers as a nihilist requires misreading them; and, in any case, both Sartre and Nietzsche are veritable humorists seen alongside the resolute commitment to nihilism and pessimism in figures like Leopardi, Zapffe, and Cioran.

Take Cioran's most unwavering work, *De l'inconvénient d'être né*, translated as *The Trouble with Being Born*, though *inconvénient* could also be the stronger "disadvantage" or even, in a sense, "harm."[28] It is a visceral tour of the dark corners of our psyche, our existential condition, and ontology itself. A treacherous read, it makes the clear, structured argumentation of David Benatar's *Better Never to Have Been* appear utterly disengaged and sterile in comparison, a mere thought experiment. A person can, I suspect, read Benatar and then go happily home to dinner with his children; a person reading Cioran risks heading home to lock himself in the garage with the car running.[29] Cioran paints a picture that is utterly uncompromising in its pessimism and nihilism. Thus, although an heir of sorts to Nietzsche's death-of-God aphoristic meditations, he accuses his predecessor of pulling up short, balking before the abyss.

> I hold [Nietzsche's] enthusiasms, his fervors against him. He demolished so many idols only to replace them with others: a false iconoclast, with adolescent aspects and a certain virginity, a certain innocence inherent in his solitary's career. He observed men only from a distance. Had he come closer, he could have neither conceived nor promulgated the superman, that preposterous, laughable, even grotesque chimera, a crotchet which could occur only to a mind without time to age, to know the long serene disgust of detachment.[30]

For Cioran, "sobbing negation" is the only acceptable form of negation.[31] No joyful "Dionysian pessimism" for him. As Eugene Thacker writes: "Kierkegaard: life is a tightrope. Nietzsche: life is a jump rope. Kafka: life is a trip rope. Schopenhauer: life is a noose. Cioran: life is a noose, improperly tied."[32]

Cioran views birth as both insignificant and intolerable—a disaster, a tragedy, an actual evil. Children should be "strangled" at birth—as a mercy one supposes—or, if they are to live, should be taught that there is "nothing to be hoped for from life."[33] Any distraction from this truth is inauthentic and self-deceptive. Progress and other such hopes, personal or collective, are "the falsest and stupidest of superstitions."[34] Life is simply to be endured. Nothing is worth defending. Profound and unbroken melancholia is, for the honest person, inevitable and incurable. Even when he finds himself on the verge of a sort of Proustian epiphany that might validate some joy, some meaning in the chaos, he demurs, insisting on the indifference of reality and the meaninglessness of existence:

> I was walking late one night along a tree-lined path; a chestnut fell at my feet. The noise it made as it burst, the resonance it provoked in me, and an upheaval out of all proportion to this insignificant event thrust me into miracle, into the rapture of the definitive, as if there were no more questions—only answers. I was drunk on a thousand unexpected discoveries, none of which I could make use of. . . . This is how I nearly reached the Supreme. But instead I went on with my walk.[35]

Cioran's pessimism bridges the existential angst of earlier thinkers and the cosmic pessimism of contemporary figures like Thacker and Brassier. It moves beyond Auden's wistful "nothing now will ever come to any good"[36] to the deeper and darker "nothing comes to anything" or, better, "everything comes to nothing":

> In five hundred thousand years, it appears that England will be entirely submerged. If I were an Englishman I would lay down my arms at once. Each of us has his unit of time. For one it is the day, the week, the month, or the year; for another it is a decade, or a century. . . .These units, still on the human scale, are compatible with any plan, any task. There are some, however, who take time itself for their unit, and sometimes raise themselves above it: for them, what task, what plan deserves to be taken seriously? A man who sees too far, who is contemporary with the *whole* future, can no longer act or even move. . .[37]

Each day the long arc of pessimism is cut into the flesh of the world with increasing depth by the blades of our impotence in an indifferent universe. We act "as if" our actions matter; but we face a common doom with all that exists in the absolute and final victory of thermodynamics, the silent and infinite spaces between stars that so terrified Pascal.[38] In the face this "awful power [which] neither hates nor loves, but rolls all things together meaninglessly into a common doom,"[39] nothing matters, which leads Leopardi and others to characterize pessimism as a philosophy that is "grievous but true."[40]

From the perspective of deep time, it seems that all hope is disappointed. Therefore, abandon all hope, ye who find yourselves here. Cioran, Thacker, Brassier, and others see in the inexorable working of the second law of thermodynamics an *absolute* limit, an end that undermines *all* purpose, meaning, and hope. Finally, when we take "finally" seriously, nothing matters. Being itself is "all sound and fury, signifying nothing."[41] We could endure the sound and the fury; but the "signifying nothing" makes the last and deepest cut, leaving the incurable wound. Life that signifies nothing has no significance; it is life without meaning. And Camus's Sisyphus notwithstanding, it is meaninglessness that we cannot endure, meaninglessness that raises the specter of despair and suicide.

Cioran is only a particularly clear example of a much more widespread temperament in philosophy and literature. A gloomy disposition, a fascination with and fixation on the negative, has come to serve as a watermark of sorts for serious continental philosophy. Plato claimed that philosophy begins in "wonder"; but Simon Critchley points out that philosophy today beings in the "experience of *disappointment*."[42] And this is true not only for the standard-bearers of pessimism and melancholy, like Cioran, but for the tradition taken as a whole. Exceptions exist, but simply serve to prove the rule. Otherness, alienation, inauthenticity, angst, anxiety, dread, melancholy, finitude, mourning, and death—such are the watchwords of continental philosophy, the *bona fides* that mark authentic thinking about the human condition.

Philosophers seem loath to embrace a more positive view of reality and human existence for fear of seeming unforgivably naive, indefensibly sanguine, or unreflectively privileged. Like Mr. Ramsey, we feel guilty reflecting on, much less embracing, joy:

> [Mr. Ramsey] turned from the sight of human ignorance and human fate and the sea eating the ground we stand on, which, had he been able to contemplate it fixedly might have led to [further philosophical insight]; and found consolation in trifles so slight compared to the august theme just now before him that he was disposed to slur that comfort over, to deprecate it, as if to be caught happy in a world of misery was for an honest man the most despicable of crimes.[43]

No success—economic, political, professional, romantic, or otherwise—is a secure bulwark against the encroaching night. As Heidegger points out, we cannot understand human being and human possibility without taking account of the central role played by mortality: the eventuality of not-being and of impossibility.[44] Death is not so much something that happens to us, but is rather something that we are: being-toward-death is constitutive of our way of being. So it is understandable that nihilism and pessimism hang like a pall over the human condition, why a mood of despair and desperation keeps popping up like a bad penny, and why melancholy tends to settle on the shoulders of those of us who dwell too long on the darkness between the stars or the "vast and trunkless legs" of Ozymandias.[45]

Needless to say, one might reasonably object that there are philosophers, writers, and poets who are not prone to pessimism or despair, either in their lives or in their work. Some plow fields in which the meaningfulness or meaninglessness of life is not at issue. It's hard to imagine drowning in despair as a result of one's ruminations on set theory. One can also point to relatively sanguine figures, those who do consider the value of life and find, on the whole, something worth celebrating. All generalizations are open to such counterexamples. Nevertheless, the cases above—which include the luminaries of continental philosophy—suggest that there is a strong tendency in 20th century philosophy and literature to focus on what we might call the darker aspects of reality: evil, finitude, fallenness, sin, the silence of God, gratuitous suffering, inauthenticity, absurdity, loss, alienation, tragedy, and the like. If it is true that there are philosophers and poets who possess a sort of temperamental optimism as well as those—seemingly more prevalent—who are possessed by temperamental pessimism, it also seems true that philosophy itself is prone to particular manifestations of "speculative melancholy."[46]

Such gloomy themes and concerns are not merely "topics" for continental philosophy. Continental negativity is more than an aesthetic bias, such as a taste for tragedy, or a psychological state, like the mourning of loss. What I'm diagnosing is something closer to an ontological mood that characterizes continental thinking per se. That is to say, this "melancholy" is not, or is not merely, a subjective state of mind "added to" a preexisting perception of an objective world; rather, it structures the hermeneutic lenses through which we understand and, indeed, "construct" the world. It shapes our attunement to the world and to things, and it constrains the ways in which we project our possibilities in the world. And to this degree, the world of despair is actually different from the non-despairing world.[47]

There are, of course, good reasons to feel dissatisfaction with things. Life will, in some way, disappoint everyone. Some events rightly cause us sorrow; ennui is an understandable reaction to certain situations; and angst is sometimes warranted. Everyone suffers. Everyone dies. And it may well be that a certain degree of melancholy is appropriate in light of the human condition. But when these gloomy states become fixed, obsessive, or all-encompassing in such a way that they occlude other phenomena, other experiences, other truths, they become the type of fetish that is my concern here: an obsessive negativity run amok, a zealous cynicism, a miserabilism that narrows our vision and restricts our experience.

## 4. After dark

But is that the full picture? Why is it, wonders Thoreau, that "in the lives of men we hear more of the dark wood than the sunny pastures?"[48] The world, and our experience of it, is made up of both. On reflection, it is clear that our *emphasis on* and *relationship to* nihilism, the seeming ease with which we give in to pessimism, and our tendency to melancholy and even miserabilism, are in some measure contingent—they could have been, and could be, otherwise.

We each inherit and inhabit specific worldviews, certain ways of looking at and engaging the world. These existential moods prime us to experience reality in particular ways, and so profoundly and fundamentally that they often escape our notice. For those of us in dialogue with

Western cultural traditions, our assessment of the world takes place in the context of the generational trauma of the 20th century and a philosophical tradition that reminds us, incessantly, that God is dead, humanistic values fail to prevent or repair evil, technology is incapable of solving our most fundamental problems (often creating new problems in the process of solving old ones), and, in any case, that no matter what we do we are all going to die shortly. The canonical writers of continental philosophy worked in a cultural milieu shaped by the First World War and the "lost generation," by the Second World War and the Holocaust, and by the Cold War, totalitarianism, and the specter of nuclear annihilation. When the "war to end all wars" merely sets the stage for more conflict, when one of the "high" European cultures descends into barbarism and genocide, and when one lives under the threat of total annihilation by weapons of mass destruction, it's bound to effect one's worldview.[49] Additionally, many prominent philosophical and literary figures were also younger people who gravitated toward the political left, and thus were also subject to seeing their political ideals—socialism or communism—warped to horrific effect in the Soviet Union, which mimicked, at least in terms of barbarity, the fascist totalitarianism of the 30s and 40s. When a person's deepest political passions and commitments are cut out from beneath her, shown to be as capable of brutality and Orwellian newspeak as the regimes she most reviles, it's easy to see how one might abandon faith in the existence of any humanistic truth at all. It is inevitable that such experiences would shape the thinking of scholars, intellectuals, and authors, influencing what they took to be most compelling and most significant about the human condition, such that the 20th century reaches an apotheosis of sorts with respect to melancholic thinking, pessimism, and nihilism.

Given this history, it is clear that the particular forms of negativity and specific flavor of pessimism we inherit through continental philosophy and literature are contingent. They could have been otherwise. As Albert Camus told the very generation in question: "everything is not summed up in negation and absurdity. We know this. But *we must first posit negation and absurdity because they are what our generation has encountered* and what we must take into account."[50]

The contingency of our melancholic inheritance does not mean it is without value, nor does it eliminate the reasons to despair particular to our time and place: the COVID-19 pandemic; an accelerating climate crisis; population pressures; resource depletion; widening economic inequality; resurgent extremism; school shootings; a wave of populist xenophobia; nuclear proliferation; and so on. After all, every culture, every tradition, and every individual is the inheritor of equally contingent moods and orientations, and encounters its own particular reasons to despair. But it does mean we ought to ask ourselves what our contingent patrimony *reveals* and what it *conceals*—what it makes apparent and emphasizes, but also what it downplays or overlooks. What truths have we seen more clearly as a result of our traditions, and which ones have we misunderstood or ignored? How much of our own despair and melancholy is a consequence of immutable facts about the world and the human condition, and how much is the result of what we've been taught by our culture, including our philosophical and literary inheritance? For the latter not only offers us arguments—direct or indirect—for nihilism, absurdity, meaninglessness, and pessimism; it also colors our reception of philosophy, theology, history, literature, and, indeed, the very facts that describe our world, informing our assessment of reasons to despair, now or in the future.[51]

Reality seems to counsel despair, and we are, seemingly, all-too-ready to heed that counsel. But is despair the last word? Or the only word?

In the following chapters, I will propose that we can, and should, teach ourselves to live more appropriately "after dark," that is, after we lose our naive and juvenile faith in the foundations of our happiness and darkness falls on our world. That darkness need not set us on the road to despair; we can learn to see and to appreciate the positive alongside the negative: life against the background of death, beauty in the stellar darkness, the gift of being within the framework of inevitable loss. I don't intend to "save" us from the darkness, which would require a theology much more robust than I am willing to offer here. Nor do I intend to "get beyond" the darkness, as if this dark night of the soul is merely temporary, an eclipse on our journey to the Elysian Fields. Living well after dark is not a matter of what happens after the darkness has gone, once we've gotten through or past the darkness and the sun, *sol invictus*, rises again; nor is it about whistling in the dark, seeking to feign courage by pretending that the dark is not, after all, quite so overwhelming. It is, rather, about what happens after darkness falls—once we become aware of the nocturnal murmurations beyond the perimeter of light cast by our fragile hearths and campfires, and once we become cognizant of the fact that the wood will not last until dawn.

We perish, each alone.

Once we are exposed to the darkness, it puts an end to the naive joy that allows us to affirm, too easily, that "God is in his heaven— / All's right with the world!"[52]: the innocent joy of youth; the unreflective joy of security, affluence, or success; the drunken joy of flowering health or new love. In short, the privileged joy of occupying, for the moment, a place in the sun: love rather than heartache, health rather than illness, security rather than instability, life rather than death. But sooner or later darkness falls. Once we catch a glimpse of the dizzying, indifferent vacuum between the stars and realize its relevance, once we recognize that we and everything we care for are doomed to die, our initial, naive, soaring joy in the world is brought back down to earth.

> For like the rain that comes now
> to the roof and slides down the gutter
> I am headed to the earth.
> And like the others, all the lost
> and all the lovers, I will follow
> an old path not marked on any map.[53]

In the aftermath of this awakening, denial is the first response of many people. Some try to ignore what they've seen, seeking to recapture their naive joy. This can take a variety of forms, from trivial distractions to frantic leisure pursuits, from hedonistic consumption to self-medication. Others choose to rage against the darkness they formerly ignored, fulminating against God or cursing the indifference of the universe. Yet others wallow in the darkness and resign themselves to the ambivalence, ennui, and anomie it seems to demand. Each of these is a predictable response to the loss of naive joy in the world—predictable both because one can see why they might be tempting and also because others have flirted with or embraced each of these options.

But there is another option. We can opt for a new and different joy, one made possible by a "new naiveté" about the world. Not a futile attempt to regain the joy of lost innocence, the "first naiveté" that was lost to the darkness, but rather a freely adopted "second naiveté", a deliberate choice to acknowledge and reaffirm that wonder, beauty, joy, hope, and love exist alongside and within the darkness.[54]

This, I hasten to point out, is far from some saccharine New Age cheerfulness or the magical thinking of the supposed "law of attraction," which are merely contemporary methods of fleeing from the darkness. Unlike the joy of first naiveté, which is possible precisely because one remains ignorant of the harsher realities of the world, and unlike myriad forms of self-deception that seek to obscure, minimize, or forget those harsh realities, this second naiveté chooses to recognize and embrace the goodness of being with full awareness and appreciation of the persistent threat of non-being. Such a choice is not, ultimately, reducible to a choice for optimism over despair, or cheer over gloom. It is fully compatible with a certain kind of melancholy. It is, rather, a conscious decision to acknowledge, engage, and appreciate the heartening aspects of existence alongside the baleful. It is possible, standing at the edge of the abyss, after looking the reasons for nihilism and pessimism straight in the face, after acknowledging the persistence of irredeemable and inexplicable suffering, after accepting the long, dark, inhuman indifference of deep time, to turn again to the world and say: "yes, I will take you / I will love you, again."[55]

This form of second naiveté is a hermeneutic wager on the stubborn persistence of goodness, beauty, life, and meaning; and—we might as well get this out of the way at the outset—such a wager constitutes a certain kind of faith. When it comes to the meaningfulness or meaninglessness of life, we are always leaping, always operating on faith. The contours of the type of faith I have in mind will become clear in what follows; but, for the moment, think of this in quite broad terms: "faith without dogma or definition"—other, perhaps, than a commitment to the assertion that being is better than non-being.[56] The "faith" I have in mind is just as compatible with "I am an atheist" or "I am a humanist" as it is with "I am a Catholic" or "I am a Hindu." But it is not ultimately compatible with "I am a nihilist." Nor is it very congenial to "I am a pessimist," if by pessimist we mean the belief that the worst (*pessimus*) will come to pass. I recognize that this is likely to irritate people. On one hand, some theists will be angered by the suggestion that a mere "wager on meaning" constitutes faith, and they may object to my bracketing other-worldly transcendence, my rejection of theodicy, or my call to a certain form of paganism. On the other hand, some atheists will no doubt chafe because faith seems incompatible with their rejection of religion, and they may object to the use of Judeo-Christian tropes to frame and engage the "problem of evil." But I am not suggesting that all knowledge, argument, opinion, or belief is religious, or even faith. I am simply pointing out that when it comes to the meaningfulness or meaninglessness of being we fall back on first principles on which we base our "way of life," and that we *argue from* rather than *argue for* these first principles.[57] That's faith.

I don't want to make too strong a point of this, because the current book is not a work of theology, or even of philosophy of religion in any traditional sense; but we cannot avoid the subject entirely. As William James observes, pessimism is "essentially a religious disease"[58] resulting from the non-correspondence between the world we have and the world we expect, hope for, or desire. And, obviously, people from essentially every culture and creed experience some version of this non-correspondence. Eugene Thacker makes a related observation regarding contemporary culture: "Pessimism is the philosophical form of disenchantment."[59] Disenchantment is the wager that the world is nothing but dead, meaningless, senseless matter, and the consequent experience of it as such. Enchantment, in contrast, is the experience of the world as shot through with vital forces and saturated with meaning. As Emerson writes, "To the dull mind nature is leaden. To the illuminated mind the whole world burns and sparkles with light."[60] There is simply no honest way to take up the questions of pessimism, despair, and melancholy without acknowledging faith taken in a broad, postmodern sense that extends to all hermeneutic wagers on meaning or meaninglessness, value or disvalue, hope or despair.[61] No one can escape such wagers. I trust, therefore, that the charitable reader will accept the need for something like faith in affirming meaning. This minimal faith frames a tent large enough to include many people who call themselves theists as well as many who call themselves atheists, and a wide variety of folks in between.

In what follows, I intend to make a start toward repolishing, perhaps even regrinding, the philosophical lens through which continental philosophy engages living, experiencing, and being, thinking anew the significance of wonder, vitality, beauty, and love, as well as that of tragedy, suffering, and loss. In doing so I will borrow freely from literature and poetry as well as philosophy; for if the latter attempts to think about the meaningfulness or meaninglessness of life in a manner that aspires to a degree of rigor and clarity, the former give voice to these matters in a manner that is immediate, raw, and candid, and thus give expression to the lived experience of meaningfulness or meaninglessness.

Because, as James notes, optimism and pessimism are in large degree temperamental dispositions, the plausibility of my alternative will depend to some degree on the temperament of the reader. I find in myself a rather significant tendency toward the melancholic; but alongside intense experiences of desolation I've had profound experiences of joy, wonder, beauty, and goodness, the number and significance of which I cannot deny. I hope most readers will, on reflection, find similar experiences in their own backgrounds, which will make what follows much more comprehensible; but in the end, following Erazim Kohák, I must warn the reader that: "I [do] not [seek] to 'prove a point' but to evoke and share a vision. Thus my primary tool [will be] the metaphor, not the argument, and the product of my labors. . . not a doctrine but an invitation to look and see."[62]

# Chapter 2
# Joy and the Myopia of Finitude

## 1. Evil

Late one night, in a country pub in County Sligo, Dr. Harte walks across the room to where the parish priest, Fr. Lavelle, sits alone in a booth. Smirking mischievously, he sips from his pint and begins, softly and slowly, to tell a singularly disturbing tale. Not a supernatural story, something that can be held at a distance because it is unreal, but a tale so banal and ordinary that its horror shakes the very foundations of Lavelle's efforts to cling to the goodness in the world, and ours.

Shortly after finishing his medical degree in Dublin, Harte saw a three-year-old boy brought into the hospital for a routine operation. Nothing special or alarming, the kind of thing that happens every day in a major city. But, in this case, there was a mistake with the anesthesia; the little boy slipped into crisis, suffered brain damage, and was left permanently deaf, dumb, blind, and paralyzed. A terrible tragedy. But Harte does not stop there. Highlighting the unspeakable horror, he asks Lavelle to imagine what it would be like for the young boy once he regained consciousness, alone in the dark. Confusion, certainly. But probably confusion softened by the expectation that things would soon become clear. After all, his parents had lovingly reassured him, told him that such a minor procedure—a tonsillectomy perhaps—was trivial, an utterly normal event that happened to little boys every day, all over the world. Like a dental examination or medical checkup. Nothing to worry about. Just like going to sleep, and afterwards a week of ice cream to soothe his healing throat. Awakening in the dark like this is probably normal, just like waking early at home, before the sun was up. That's what the boy would tell himself in that strange, disquieting silence. He could call out to his parents and they would come, groggily to turn the light on and sweep him up in a warm embrace, perhaps to nestle in their own bed. But, Harte continues, think about what happens next. The boy calls out, but cannot hear his own voice. He calls again, louder. Nothing. Now he is really confused, and frightened. He bolts up, shouting, to run to his parents' room. Only he doesn't. He can't move; he doesn't make a sound. Panic washes over him, but there is nothing he can do. He is entombed in his own body, alone in the dark, "howling with terror."[1]

In this powerful scene from the 2014 film *Calvary*, Harte rubs our noses in the blind, stupid, indefensible cruelty and suffering of the world, ripping away any appeal to compensation or comfort. A three-year-old boy, condemned to a life—a long life given his age—alone, *utterly* alone, in the dark. There is something irredeemable in such tragedy.

Harte's story confronts us with "the problem of evil," a problem with a long history, but which has perhaps been formulated most powerfully by the Judeo-Christian tradition. It's easy to see why. Take a personal God who is, supposedly, omniscient, omnipotent, and omnibenevolent and, holding that thought in mind, survey the diverse and disturbing manifestations of evil on offer in the world, which are pervasive and inescapable. The silence of God is thunderous.

> Impossible to pin down, he has fallen
> as silent as the infinite spaces
> that rendered Pascal mute:
> gaps unplugged in the universe.
> Silent as the contemplative order
> sedated in the terminal ward.
> Silent as the tongues of dusty shoes
> dumbfounded in the Holocaust Museum.[2]

The Greeks suffered evil, but they did not suffer that evil wondering about abandonment by a benevolent, personal God. Apollo's attempted rape of Daphne is not surprising for the Greeks, whose myths included both strikingly fallible divinities and fates that the gods themselves could not avoid. The Greek gods are neither omniscient, nor omnipotent, nor omnibenevolent; and so evil and tragedy, while lamentable, are not obscenities. In contrast, the parents in Harte's tale, presumably Christian, must wonder: where is God? Where is the Christ who healed the sick and raised the dead? The God for whom all things are possible? For Christians evil always reeks of betrayal, taking place against the background of a personal God who knows about it, could have prevented it, and presumably would want to do so.

But I noted in the last chapter that I mean for both my diagnosis of our problem—a temperamental imbalance that obscures certain truths and borders on despair—and my response to that problem to be accessible and meaningful to people regardless of creedal belief or disbelief. So, let's take a step back.

The presumption of religious belief is not a prerequisite for considering my concern here. To make this clear, I'll go further to say that even the atheist cannot escape the problem of evil, and not only in the sense that the atheist, like the theist, will suffer evil in all its diverse manifestations, but also in the sense that evil represents an epistemic and metaphysical problem with which the atheist must wrestle. True, the atheist does not feel the sting of evil as a personal betrayal; nevertheless—as we've seen with Leopardi, Zapffe, and Cioran—the atheist too can rebel against a universe that, as poet Dennis O'Driscoll says, "never lives up / to its billing."[3] Harte's story is presented as an indictment against God; but it is merely one example of a much larger class of reasons to lose faith, not only faith in God, but faith in life, in the world, in existence itself.

In her book, *Evil in Modern Thought*, Susan Neiman argues that any normative claim leads, more or less inexorably, to the problem of evil: "Every time we make the judgment *this ought not to have happened*, we are stepping onto a path that leads straight to the problem of evil."[4] The problem of evil—the problem of why things *are not* as they *ought to be*—is something that, in a broader sense, plagues not only the traditional theist and her personal God, but also the philosophical theist (e.g., Aristotle) and the atheist (e.g., Camus). Therefore, when considering both the problem of evil and responses to it, we need to dig deeper than monotheism, deeper than religion, all the way down to human nature itself. "The problem of evil is not derived from religion"—that is, it is not a consequence of religious presuppositions—"[rather]

religion is one kind of attempt [among others] to solve the problem of evil."[5] As Levinas says: "The first metaphysical question is no longer Leibniz's question *why is there something rather than nothing*? but *why is there evil rather than good*?"[6]

## 2. Strong theology, strong theodicy

The problem of evil is an enormously complicated one; and if we extend this problem, even in an attenuated form, beyond traditional theologies to include all cases in which someone asserts that the world is not what it ought to be, things become more complicated still. Therefore, following Ivan Karamazov in his infamous indictment of God (in the "Rebellion" chapter of Dostoevsky's *The Brothers Karamazov*), I propose to "keep things simple" by focusing on a narrower and particularly troubling class of examples.

As traditionally formatted by Christianity, evil comes in two forms: radical evil (evil resulting from human acts), and natural evil (evil from "natural" causes, so-called "acts of God"). Radical evil, it is commonly understood, is an unavoidable consequence of free will. God made humans with free will, which is the gift of autonomy. We are neither objects without agency, nor agents governed by mere programming or instinct. We can freely choose our goals. But if free will is truly free, it harbors the possibility that it will be used for evil. If God steps in to change our will and prevent people from choosing evil, or if we are created so as to be free with the caveat that we cannot choose evil, we become nothing more than fancy robots, not free at all.

Precisely because actual freedom must, logically, include the freedom to err, radical evil is to my mind the less problematic species of evil, at least in terms of giving an account of its existence. If people are free to decide how to act, some of them will decide to act badly. So, following the goal of keeping things simple, let's bracket radical evil for the moment. For Dostoevsky's Ivan, keeping things simple meant focusing on the unjustified suffering of innocent children. Perhaps my own suffering is, in some measure, just deserts for my own faults and failures, which are many; but "pray tell me what have the children got to do with it? It is quite incomprehensible why they should have to suffer, and why they should buy harmony with their suffering. Why do they get thrown on the pile, to manure someone's future harmony with themselves?"[7]

However, Ivan's key example, a girl tortured by her own parents, complicates things by telling a tale of radical evil. Harte's example is also open to such an interpretation. Was the anesthetist drinking the night before the surgery? Was she insufficiently studious in medical school? Did she allow herself to be distracted during the procedure? Therefore, let's modify Dr. Harte's story in a manner that places the source of the evil well out of the sphere of human freedom, something that is purely a consequence of the manner in which the world is structured: no mistake by an anesthetist, just a random, inexplicable stroke. A lifetime of solitary torture because of a ruptured aneurism at three years old. Thus modified, Harte's provocation—both a taunt and a lament—is one that clearly and compellingly undermines the notion that the universe is benevolent or just.

Natural evil—death, disease, tsunami, earthquakes, and even the very structure of life itself, based as it is on predation and parasitism—is not the result of human free will but rather of the structure of the world, which for the theist is tied directly to divine action (or inaction). If God, omniscient and omnipotent, creates the world *ex nihilo*, surely God is the author of all the things in the world, their nature, and their modes of interaction. And, therefore, God is the one who designed Ebola to aggressively attack human organs, tectonic plates to shift abruptly enough to cause tsunami, and human neurons to be susceptible to the degeneration that causes Alzheimer's Disease. As Paul Valéry wrote, "God made everything out of nothing, but the nothingness shows through."[8]

The most common secular response to the problem of evil is a kind of "weak nihilism" coupled with a "shallow hedonism." Weak nihilism is the result of dismissing "evil" by asserting that there is, in fact, no way the world *ought* to be and, therefore, that there is no failure or misfortune in a world that falls short of what it might be. But this nihilism is "weak" precisely because while some people assert it, when put to the pins no one really cleaves to it. Despite their avowed nihilism, such people still speak and act and feel in a way that reveals an underlying belief that things ought to be otherwise. They protest when they themselves are the victims of injustice. They ask, "why me?" If we take their actions to be revelatory, they believe some things are more valuable than others, and that some things are intrinsically valuable. But for the avowed nihilist, that is a contradiction. If one claims to be a nihilist one can, at best, express a conditional preference for some alternative; one cannot say that we "ought," for example, to have justice or freedom, or even that they are "better" in any meaningful sense. In the end, nihilism is a temptation and a fear—indeed, it is probably an unavoidable dark night of the soul for any intelligent and reflective person—but it is not a lived disposition. Clever undergraduates stretching their intellectual wings may claim to be nihilists; but, in the end, no one—not Leopardi, not Zapffe, not Cioran—really *lives* as a nihilist.[9]

Perhaps the weakness of this nihilism is the result of the fact that, as John D. Caputo makes clear, there is a great deal of "religion," of a peculiar sort, in people who "quite rightly pass for atheists." A weak nihilist asserts the meaninglessness and indifference of the cosmos; but such people remain "haunted," as Caputo says, by "God," or by "something that passes under the name of God"—that is, by a kind of faith that is the promise of something to come. The result? Weak nihilists need to find a way to cope; they suspect the world is meaningless but cannot live without meaning. And so, to drown out the sound of the wolves of entropy howling outside the door, they attempt to distract themselves with trivial news and gossip, or politics, or finance, or some version of eating, drinking, and merry-making—that is, through hedonism of a rather shallow sort—happy to sin, but too timid to sin boldly.[10]

On the religious side, at least in the monotheisms of the West, the problem of evil is expressed in the apparent incommensurability between (1) God's nature as (a) omniscient, (b) omnipotent, and (c) omnibenevolent, and (2) the existence of evil. The problem can be "solved" or defused by eliminating one or more of the claims in the formulation of the problem. For example, if God is omnibenevolent and omnipotent but not omniscient—perhaps God created, rested on the proverbial seventh day, and is still resting—there is an explanation for evil: God would want to eliminate evil (omnibenevolent) and could eliminate evil (omnipotent), but is simply unaware how things have gotten out of hand (not omniscient). Alternatively, and terrifyingly, God could be omniscient and omnipotent without being omnibenevolent. Here we would have an explanation not unlike the Greeks and Romans. The gods are powerful and clever, but they are perfectly willing to endorse, and even commit, myriad evils. Take, for example, Zeus's rape of Leda in the form of a swan, Hades' kidnapping of Persephone, or the involvement of various gods in the butchery of the Trojan War. As Shakespeare's Earl of Gloucester has it, "as flies to wanton boys are we to th' gods. They kill us for their sport."[11]

In the Judeo-Christian tradition, the problem of natural evil is generally addressed through some form of theodicy, which seeks to eliminate the contradiction in the problem of evil by denying evil itself rather than limiting God in any way. What we take to be evil is, on this account, merely a lack of goodness, which we misunderstand largely due to our limited perspective. When Job decries the afflictions that have beset him—the death of his family, the diseases that plague him, and so on—God rebukes him by pointing out that he complains "without knowledge" (Job 38:2) and asks, clearly rhetorically, "Shall a faultfinder contend with the Almighty?" (Job 40:2). Things may look imperfect to us, when viewed from our finite and self-interested perspective; however, if viewed from the absolute perspective of God, it would become clear that reality is unfolding according to a perfectly benevolent plan that we, as finite beings, cannot perceive. It's a bit like a mother insisting that her less-than-enthusiastic daughter develop a taste for vegetables rather than candy—the child rails against the indefensible injustice of the world, while the mother knows (and the daughter will herself acknowledge as an adult) that this is for the best. Neo-Platonists gave this logic justification by explaining that evil is merely an absence of the good. Because God is the author of all that is, and because God is perfectly good, "evil" as such does not exist; things are flawed simply as a result of having fallen away from their created perfection, becoming "less good." Thus, Augustine says "evil is only the privation of good,"[12] and Boethius insists "evil has no existence."[13]

But theodicy is a bitter draught. For the theist, it means accepting, and even endorsing as part of God's incomprehensible-but-perfectly-good plan, horrors like Harte's locked-in child. And, as Ivan Karamazov fumes, the "perfection" of the world bought at such a price remains "too high a price to pay."[14] Although things might appear somewhat easier for the atheist, a commitment to accepting the world "just as it is" is likely to lead us to endorse things we really ought not endorse. Nietzsche—otherwise a fine example of someone who seeks to live joyfully "after dark"—falls into this quagmire with his doctrine of eternal recurrence (*ewige Wiederkunft*), which we will take up in due course.

Both theodicy and eternal return require us to assert that evils are not, in fact, evil; they merely seem evil as a consequence of our narrow, self-centered, all-too-human perspective.

The source of this difficultly lies in the legacy of what Caputo calls "strong theology."[15] Strong theology is theology based in certainties; it "trades in the hard and fast, the dogmatic"[16] and "belongs to the sovereign order of power and presence and favors a grammar of great omni-nouns and hyper-verbs."[17] Strong theology not only confines God in determinate and fixed religious symbols ("my way of thinking about God is the only true way"), it also, at least in the West, tends to view God in terms of absolute power. That is to say, strong theology is theology that emphasizes the power of God (omnipotence, omniscience) rather than the justice to which God—or better, for Caputo, "the event harbored in the name of God"—calls us. And this is an epistemic and existential legacy that even the atheist inherits.

But strong theology requires strong theodicy. If we insist on the "Omni-God of celestial Might,"[18] we have to account for blasphemous evil in a world governed by a perfectly good God. Why do we die? God could have made it otherwise.[19] Why do we suffer so reliably and so persistently, often in ways that are totally unrelated to the exercise of free will? Many of these sources of suffering could be eliminated without harming the greater whole and without needing to radically alter fundamental aspects of the human condition—reason, free will, and so forth—on which we have traditionally been so fixated. Since the strong theologian is not going to weaken God, she must weaken evil; and since the strong theologian's God is *absolutely* powerful, evil must be *absolutely* weak, weak to the point of nonexistence. But, again, this sort of theodicy is a pretty hard pill to swallow in cases like our modified version of Harte's story. I am far from omnipotent, omniscient, or omnibenevolent, but surely there are possible worlds that are like this one in every respect save one: childhood strokes do not occur. And surely such a world would be better than this one.

Recent movements in philosophy of religion suggest that strong theology is not our only option, even in the monotheistic traditions of the West. As an alternative, Caputo suggests a "weak theology" governed by the grammar and logic of "perhaps" in order to salvage "the event harbored in the name of God" from ossification in strong theologies.[20] On this account, "God is not a powerful doer and mysterious undoer but the powerless power of the event. That is why it is futile to blame God for doing us wrong and unnecessary to exonerate God's ways before human courts."[21] God does not do things (like fight evil, cure disease, address climate change), but calls us to do things (like fight evil, cure disease, address climate change). Similarly, Richard Kearney calls us to an "anatheistic" faith, which is a wager on a God who "may be" if we respond to the call to justice and hospitality, an account that is willing to give up on classical narratives of God's omnipotence in order to avoid the pitfalls of theodicy.[22] Such a God does not help us through mighty demonstrations of power—magically clothing the naked, sheltering the refugee, or curing disease; rather, God is a cry in the wilderness, a shout in the streets, that *calls us* to clothe the naked, shelter the refugee, and tend to the diseased. Such miracles are distinct from the magic of strong theology; they are the possibility of the impossible, which happens all the time when otherwise all-too-human people respond to the call of God. As Etty Hillesum, who wrote from the depths of the Holocaust, said: "You [God] cannot help us, but we must help you and defend Your dwelling place inside us to the last."[23] Both Caputo and Kearney suggest that God's power is powerless to right the wrongs of the world, which is, precisely, a call to *human* responsibility, capability, and power as an answer to God's call to goodness.

What if we call into question strong theologies and consider a God whose strength may be in weakness, a God who "may be" if we respond, a God who transfigures creation—or, better, calls us and our fellow creatures to transfigure it—rather than micro-managing it?[24] What then becomes of evil? Well, at the very least, the problem of evil becomes less explosive. When we deemphasize omnipotence, we disarm evil, at least as a problem. If we adopt an alternative theology—one that thinks of God not in terms of absolute power, but rather in terms of creativity, love, wonder, and solidarity—the evils of the world, though they remain something to struggle with, no longer seem like betrayals or inexplicable obscenities.

Note, however, that having extended the problem of evil beyond the boundaries of formal religions to darken the door of anyone who thinks the world is not what it ought to be, escaping the obscenity is not, yet, escaping the problem. While theodicy proper is tied inextricably to a monotheistic view of God as omniscient, omnipotent, and omnibenevolent, the general structure of theodicy holds even for atheists who reject the "*theos*." The echo of theodicy is audible in every argument against anthropocentrism as constituting a too-narrow and too-self-interested view of things. The deviation of Earth's temperature by 2°C, or 4°C, or even 10°C from the recent historical average is not "evil"—the Earth couldn't care less, if it cared at all—it is merely our anthropocentric view of things that thinks it so. But when, for example, certain deep ecologists remind us that climate change is not a threat to the Earth—or even to life, which will keep chugging along quite well, thank you—but rather a threat to the kind of Earth that supports human civilization and on which we are able to flourish, and each time they suggest that might not be an obviously or entirely bad thing, they repeat the logic of theodicy. As if Gaia, rather than God, screamed from the whirlwind: "Where were you when life arose from inorganic matter? When natural selection began to drive evolution? When consciousness arose in life? Do you imagine all this was orchestrated just to lead to your existence, your flourishing? What about the Leviathan? The Behemoth? What about the butterfly, the maple tree, the sea slug? What about *cochliomyia hominivorax*, *ascaris lumbricoides*, *naegleria fowleri*? Did they not evolve in the same manner? Is the earth not theirs, equally? What makes you think that something is wrong just because it seems so from your all-too-human perspective?" The danger of such "non-theistic theodicies"—Nietzschean, deep ecological, or otherwise—is that they ask us to accept some evils that we *ought* to repudiate.

We have to try to hold together the paradoxical notions that (a) we cannot, and ought not, expect the world to conform to our every desire—there are some "evils" that are structurally part of reality, and which both prudence and propriety demand we accept—and (b), nevertheless, there are particular instances of evil that we must denounce and resist. Wisdom suggests I learn to accept human mortality; it does not demand that I accept the fact that children in the developing world die daily from diseases that could be cured with a trip to the corner pharmacy in the global north. Maintaining this distinction does not dictate any particular view of reality, theistic or atheistic, in advance; but it does remind us that there are goods we can experience and evils with which we have to contend.

Many traditional theists will no doubt scoff at the notion that God does not micro-manage creation, dictating each moment down to the details of who will become ill and, then, who will recover. And many atheists will surely bristle at being told their hope for the future and their preference for justice rather than injustice constitute a strange "religion without religion." Yet a weakened theology points toward a way in which we can grapple with evil while avoiding two common pitfalls. The first pitfall places the solution to evil in the hands of God or whatever goes by the name of God: the state, the revolution, progress, or whatever. The problem here is that if the solution to evil is in the hands of God, but we still suffer evil, then God is complicit in that suffering. The second, related pitfall seeks to explain away evil as an illusion—either part of God's perfect plan (theodicy) or an artifact of our anthropocentrism (an "ecodicy" perhaps?). The problem here is that we are asked to accept evil, or even endorse it, as part of the proper and harmonious operation of the universe.

While death, fallibility, finitude and other such evils remain inescapable for both the strong theologian and the weak theologian—whether she quite rightly passes for a theist or an atheist—if we choose to adopt a weaker theology it becomes easier to view evil as part of the *mystery* of being rather than the *problem* of evil.

## 3. The problem of evil and the mystery of the good

What if the way to deal with the problem of evil is not to work out some elaborate way of explaining or justifying evil (strong theodicy), nor to resign oneself to the existence of evil (weak nihilism), but rather to rethink the question we are asking? What if the matter at issue in the problem of evil is not evil per se, but the problem: the problem with the *problem* of evil?

Gabriel Marcel argues that problems are (a) solvable and (b) tied to *technics*.[25] That is to say, a problem is something we can, at least in theory, defeat or move past, and that the means which we employ to do so are generally technical in nature, whether that technique has to do with technological innovation, or social organization, or some standardized set of procedures. Because of this technical approach to problems, the identity of the person seeking the solution is not at issue when dealing with a problem; it makes no difference who is asking the question because all the relevant facts are external to the questioner:

"when I am dealing with a problem, I am trying to discover a solution [invariably a technique of some sort] that can become common property, that consequently can, at least in theory, be rediscovered by anybody at all."[26] For example, there is a standardized procedure—or perhaps a few options among sets of standardized procedures—for replacing a sink and faucet, and these procedures are more or less the same for every person who ever installs a sink and faucet. Likewise, if a person is trying to lose weight, she will employ a technique that is more or less indifferent to her individuality: burn more calories than are ingested. Even if some diet regimes work better for some people than others, any diet one adopts can be employed by many other people seeking the same solution to the same problem. So, when encountering problems, we seek some object or outcome that will serve as a solution; and those solutions are generally achieved through the application of some specific technique, a technique that is, in principle, of use to anyone else desiring the same object or outcome.

Mysteries, however, cannot be solved with techniques, because when dealing with mysteries the identity of the questioner *is* at stake and is not incidental to the matter at issue. If my being—my unique particularity, my *haecceitas*—is at stake in any mystery, it goes without saying that the response to that mystery cannot be something technical, something which would be, by its very nature, indifferent to the being of the person employing the technique. My being is not at stake in laying the stonework outside my house, which—however creative I may strive to be—takes place using techniques that are basically the same for anyone doing a similar task. But if I ask myself if I am in love, or if life is worth living, or if being is justified by the goodness in it, then the answer cannot be generic, formulaic, or technical, because *I* am the one who is loving, living, or being. Whatever resources I use to discern whether or not I love someone, they will not be precisely the same resources you use to determine whether or not you love some other person.

Mysteries, in fact, are not something one "solves" at all; they do not present us with an obstacle to some desire or a gap in our knowledge; as Marcel says, "the mysterious is not the unknowable, the unknowable is only the limiting case of the problematic."[27] The mystery of being—including the existence of evil—is a reality we experience, not a problem we can solve. We may cure cancer, extend life, reduce poverty, and promote justice—and I hope that we do—but any technical responses to evil are, of necessity, partial, local, and incomplete. We will never eliminate evil per se with techniques, whether technological or cultural. Therefore, our response to evil cannot, or should not, be based solely in technics. Evil is an unavoidable aspect of the mystery of being; and part of wisdom is learning to deal with evil that cannot be entirely eradicated or explained away.[28]

This goes some way toward addressing the reason that evil scandalizes Ivan Karamazov, who is outraged by the attempt to explain evil: "I don't understand anything. . . and I no longer want to understand anything. I want to stick to the fact. I made up my mind long ago not to understand. If I wanted to understand [evil], I would immediately have to betray the fact. . ."[29] Ivan rejects any explanation of evil that would somehow suggest that particular cases—the facts with which he provokes Alyosha (e.g., the young child tortured by her own parents)—could be justified as part of some better order: compost to fertilize future happiness or utopia. He is scandalized by the "but"—he says so explicitly—as in, "the torture of a young child is a monstrous evil, *but*. . .". Which is something like someone saying "I'm not a racist, *but*. . .," in which the "but" often indicates that we are about hear something racist. The "but" is an attempt to qualify or justify evil, to remove its sting and its scandal. And for Ivan there is no qualification, no excuse, no theological jujitsu that can justify or expiate the kind of evil laid bare by Harte's example, or by countless other non-fictional horrors, historical and contemporary.

Ivan, however, is still grappling with the *problem* of evil within the paradigm of *strong* theology. And we've seen that it might be wise to give up thinking of evil in terms of a problem and to acknowledge its essentially mysterious nature. As a problem, evil per se remains incomprehensible and intractable, something we can neither explain nor eradicate. But if we give up that fool's errand and recognize the mysterious nature of evil—itself part of the more comprehensive mystery of being—what new horizons might open up for us philosophically and, perhaps more importantly, existentially?

*Pace* Ivan, let me suggest that we can better cope with evil *precisely by sticking to the facts*, because while the facts include contingent evils such as child abuse, systematic rape, genocide, and other horrors, as well as seemingly unavoidable evils like finitude, death, and entropy, they also include ineluctable goods that elicit wonder, joy, and love. Ivan rejects any "but. . ." that would explain or justify evil, as in "evil is monstrous, but. . . ." Fair enough. However, I think we might get somewhere if we are careful not to forget the "and," as in "evil is monstrous, *and*. . . ." And what? And, nevertheless, the glory of life, love, beauty, joy, and wonder are, seemingly, inextinguishable: "There are a thousand thousand reasons to live this life, every one of them sufficient."[30] The "and" is not scandalous in the way that the "but" is, because the "and" does not minimize evil or suggest that it is justified in some economic calculus when weighed against the good.

The understanding we glean from the "and. . ." is unlike the explanation proffered by the "but. . .," the explanation of theodicy. The "and. . ." does not claim we can escape, solve, or explain evil. It does not downplay or dismiss the reality of suffering. At best it helps us to cope with evil by reminding us of the background of goodness against which it takes place.[31] This entails coming to grips with the inescapable and inexplicable nature of evil—which we will never fully eliminate—as well as resisting and struggling against particular instances of evil that we can ameliorate; it also means accepting that reality is, and always will be, imperfect, even as we affirm the fact that it is somehow, mysteriously and fundamentally, good.

## 4. Joy in finitude, or "in-finite" joy

What shall we say about evil when we can no longer lay responsibility for it at the feet of a divine caregiver who could, but does not, eliminate it? When evil becomes simply part of the warp and weft of being rather than some divine oversight or lapse in judgment, we can step back from the question of why God "allows" myriad evils and see that there is much to do besides, or at least in addition to, lamenting the evils of the world. What do we miss when we focus so obsessively on evil?

> Cruelty is a mystery, and the waste of pain. But if we describe a world to compass these things, a world that is a long, brute game, then we bump up against another mystery: the inrush of power and light, the canary that sings on the skull. . . . There seems to be such a thing as beauty, a grace wholly gratuitous.[32]

## 4.1 Erazim Kohák: Time and eternity

In *The Embers and the Stars*, Czech philosopher Erazim Kohák argues that: (1) being is intrinsically good; (2) human being is distinguished by its ability to recognize this goodness and its responsibility to foster it; and (3) when humans recognize this goodness "eternity" intersects normal time. Here we cannot survey the complete argument of this underappreciated classic; however, the architecture of Kohák's account will be useful for developing a less-gloomy response to the problem of evil.

Kohák argues that, in our lived experience, the meaningfulness and goodness of being is "so utterly basic. . . [that it is] never absent from all the many configurations of life's rhythm," even the experiences of suffering and pain.[33] One way to think of this is to say that the "problem of evil," which so many people see as a reason to deny the goodness of being, is, at root, really the "mystery of the good." That is to say, the problem of evil arises from the presence of evil in a world that is so obviously, undeniably, primordially good. We have a natural affinity for being, evident in positive experiences such as wonder, beauty, and joy. And while it is clear that this affinity can be, and all too frequently is, smothered, neglected, or denied, it remains part of our basic nature and can never truly be silenced.[34]

Kohák draws a distinction between two overlapping but distinct orders—the order of temporality and the order of value—and suggests much of our dissatisfaction with the world arises from confusing the two. The order of temporality is a causal one that we experience in mechanistic and utilitarian terms, which connects the present to the past from which it came and the future into which it will flow. Thus, for example, we plan for the future like the eponymous ant of Aesop's "The Ant and the Grasshopper"; this despite the fact that such planning cannot prevent loss in the flow of time, "where moth and decay destroy, and thieves break in and steal" (Matthew 6:19). In contrast, the order of value is revealed when we glimpse the present "not in its relation to what preceded and what will follow it, but in its absolute being—in its relation to what, clumsily, we describe as eternity."[35]

These glimpses take place when time, as the saying goes, "stops" in moments of harmony with others or the natural world. In such moments—which most often come on us by surprise—we forget the wolves at our door and desire is, for the moment, laid to rest.[36] More, we forget ourselves, overcome with feelings of union or fulfillment and, often, a sense of goodness and rightness associated with the world and our place in it. And in suspending or transforming our sense of our own existence, we find ourselves unburdened of the being-toward-death that is characteristic of that ek-sistence.[37] Unburdening ourselves in this way is not a flight from mortality in the sense of ignoring or denying it. It is, rather, the full assumption of our creatureliness, finitude, and mortality. In losing ourselves as sovereign, monadic egos aspiring to omnipotence and denying our mortality, we gain ourselves as good creatures or animals, embracing and even celebrating our finitude: the experience of joy, or wonder, or vitality is the experience of the "not yet" of our inevitable death. The sufficiency, the plenitude, of such moments is the effect of eternity erupting in the flow of the temporal, the extraordinary in the ordinary, heaven on Earth: "We have but a single moment at our disposal. Let us transform that moment into eternity. No other form of immortality exists."[38] And while, absent a different faith, these experiences cannot quite bring us to "mock" the victory of death in the order of temporality, attending to them can certainly lessen or remove death's "sting" (cf. 1 Corinthians 15:55).

When we ask why "nothing gold can stay"[39]—or, rather, when we fixate on this transience—we misunderstand the nature of meaning and of goodness, which are expressions of value and, therefore, part of the eternal rather than temporal sphere. Finitude is a temporal phenomenon; joy is a "moral" one.[40] To be sure, manifestations of goodness come to be and pass away in the flow of temporality, because that is the nature of objects and of temporality; but goodness itself, existing in the order of value, is "eternal." To speak of a "transient good" is in this sense an oxymoron. And so, when we glimpse goodness, when we experience joy or wonder, we experience eternity, which the flow of time cannot unmake.

When Ivan Karamazov furiously demands, "what about the children?", Kohák responds, "the intense anguished beauty of children playing in the sun by the river, heedless of the horizon about to close in upon them, is bearable *only because* it [i.e., the goodness it manifests] is forever inscribed in eternity."[41] Note that this does not explain away the suffering of the children; nor does it seek to justify it on some cosmic scale of reckoning. Kohák sees, he cannot forget, the horizon closing in on those unsuspecting innocents: loss, tragedy, suffering, and death. He is not suggesting that the suffering of the children will purchase some "future" happiness, which would be to speak of things in temporal terms. If goodness somehow "compensates" us for evil, it is not in some quasi-economic sense in which we receive "twice as much" as we lose (cf., Job 42:10). Nor is there any guarantee that on a long enough timeline "the arc of the moral universe. . . bends toward justice."[42]

We don't need to wait for God to put his thumb on the scales of reckoning; the goodness of the universe and the horror of the universe cannot be weighed on the same scale, as if they were commensurable objects to be measured by some third, neutral unit. Defect and loss are inevitable features of the temporal sphere, in which things submit inexorably to the second law of thermodynamics. But goodness, beauty, and similar phenomena are manifestations of a different order. No amount of deferred goodness can justify the evils of this world; but no amount of evil can ever fully obscure the goodness of being, or the myriad opportunities for wonder and joy that it offers us.[43] The "compensation" of joy is nothing more than this: considering together, recognizing, and acknowledging the glory of "all things shining" amidst the wreckage and carnage of "nature, red in tooth and claw."

## 4.2 Terence Malick: All things shining

Terrence Malick's *Palme d'Or* winning *The Tree of Life*, grapples, like much of his oeuvre, with the tenacity of goodness—beauty, wonder, grace, and glory—in a world that is often cruel, brutal, and senseless. The overall vision of the film can be summed up as follows. First, at a fundamental level, we have no idea what is going on: what it all means; whether it means anything; why evil exists; why we suffer; why we ourselves perpetuate evil; why love and goodness seem weaker than violence and egoism; why loss and tragedy have, apparently, the last word. Second, despite this, the world is full of wondrous things: life, beauty, and goodness. And, third, the proper response to this situation—the presence of beauty and wonder in a world that is inscrutable and often brutal—is wonder, joy, and love.

Drawing on medieval monk and mystic Thomas à Kempis, Malick's film contrasts two different ways of being, exemplified respectively by Ms. and Mr. O'Brien: the "way of grace" and the "way of nature."[44] The way of nature leads a person to focus on himself, to look to his own benefit or advantage, his own profit, reward, or recognition. It interacts with others and with the world with this goal in mind, and so it seeks to control or dominate; it is occupied with planning, scheming, and struggling. It takes more than it gives. In contrast, the way of grace is satisfied with little, and takes joy in simple things—a child, a friend, a leaf, a ray of light—each day sufficient unto itself. Grace is generous; it does not desire domination over any creature. It is unpretentious, grateful, and quietly joyous.

Nature disposes a person to strive; Mr. O'Brien always wants something more or something else, looks at the world with an eye toward what is lacking or unsatisfactory. Grace, in contrast, disposes a person to love; Ms. O'Brien sees the world with eyes attentive to the miracle of being and the gift of beauty. From the perspective of grace, the way of nature surveys the world looking for reasons to be dissatisfied or miserable rather than content or awed. Naturally, Ms. O'Brien is not immune from suffering or tragedy; her way of being neither inures her to nor shields her from the tragic consequences of finitude. She endures an occasionally hostile marriage to a man whose mercurial emotions reflect both his ambitions for his future and his regrets about his past, his love for his family and his desire to secure them in a world he views as fundamentally hostile. She also suffers the loss of a child by suicide.

Nevertheless, it is clear that the way of grace allows Ms. O'Brien to experience joys that are closed to Mr. O'Brien, even in the moments when his drive and ambition seem like they might be satisfied, and helps her to endure the suffering that lays her husband low. The impoverishment of the way of nature reveals itself when Mr. O'Brien, suffering a final, devastating professional failure, awakens to the error of his ways. Here Malick draws on Dostoevsky rather than Thomas, and O'Brien laments his delusion in words that echo, almost word-for-word, Markel's confession in *The Brothers Karamazov*: "There was so much of God's glory around me: birds, meadows, sky and I alone lived in shame, I alone dishonored everything, and did not notice the beauty and glory of it all."[45]

A parallel line of reflection runs through Malick's *The Thin Red Line*, a story framed by the carnage of the Pacific Theater in the Second World War.[46] Here, Lt. Col. Tall represents one extreme of human perception of being. For Tall, the cruelty and violence of nature is blindingly obvious, an overdetermined case. He furiously reprimands one of his officers,

Capt. Staros, for being soft-hearted, unwilling to send waves of enlisted men to their death in a frontal assault on a hill. From Tall's perspective, an inappropriate concern for life is evidence of misunderstanding of the laws of nature. Nature is violent and brutal, so we must be equally cruel, hard-hearted, and willing to do whatever is necessary to achieve our aims within it. First Sergeant Welsh—a similarly pragmatic if somewhat more conflicted character—expresses a related point of view while disciplining Private Witt for going AWOL and living, happily, among the indigenous Melanesians. Welsh advises Witt to get his act together. The world is tearing itself apart in an orgy of violence, and the only sensible thing to do is to keep one's head down and try to protect oneself, hunker down and endure it. There is nothing else to do because, as Welsh asserts, this is the world we've got, the only world there is. But Witt remains unbowed—despite the threat of court martial and the certainty of punishment—and responds softly and simply, as if testifying to a revelation, "You're wrong about that Top. I seen another world."[47]

Tall and Welsh insist, for different reasons, that it is best to conform to the inscrutable cruelty of the world; but Witt—and, to some degree, Capt. Staros, Pvt. Bell, Pvt. Train, and others—recognize that there is "another world." This is not to suggest that turning from "nature" to "grace"—to retain the somewhat unfortunate dichotomy of the *Tree of Life*—is easy. As the narrative unfolds, we see plenty of obstacles between our suffering and the glory that seems tantalizingly—permanently, tauntingly—just out of reach: the soldiers' lives are comprised of one part ache (mindless boredom, extended separation from loved ones, etc.) to two parts agony (meaningless slaughter, violent death, moral collapse). At one point, having been unhinged—or perhaps enlightened—by the carnage, Sgt. McCron sits on a hillside, madly crumbling clumps of soil: "We're just dirt," he raves. In one of the oft-referenced voiceovers in the film, Pvt. Train expresses confusion about the evil that seems to threaten and overwhelm the "glory" at every turn. Given the evident goodness of the world, how did evil slip in? How did we lose hold of the gift that we were given? Why did we turn on each other in competition and conflict? What keeps us from experiencing the "other world" that Witt glimpsed?[48]

Throughout the film, Witt seems to suggest, in his words and in his actions, that we are capable of reaching out and touching the glory. But his death leaves us, and his companions, wondering if such an act, such a connection, is actually possible. Skeptical as to whether the glory is real. Kneeling over Witt's hastily-dug grave, Welsh gives voice to a complicated mix of uncertainty, resignation, and anguish. The loss of Witt's life and light is a sorrowful confirmation of Welsh's fear that the world is simply brutal and meaningless. Despite his beatific reveries, Witt lies rotting in a shallow grave far from home, friends, and family, just like thousands of other young men.

But the film does not end with Witt's burial; it ends with the surviving men transported back to a ship and, it must be acknowledged, an uncertain fate. As Guadalcanal shrinks on the horizon, there is one last voiceover from Pvt. Train. Reflecting on the chiaroscuro of darkness and light in the palette of the world, and on the struggle between the propensity to violence and the capacity for love in the hearts of men, he offers a whispered plea or prayer to be able to look at the world and see "all things shining." Given the savagery and carnage that occupies much of the story, it would be inappropriate to suggest that seeing or feeling the glory implies anything like victory over the darkness or immunity to strife. What Train and Witt want, given their inability to *escape* the world, is to *see the world otherwise*, to experience the world as it is at the intersection of eternity and time, to feel the beauty, grace, glory, and love that shine through all things. Not a deferred eschatological world, but another world inside this one.[49] All things shine, if only we know how to look.

## 4.3 Virginia Woolf: Moments of being

Virginia Woolf offers a vision that is remarkably similar in many respects, and her staunch atheism—as well as her experience with profound depression—contrasts starkly with Kohák's avowed Christianity and Malick's ambiguous spirituality and religiosity, illustrating that an attunement to joy and the goodness of being does not hinge on a traditional religious orientation.[50]

Woolf's vision of "eternity" erupting in the order of time is expressed most compellingly in *To the Lighthouse*. Take, for example, her description of the evening meal that forms one of the focal points of the narrative. Ms. Ramsey, whose particular gift it is to bring people together in just the right way, arranges a meal in which everything—the food, the company, the conversation, the setting, the time and rhythm—falls into place. She and her guests experience a moment of grace, with overtones of "security," "joy," "stillness," and "safety," that "partook. . .*of eternity*."[51]

> [She felt] a coherence in things, a stability; something. . . is immune from change, and shines out. . . in the face of the flowing, the fleeting, the spectral, like a ruby; so that again tonight she had the feeling she had had once today already, of peace, of rest. Of such moments, she thought, the thing is made that endures. This would remain.[52]

Here Woolf depicts a rather common experience for those sensitive enough and reflective enough to notice it. This miracle of eternity erupting in the everyday order of time, and the joy it brings to those open to it, does not require hosts of angels, at least not as we've come to expect them. It requires, rather, something like receptivity to the miracle of the everyday. And while we cannot create or force such moments, we can prepare ourselves for them in acts of a loving creativity like the dinner party Ms. Ramsey plans.[53]

Woolf's aesthetic and ethic suggest a similar affinity, one not too far from what the Japanese describe as *mono no aware*. Often translated as "the pathos of things," the phrase expresses the bittersweet feeling associated with a brief moment of transcendent beauty, echoing, in the West, Virgil's *lacrimae rerum*.[54] Here both the transcendence (beauty, goodness, eternity) and the brevity (fragile, finite, ephemeral) are essential to the experience. Of course we want such moments to endure; but that desire is born of a misunderstanding of the difference between the order of value and the order of time: "*Verweile doch*! Last forever! Who hasn't prayed that prayer? But the *augenblick* isn't going to *verweile*. You were lucky to get it in the first place. The present is a freely given canvas. That it is constantly being ripped apart and washed downstream goes without saying; it is a canvas nonetheless."[55] Ms. Ramsey, whose life is, in part, committed to creating such "moments of being,"[56] is wise enough to realize their fragility and transience. She feels acutely the suffering her children will endure as they come into adulthood. And the very dinner scene that shone forth like a ruby, revealing eternity, comes to its inevitable end:

> It was necessary now to carry everything a step further. With her foot on the threshold she waited a moment longer in a scene which was

> vanishing even as she looked, and then, as she moved and took Minta's arm and left the room, it changed, it shaped itself differently; it had become, she knew, giving one last look at it over her shoulder, already the past.[57]

One of the Ramseys' guests, Lily Briscoe, struggles later in life to capture this insight of the epiphany-of-the-everyday on her own canvas, asking again the "old question that [traverses] the sky of the soul perpetually": "what is the meaning of life?"[58] She admits, "the great revelation had never come," and realizes that, perhaps, the "great revelation" never would come. "Instead there [are] little daily miracles, illuminations, matches struck unexpectedly in the dark; here was one."[59] Such an epiphany may not be "great" in the sense of imposing or powerful, but it is profound, even decisive. As Emerson reminds us, "the invariable mark of wisdom is to see the miraculous in the common."[60] In such moments, life stands still, revealing "something permanent."[61] This is not to say that these phenomena do not pass away in the order of time; the characters themselves recognize the transient nature of these experiences as they occur. The point, rather, is to recognize, as Ms. Ramsey feels in the midst of one such moment: "It is enough! It is enough!"[62]

## 4.4 Jack Gilbert: The faint sound of oars in the silence

We can find a final description of the sufficiency of such moments in the work of poet Jack Gilbert, whose "A Brief for the Defense" captures the essence of Ms. Ramsey's feeling. The poem begins by acknowledging the omnipresent suffering and consequent sorrow in the world, cataloging starving children, poverty, illness, servitude, injustice, and mortality, which, with other assorted ills, are woven into the tapestry of life—past, present, and future. We've suffered, and we will suffer more. Nevertheless, Gilbert insists that we must stubbornly embrace the experience of delight in the "ruthless furnace of this world."[63] This is good advice; for without joy, nihilism becomes irresistible.[64]

The unavoidable evils and tragedies that mark, in some measure, all human lives cannot extinguish or fully obscure the beauty of the world and the goodness of being; and so, in addition to whatever else we do, we should enjoy life: embrace our happiness in this world;

laugh and celebrate with others; appreciate and give thanks for the moments of wonder, joy, and vitality. As Paul Ricoeur says, "Man is the joy of yes in the sadness of the finite."[65] Wrestling with the tension between the suffering and injustice that threaten to overwhelm us, and the moments of happiness, wonder, and joy that seem to offer respite, Gilbert concludes:

> We stand at the prow again of a small ship
> anchored late at night in the tiny port
> looking over to the sleeping island: the waterfront
> is three shuttered cafes and one naked light burning.
> To hear the faint sound of oars in the silence as a rowboat
> comes slowly out and then goes back is truly worth
> all the years of sorrow that are to come.[66]

On one reading this sounds like a straightforward theodicy, a "defense" of sorrow and suffering on the basis of some good that makes it "truly worth" it.[67] But there is another reading of this poem, one aligned with my reading of Kohák, Malick, Woolf, and the other thinkers we have considered through the lenses of "weak theology" or "anatheism."[68] The world is not "worth" it because the sound of the oars in the silence outnumber or outweigh death, suffering, genocide, sectarian religious violence, systematic rape, economic injustice, and the rest of the litany of human woe, to say nothing of the suffering and sorrow inflicted on the more-than-human world.[69] The world is worth it because, despite those things, *goodness remains* and *we can witness it*: "the point is not only does time fly and do we die, but that in these reckless conditions we live at all, and are vouchsafed, for the duration of certain inexplicable moments, to know it."[70] We can hope, and live, and love, and laugh without cheating the hardness of reality, death, and the second law of thermodynamics, and without endorsing them in the dream of eternal recurrence. The goodness of being and the meaningfulness of existence do not rest on the victory of goodness over horror or indifference in the order of time. The victory of the good—of beauty, love, life—is in the "order of eternity," the order of value and of meaning, which can become manifest in almost any moment and to which humans are particular, perhaps unique, witnesses.[71] Joy does not deny the absolute *reality* of death, dissolution, and evil; it denies their absolute *significance*.[72]

# Chapter 3
# From Mortality to Vitality

## 1. Living deeply

Autumn comes quickly to the High Sierra. At 8,500 feet above sea level, the long, warm days of summer give way early to crisp mornings, long shadows, and the first flurries of snow on the ridges and peaks. There are huge swaths of isolated terrain here, even in the summer; but after Labor Day the crowds begin to thin, and after the equinox one can find deep silence and solitude in the hushed *diminuendo* before the long silence of winter. In this transitional period, one finds the Sierra at its finest, its dappled landscape a sweeping testament to Donne's contention that "in heaven it is always autumn."[1]

Early one morning, some years ago, I hiked alone into the Cathedral Range, just south of Tuolumne Meadows, an area dotted with striking granite peaks soaring toward heaven from the subalpine landscape. Over the course of the day I climbed and traversed over a dozen distinct summits, spires, and ridges before turning north again and hiking out to the road. With nothing other than a tiny daypack to hold my climbing shoes and some water, now long gone, my body glided lightly over the trail, weaving in and out of Sierra lodgepole, alongside a stream drawn down by the summer, and across granite slabs shining with glacial polish. As the trees thinned approaching the meadow I slowed down so as to prolong the moment, my body flushed with the radiance of exertion, which was mirrored by the rosy alpenglow on the granite domes and, in the distance, on the summit of Mt. Conness. Minutes later, arriving at the road in the waning light, a lone car sped past me, heading east into the dusk and the long descent into Owens Valley. The noise of the engine, rising and falling with the Doppler shift, was not exactly jarring, but incongruous; it pulled me from one world into another, as if waking me from a dream or reverie.

Later that evening, camped with a murmuring creek at my feet and the brilliant river of the Milky Way above my head, I thought about the day. I realized that while I'd been on the move for many hours, hiking and climbing thousands of feet of moderately technical ground, what stood out was not a clear, linear narrative of events. My recollection was rather of a deep sense of connection to the place and with the moment, an intimate experience of my body engaged with the terrain, and a kind of global sensuous experience of the environment.[2] True, in retrospect I could, and did, frame the events in a narrative, intoning the names of the peaks I'd climbed and the topographic contours I'd followed to enchain the summits. Likewise, I could abstract and recollect individual scents, sounds, or sights that had been part of my immersion in the environment: the soft whistling of a hermit thrush, the resinous odor of pine, the invigorating chill of an afternoon dip in an alpine tarn, the view of south toward the Minarets from the summit of Matthes Crest. However, that narrative sequence and those abstract sensory elements were not what I had actually experienced during large portions of the day.

The difference was more than that between reflecting on the activity and engaging in the activity, though that was certainly part of it. During the day I had, for a while, been more deeply immersed in and connected with the world than was the case on either rest days or on other, more challenging climbing routes that occupied me that summer. I'd experienced this before: on the polished floor of a *dojo* in Japan; gliding across the face of a wave in Indonesia; carving long turns on skis deep in the San Juan Mountains. Different places, different moments, but always the same kind of experience: thoroughly engaged but somehow effortless; wholly aware without being consciously analytical; intimately in touch with my body; immersed in the environment; and fully, vibrantly alive. And always the same feelings: joy, wonder, connection to the particular place, and a deep appreciation for the gift of life and the goodness of being.

In this chapter, I want to reflect on these and similar experiences, which I will call examples of *vitality*. Despite common misconceptions, these experiences are not frivolous diversions from more serious endeavors. Nor are they distractions from the pursuit of truth by some ideal and disembodied reason. Nor again are they an attempt to ignore or cheat death. They are, rather, one of the ways in which we can experience and understand our fittedness for this world and the goodness of being, and in which we can live life to the fullest in the shadow of our common doom.

The significance I will attach to experiences of vitality is neither idiosyncratic (they overlap major themes in Chinese philosophy and elsewhere) nor mere romanticism (contemporary psychology lends credence to these accounts). Nevertheless, vital experience has received relatively little attention from philosophers. The reasons for this lacuna are, no doubt, complex; but they are not entirely surprising. As Aldous Huxley observes, "in a world where education is predominantly verbal, highly educated people find it all but impossible to pay serious attention to anything but words and notions."[3] Philosophers, like the majority of academics, are for the most part intellectual creatures. And if continental philosophy has laid to rest Cartesian dualism with the rise of existential phenomenology and hermeneutics, the news seems not to have reached a great many philosophers. Most academics, after all, live the "life of the mind." And for many, if the body is not quite a prison-house it remains something of secondary import outside of discourse about race and gender, or about distinctly epicurean concerns.[4] A colleague once confided to me that he thought of his body mainly as tool to carry his brain from one room to another; and some futurists go so far as to anticipate with relish abandoning the body entirely and merging with machines—casting off our carnal shell like some vestigial relic of our animal origins, no longer adaptive in an increasingly information- and data-oriented world and superfluous to our post-human selves. Obviously, such hyper-intellectual dispositions color the sort of experiences and phenomena one finds philosophically interesting.

Moreover, as we have seen, philosophy has a remarkable interest, even an obsession, with mortality, finitude, and related concerns. From Plato to Heidegger, we hear the unceasing refrain, "*momento mori*." This fascination with death, including the question of what happens to us after we die, tends to interfere with giving carnal embodiment and vital life experiences the full attention they deserve; and it is easy to see how continental philosophy might find it difficult to think clearly about the experience of an active, physical life and the joys associated with it.

There has been a great deal of philosophizing about the quality of life *after* death, but perhaps we ought to be more concerned with the quality of life *before* death.[5]

In this chapter we will take a closer look at vitality, asking what such experiences teach us about ourselves and our world, and to what degree they might contribute to a wisdom that, without losing sight of reasons to despair, finds cause to embrace an outlook that is less relentlessly gloomy than that commonly on offer in philosophy.

## 2. Analogues of vitality

One way to get at vitality is to begin with more well-known accounts with which it shares some characteristics: Abraham Maslow's notion of "peak experience," Mihaly Csikszentmihalyi's account of "flow," the Taoist concept of *wu-wei*, and related Japanese adaptations of Tao in various *dō* (ways).[6] What all these concepts have in common—not to conflate them or engage in reductivism—is a way of being in which action flows effectively but without conscious effort and, as a consequence, one has the feeling of "naturalness" or being in harmony with the world.

### 2.1 Flow

Flow, for example, is the experience of being deeply engaged in an activity in which "a person's body or mind is stretched. . . in a voluntary effort to accomplish something difficult and worthwhile."[7] It generally occurs in an activity or undertaking that is neither too easy nor too difficult, but rather, following a kind of Goldilocks principle, "just right." The experience of performing well at one's limit, where one's skills are well-suited to the challenge at hand, can bring about a particular state that affects both the mind and the body. It also produces a very special sort of enjoyment, one that is qualitatively different from the pleasures and successes of everyday life. These are the magical moments of life when it seems that we are working in perfect synchrony with the world, as if we are doing precisely what we were meant to do.

Csikszentmihalyi observes that flow can come about from a very wide range of activities: almost any sport, many games, playing music, painting, prayer, reading, and even social conversation. And the characteristic joy associated with it seems to be correlated with all or most of the following: challenging activities that require some sort of skill; activities that require all of our attention or "psychic energy," so that they completely absorb us; situations over which, with proper training and discipline, one feels able to exercise some control; endeavors with clear goals and immediate feedback, which demand our focused concentration, to the point that we experience a "loss of self-consciousness and [a] participatory engagement with the activity and the world."[8]

Flow is an "autotelic" experience, that is to say it is an intrinsic good; it is its own end, without requiring another goal or reason to pursue it.[9] Aristotle saw such "ends-in-themselves" as central to understanding happiness or flourishing (*eudaimonia*). For most people, flow experiences stand in stark contrast to the highly routinized and largely monotonous nature of day-to-day life. Csikszentmihalyi observes, "One of the most ironic paradoxes of our time is this great availability of leisure that somehow fails to be translated into enjoyment."[10] However, some people are able to become better and better at achieving flow, benefiting from an acutely heightened awareness of and appreciation for the present moment. As in the experiences of "eternity" extoled by Kohák and Woolf, time seems to stop or radically slow. In such moments, the darkness between the stars is no longer menacing and one's anxieties and problems, even one's suffering, lose their importance. In such moments, nothing else seems to matter. Is it any surprise that such experiences are closely correlated with joy?

## 2.2 *Wu-wei*

The Taoist concept of *wu-wei*, or "action without action," also shares some characteristics with vitality. *Wu-wei* emphasizes the degree to which a person is acting in harmony with "heaven" or the cosmic order (*Tao*). Rather than focusing on individual challenge, *wu-wei* stresses "peaceful, relaxed absorption into something larger than the self," something closely identified with virtue and the good.[11] To achieve this state, it is, paradoxically, essential *not* to try. Needless to say, just exactly how one is supposed to achieve success through "trying not to try" is a vexing question, and different accounts offer different sorts of advice.[12]

For example, Confucius argues that it is only after a lifetime of focused, conscious effort—including scrupulous attention to detailed rituals circumscribing one's action in almost every imaginable sphere—that our desires and values will be ordered such that we can act virtuously without effort. Thus, in one famous passage of the *Analects*, we find the following:

> The Master said, "At fifteen, I had my mind bent on learning. At thirty, I stood firm. At forty, I had no doubts. At fifty, I knew the decrees of Heaven. At sixty, my ear was an obedient organ for the reception of truth. At seventy, I could follow what my heart desired, without transgressing what was right."[13]

On this account we can only trust effortless action if we have subdued, trained, and domesticated our "natural spontaneity," replacing it with a "cultured spontaneity." As in Aristotle, it is habituation that, eventually, makes virtuous action our "natural" disposition.

The *Zhuangzi* and *Laozi*—the foundational texts of Taoism—emphasize precisely the opposite strategy. Achieving effortless action and experiencing the loss of self in a greater whole come about not through conscious effort and striving, but rather through simply "letting go," emptying yourself so that the Way (*Tao*) can become manifest in you.[14]

> There are those who want to take the world and run it:
> I see they will not succeed.
> The world is a spiritual vessel and cannot be run.
> One who runs it destroys it; one who seizes it loses it . . .
> For this reason,
> The Sage rejects extremes,
> rejects excess,
> rejects excellence.[15]

Finally, Mencius offers a position between conscious, disciplined Confucian training and the Taoist celebration of natural flow. He suggests that the beginnings of virtue are in us naturally as "seeds" that we must help to grow: "the heart of compassion is the germ of benevolence; the heart of shame, of dutifulness; the heart of courtesy and modesty, of observance of the rites; the heart of right and wrong, of wisdom."[16] He agrees with Laozi that virtue is in us by nature, but asserts that its initial form is inchoate and in need of development. Thus, he agrees with Confucius that at least some degree of growth or transformation is necessary for us to arrive at the point where we can fully trust our inclinations and act spontaneously. It is only when the seeds of virtue have sprouted and grown that we serve Heaven and can allow our spontaneity completely free reign.

Whether we are speaking of flow, or *wu-wei*, or other similar accounts, what these experiences have in common is a type of action that is somehow both effortless and focused, one that brings about the loss of self and the feeling of participation in something larger, and which gives rise to a particular form of joy or contentment. However, while flow is possible in many activities, the flow of solving a mathematical proof and the flow of good conversation over good food are not quite the same; and the flow of trail running in the foothills near my home is, despite similarities to the first two cases, different again. Each of these activities—their respective effects on the body and the mind, the sort of engagement they elicit, and so forth—leads to a different sort of experience, even if all are done with *wu-wei* or flow.

"Vitality," then, is a subcategory of flow or *wu-wei* that is distinguished by, among other things, a particular sort of active and bodily engagement with the world. It is not unconnected to flow, but a specific manifestation of it. Vitality is not limited to stereotypically vigorous activities such as running, hiking, swimming, and the like—although those remain, in a sense, archetypal examples. Csikszentmihalyi is clear that one can achieve flow through the *vita activa* or the *vita contemplativa*.[17] Thus, in drawing our attention to vitality and the vigorous activities that characterize it, I do not intend to disparage other manifestations of flow—for example, the flow possible in music, or cooking, or contemplation. Rather, I hope to draw our attention to what our somatic engagement with the material world can teach us, and to highlight the virtues of a certain form of *vita activa* to those who may be more naturally inclined to the *vita contemplativa*.

Naturally, the body is never fully disengaged in any activity. As Maurice Merleau-Ponty, Richard Schusterman, and others have clearly demonstrated, we are embodied beings through and through; and there is a somatic component to all the multifarious aspects of our being, right down to our thinking, knowing, perceiving, and interpreting. From vigorous physical exertion to seemingly passive endeavors such as the appreciation of art or music, the body remains the inescapable "background" against which all our various modes of being unfold.[18] Therefore, the relevant distinction cannot be one of activity and passivity, or of embodiment and disembodiment, whatever the latter might mean. Rather, vitality must be distinguished by association with a certain type of activity and engagement. For while the body is always engaged, it is easier to experience vitality in some activities and more difficult, often *much* more difficult, in others. Reading about excellent food and wine is different from consuming excellent food and wine; and contemplating a mountain while enjoying that food in a valley café is different from experiencing it as you climb it.[19]

My argument is that vitality—overlooked or misunderstood by philosophy—is a chiasmus where materiality and meaning intersect and inform each other. It discloses certain truths about the world in an exemplary way, truths that shed light on the meaningfulness of life and the goodness of being in a world marked by finitude and destruction. Consequently, vitality has much to teach us about the reasons for gloom or joy in our lives.

## 3. Vitality proper

Philosophy, it turns out, has not been entirely indifferent to vitality. For example, Michel Serres's idiosyncratic and challenging work touches, in several places, on issues related to the topic.[20] Perhaps this is because Serres's own life was lived with a commitment to both the "life of the mind," as an author and professor of philosophy, as well as the "active" life, first as a young bargeman, then as a naval officer and sailor, and later as an amateur mountaineer.

> No seated professor taught me productive work; the only kind of any worth, whereas my gymnastics teachers, coaches and, later, my guides inscribed its very conditions into my muscles and bones. Do you want to write, do research, live a work-producing life? Follow their advice and example, namely, that nothing can withstand training, the ascesis of which repeats rather unnatural gestures. . .

> and makes effortless the necessary virtues of concentration. . . courage. . . patience. . . the mastery of anxiety. . . .[21]

This commitment to both the body and the mind attunes Serres to the phenomenon I am calling vitality. He recounts, for example, "rare" occasions when, climbing or otherwise engaged in vigorous activity, he became surprised by a "physically supernatural joy" in which "life superlives"[22]:

> I was suddenly inundated, filled, saturated, satiated, flooded over, thunderstruck with such lofty elation, continuous and sovereign, that I thought my chest was bursting, that my entire body was levitating, present in all the space of the world entirely present in me. Pleroma of exultation. There was nothing artificial in that experience, since it occurred at times when I was eating little and drinking only water, and since all my attention, nervous and muscular, was required so as not to fall: thus the ecstasy arose during an active period when reality, hard, was mobilizing the entire body.[23]

This, it seems to me, is a textbook account of the experience of vitality. One can imagine Serres sounding one of Whitman's "barbaric yawps" over the roof of the world. The activity mobilized his whole being, carnal and cognitive (though not abstract or analytical). He was completely absorbed in the task, which required intimate interaction with what he calls "the hard" (*le dur*)—that is, the primary, sensuous, material givenness of the world. The experience was both a kind of ecstatic self-transcending ("pleroma of exultation") and, at the same time, grounding ("present in all the space of the world entirely present in me"). Finally, the experience came upon him ("inundated, saturated. . . flooded over, thunderstruck"); he did not cause the experience but was overtaken by it.

Although not all instances of vitality require vigorous bodily activity—in this case, mountain climbing—such examples do offer us a certain kind of paradigm. Here again, we may come up against ingrained assumptions. It is easy, perhaps too easy, for intellectuals to think of athletes in casually dismissive terms. Today, few people would express unvarnished contempt for a skilled woodworker, recognizing the complex intelligence and disciplined skill necessary for her work—a different set of intelligences and skills from the philosopher or poet, but admirable in their own right. But introduce an intellectual to a footballer, sailor, or climber and the reaction is likely to be quite different. "Just a dumb jock." "He should use his head for something other than getting hit." "She's got a death wish."

I suspect the carelessness of such criticisms is, in part, the result of a lingering mind-body dualism that errs both in distinguishing too sharply between the "body" and the "mind," and in failing to recognize that the body—the carnal and somatic aspects of our lived embodiment—chooses, thinks, and possesses its own brand of wisdom. This is not to lionize the carnal or somatic over the intellectual or cognitive. Nor is it to deny that there are "dumb jocks" and young men (and women) on the fast track to early death as a result of "testosterone poisoning." There are myriad examples of both types. However, hasty generalization risks occluding individuals and groups that do not fit the type. The silent, introverted, cleaver-wielding fellow cutting steaks at the local market—denigrated as an oaf by his bourgeois patrons—could be a Taoist butcher.[24] Just so, not every fighter is a dumb brute, not every ultrarunner is a self-loathing masochist, and not every climber a suicidal romantic; some of these people are something else entirely.

Françoise Dastur's otherwise excellent *How Are We to Confront Death?* veers at times toward related caricatures. She thinks vital activity—naming "rock climbing, parachuting, and solitary navigation or exploration," among others—is not fundamentally different from drug abuse and other forms of refusing social integration: "The same lack of being is experienced in the two cases, for which one seems to compensate by heroically proving one's existence to oneself or that one tries to escape by neutralizing the feeling of physical limits."[25] In other words, it is a "stratagem that is hatched in order to escape death"—which is, of course, ultimately impossible—rather than a "true assumption of finitude."[26] On this account, the climber or the solo, long-distance sailor is seeking to deny her mortality by force of will and application of skill. By placing herself at risk of death, she believes that she can escape or cheat death. This, Dastur claims, is nothing but an "illusory immortality" based on a denial of our nature: our embodiment, our time-boundedness, our finitude.[27]

But while any response to Dastur must begin by acknowledging that there are indeed athletes and adventurers that fit this type, her diagnosis is an extreme over-generalization. Dastur herself notes that there is a paradox at play here: it is precisely in societies in which life is by and large secure that individuals feel the need to risk life and limb in "leisure" activities.[28] They are in search of "powerful feelings. . . of plenitude" which are no longer possible in their overprotected and over-managed lives. These experiences of plenitude—which seem to map nicely on to Serres's description of his own experience as well as some of Csikszentmihalyi's examples of flow—"offer the possibility of restoring meaning and intensity to life."[29] So even people who engage in these vital activities with an inadequate appreciation of their own creatureliness are seeking, in some measure, meaning. Surely then, persons who *are* in touch with the truth of their own embodiment—its powers and limitations, its finitude, its inevitable decline and death—could live these experiences in a different way.

I'm not sure about Dastur's experience, but my own suggests that people who immerse themselves deeply in such activities are often under no illusions in this regard. It is true that people with moderate amounts of experience may be deceived by the feelings of control that accompany flow, and that the addictive nature of flow, acknowledged by Csikszentmihalyi and others, can lead a person to bad decisions. It's a well-worn observation that there is a dangerous period in one's development, when one has enough skill to get into trouble but not enough to get out; and at such times there is a real danger of underestimating risk or overestimating ability. However, if one climbs, or skis, or pilots a wing for any period of time, if one is immersed in these cultures and activities, the reality of death is generally well-appreciated. As a young climber, my first encounters with death took place in one of its more shocking forms: as it struck people in the full bloom of health (unlike the later deaths of friends toward the end of a long life) and in a manner that could have been avoided (unlike, for example, an unforeseeable cancer). Few long-term climbers I know confuse the experience of flow with omnipotence; and while all of them take calculated risks, sorrowful personal experience means that few think they can "cheat" death. This, paradoxically, may be an example of precisely the sort of clarity Dastur urges us to seek, one based on the assumption rather than the denial of mortality.

Our being-toward-death is also a *death-not-yet*, something experienced powerfully in moments of vitality. We cannot cheat death; but we should not, as a consequence, turn around and cheat life. The idea that we ought not climb because, by staying at home and avoiding risky behaviors, we could thereby avoid death is nothing more than a different manifestation of precisely the illusion Dastur seeks to overcome.[30] We cannot avoid death by avoiding risk. And the conclusion one ought to draw from that fact is that we ought to live vibrantly and vitally while we can. Everyone wants to "live fully"; but, the fact is, every life is full. The question is: *full with what*?

Perhaps the vibrancy of life is enhanced, not just by flow, but by a bit of well-calculated risk. Freud may have overstated the case when he wrote that "[our conventional attitude] towards death has a powerful effect on our lives. Life is impoverished, it loses its interest, when the highest stake in the game of living, life itself, may not be risked"; but he was directly on point when he developed this line of thinking:

> Our emotional ties, the unbearable intensity of our grief, make us disinclined to court danger for ourselves and for those who belong to us. We dare not contemplate a great many undertakings which are dangerous but in fact indispensable, such as attempts at artificial flight, expeditions to distant countries, or experiments with explosive substances. We are paralyzed by the thought of who is to take the son's place with his mother, the husband's with the wife, the father's with his children, if disaster should occur. Thus the tendency to exclude death from our calculations in life brings in its train many other renunciations and exclusions.[31]

Odd examples like the "indispensability" of "experiments with explosive substances" aside, the point is that the wager of one's life runs a risk and sacrifices goods either way. Either one clings to shore and wins a chance at a longer life—but only a chance, and at the risk of losing life's vibrancy—or one pushes the boat out to sea and wins a chance at a certain kind of vibrancy at the risk of a shorter life. Leopardi, whose depressive reflections we encountered in the first chapter, felt that "Life must be vital, that is, truly life; otherwise death incomparably surpasses it in merit."[32] And, after all, no life can avoid danger entirely; that's the way of things.

Thus, it might be worth considering what goods can be bought at the price of a bit of danger and discomfort. Csikszentmihalyi's research on flow suggests "the traits that mark an autotelic personality are most clearly revealed by people who seem to enjoy situations that ordinary persons would find unbearable."[33] Of course, just what constitutes "danger and discomfort" will be relative to the person in question; and if there is a certain correlation between risk and reward, this is not to suggest that vitality is confined to solely to so-called "extreme" activities. True, vitality requires active, bodily effort engaged with the material world; but one need not engage in death-defying antics or Hemingwayesque pursuits to experience vitality.[34] Examples like sailing, climbing, and solo travel in the wilderness pop up frequently in the literature; but Csikszentmihalyi, Serres, Snyder, and others place such activities on a continuum that includes more mundane pastimes—from easy hiking, to yogic practices, to intellectual pursuits. That is to say, the difference between flow and vitality are differences of degree, not of kind.

Thus, the emphasis on strenuous activity, and even a measure of risk, is not a manifestation of some kind of virile elitism. It is, rather, a reminder that there is a difference between pleasure and flourishing, happiness, or enjoyment. The latter are entirely possible even without the former, something that is very often overlooked in popular accounts. As Huxley's *Brave New World* illustrates—with an unnerving degree of prescience, given the contemporary cultural landscape in the industrialized North—a high degree of pleasure is perfectly compatible with an utter lack of joy. Indeed, not only is joy independent of pleasure, it is compatible with suffering. This distinction is essential. Huxleyan "soma" is an addictive drug that aims to produce pleasure, but which utterly fails to produce joy. Vitality, in contrast, produces joy, even in endeavors that require suffering.[35] The analogy of vitality to drug use—whether by Dastur or others—is not, therefore, particularly apt. Vitality is addictive not because it is a drug, but because it is a good.

People enjoy, and ought to enjoy, effort and struggle, which teach us important things about ourselves and about the world. More, such experiences have significant benefits beyond the delight they bring when achieved with vitality or flow. During the Second World War something unusual was noticed about the survivors of torpedoed ships: among the survivors of the initial explosion, it was often the case that younger and fitter men succumbed in the water, while older men survived. Kurt Hahn and Lawrence Holt became convinced that this counterintuitive statistic was the result of a younger generation that lacked the grit of the older. Having never experienced deep fatigue, cold, or hunger, having never faced adversity in circumstances from which it was unclear how, or indeed if, they could extract themselves, the younger sailors lost hope and, then, their lives. Hahn and Holt responded by founding a school to form young people in challenging circumstances, outdoors and in the elements. They were convinced that there are concrete benefits to "living dangerously." When Nietzsche made a similar appeal in *The Gay Science*, it was, as elsewhere in his work, largely rhetorical—a call to self-overcoming in the face of accreted tradition. But while Nietzsche's own dangerous living was primarily intellectual—notwithstanding a youthful stint in the army and long strolls in the alpine topography around Sils Maria—his entreaty to dangerous living could, and should, be undertaken literally as well as metaphorically.[36]

## 4. The body and interpretation

If the active body teaches us something, it does not do so via logical syllogism or propositional argument. The lessons of vitality may be direct and inescapable, but their full meaning is often mysterious, and our grasp or understanding of them an ongoing process. Because vitality does not lend itself to demonstration, it is best understood with hermeneutic rather than analytic techniques. Understanding the experience of vitality is going to be more like interpreting a great novel than it is like proving a mathematical hypothesis or sequencing a genome. However, because traditional hermeneutic accounts are rooted in the metaphor of the text—the conviction that interpretation is fundamentally like "reading" a "text," even when the text is metaphorical—we are going to need alternative hermeneutic resources to explore the experience of vitality.

Grasping the meaning of a text is complicated by polysemy (words do not have a single, clear meaning), by its open character (no single account exhausts the meaning of a text), and by its ambiguity (one can give a more plausible interpretation of *Moby Dick*, but there is no proof that can definitively decide in favor of one plausible interpretation over another). However, the core of hermeneutics and interpretation cannot be reduced to polysemy, or the surplus of meaning, or ambiguity; it is, rather, the inescapable fact of perspective itself, the fact that we always have a point of view on the world. That point of view may evolve or shift;

we may abandon a particular point of view entirely. However, when we do so it is always to occupy another point of view. The necessity of a point of view itself is utterly inescapable. There is no innocent eye, no view from nowhere from which we might escape the hermeneutic circle. Other things flow from this primary hermeneutic insight, but perspectivism is the ground of it all. How is the body a perspective? There is, certainly, the obvious fact that we experience the world from a particular position which reveals some things and conceals others. For example, looking west rather than east at a given moment. But the perspectival nature of our somatic experience goes much deeper, all the way down to our perception of, and sensuous engagement with, the world.[37]

Distinguishing between narrative and nature, imagination and incarnation, is not meant to imply a mind-body dualism. We are both embodied mind and thinking body. The miracle of the body—or at least one bodily miracle—is that it is the point of mediation between nature and culture, the physical and the psychical, materiality and meaning. Serres describes this somatic nexus in terms of a "black box": "To its left, or before it, there is the world. To its right, or after it, travelling across certain circuits, there is what we call information. The energy of things goes in. . . Information comes out, even meaning. . . . Before the box, the hard; after it, the soft."[38] By "the hard" Serres means to indicate the direct, primary, sensuous, material givenness of the world—reality independent of human interests, or, as deconstructive hermeneutics would have it, reality "as if I were dead."[39] "The soft," in contrast, is the sphere of culture, language, and other human accounts of reality. The body mediates—a fundamentally hermeneutic operation—the exchange between the hard and the soft; and, crucially, it helps to effect the process by which the hard becomes soft and, perhaps more surprisingly, the soft becomes hard. But if the body transforms reality, mediating between matter and meaning, Serres is concerned that we have placed an inappropriate emphasis on softening (language, culture, the human) that obscures the significance of the hard (the given, nature, the inhuman): "when [philosophies] come across an object, they change it, by sleight of hand, into a relationship, language or representation."[40]

The concern here is not one of purity or contamination, as in some postmodern philosophies. We cannot work our way around or back to some purely hard reality, which is always-already a mixed affair. Thus, the rhetoric of the hard and soft is didactic rather than dualist. The issue is the overemphasis on the soft aspects of reality: on language, the symbolic, the constructed aspects of reality. The "first cogito" of our bodily subjectivity and insertion into the world has been obscured by the "second cogito" of language, when our understanding ought to draw on both.[41] It is not that we ought to reject the soft, but rather that we ought to remember the hard. We should not be so quick to abandon the wood for the word or the mountain for the metaphor.

What does this have to do with vitality? And with despair? Simply this. Hermeneutics is the method or practice we use to understand the wagers we make on meaning, including the meaningfulness or meaninglessness of the world. Generally, hermeneutics is thought of in terms analogous to reading a text, which helps to reveal important truths about the world. But vitality reminds us that the body itself is hermeneutic; it too shapes the way we experience and understand the world, and therefore the things we find valuable or meaningful. And it does so in a manner that is fundamentally different from language- and text-based hermeneutic accounts. As a consequence, the body reveals things that textual hermeneutics does not.[42]

Consider, for example, Annie Dillard's account of a girl, blind from birth, having her sight restored. What would it be like to see for the first time? On first seeing a tree, the girl described it as "full of light," awestruck by the extravagance, beauty, and wonder of the illuminated world.[43] Dillard herself works at trying to see the world in this way, prior to the influence of her common assumptions and presuppositions, with the wonder and gratitude of new eyes; but her senses, long habituated to more pragmatic concerns, have lost the innocence of first contact. Then, with a very *wu-wei* insight, she realizes that naive sight will never come from painstaking observation or effort; only emptying oneself and letting go makes it possible. And, eventually, after turning to the world without expectation or demand, "some undeniably new spirit roared down the air, bowled [her] over, and turned on the lights."[44] She sees with new eyes a cedar tree "transfigured, each cell buzzing with flame"[45] and "charged like wings beating praise."[46]

If we listen to the body, listen to our senses, listen to our active and vital engagement with the world, what might we find? What might we discover about our body, about the world, and about the relationship between them?

# 5. The wisdom of the body

So, the body, including the body in vitality, teaches us; and the type of understanding we associate with it is something like hermeneutic understanding, albeit of a different kind. But if the body is always engaged, and interpretation of some sort is always going on, this is not to say that the operations of the 'black box' unfold in a uniform manner in all of the body's various activities and engagements with the world. Different activities, and different ways of conducting similar activities, engage the body in different ways. The cords of vitality—to use another of Serres's tropes—connect us to both soft relations and hard reality, and they reveal certain truths about the world in an exemplary manner.[47]

## 5.1 The unity of experience

Merleau-Ponty, Shusterman, and others have demonstrated at length the degree to which our immersion in the world—evident in experiences of flow or vitality—is one of undifferentiated perception that does not distinguish between the five classical senses.[48] However, because reflection tends to break perception into constituent parts for purposes of emphasis or analysis, the fact is that we often miss this primary unity of experience. As a consequence, we are apt to overlook or forget its significance. Take taste for example, which is perhaps the most obviously synesthetic or conesthetic of the senses. When "tasting" it is difficult to disentangle taste, smell, and touch; the flavor, the aromas, and the texture are more or less indistinguishable in our primary experience of food.[49] To say that we taste food—if by "taste" we mean something independent of smell, touch, and so on—is at best an abstraction, a selective filtering of a more comprehensive primary experience as it moves through the black box. Such abstraction can serve a purpose, as when an oenophile wants to describe the complexity of oak, berries, or tobacco she smells in the aroma of a Bordeaux from the body of the wine she feels once she takes a sip; but that same abstraction is misleading if it is taken to express a primary or more veridical perception of the world.

This undifferentiated immersion of the world is inescapable, and least able to be ignored, in vitality. As Serres testifies, in vitality the "entire body" is "inundated, filled, saturated, satiated, flooded over." It is precisely the absorbing nature of vital experience that keeps us from focusing on a single sense and reveals our primary, global, sensuous immersion in the world. In vitality, our engagement with the world is more immediate: pre-reflective, pre-analytic, and pre-skeptical; we see things without the distortion or coloring of our habitual vision. Nevertheless, our new perception, like our habitual perception, always already stylizes or frames the world, only differently. So, to perceive the world in vitality is to actually experience a different world (or, perhaps better, to experience the world differently).

The unity of our experience is not only a function of our primordial perception; it is also a function of the world. And flow, wu-wei, and vitality are, again, the clearest testament to this. Rather than giving us discrete phenomena—some particular slice of the world—vitality delivers us over to the world itself, as a whole. Consider, by way of analogy, Proust's theory of voluntary and involuntary memory, famously captured in his account of a *madeleine* dipped in tea, a stumble on the cobblestones outside the Guermantes's mansion, and similar experiences rooted in bodily, sensuous engagement with the world. Voluntary memory is accomplished through conscious effort and brings to mind discrete facts, images, or events. Involuntary memory—the sort of memory awakened by the *madeleine*—operates not by conscious effort but rather by letting go; and it delivers not discrete phenomena but an entire world, the global sense of a place (e.g., one's childhood home in Combray, or the baptistery of St. Mark's in Venice). Rather than the resistance we experience in the effort of conscious memory, involuntary memory is experienced naturally and spontaneously, without effort. Consequently, the experience is one of vivification rather than resistance, of the mind being "overtaken" and of an "essence. . . called into being."[50] Here memory imposes itself upon us rather than being called into being in a narrative structured, consciously or unconsciously, by our will. The experience is "indisputable."[51] In a parallel manner, vitality delivers over an entire world, not one of imagination or memory but that of some particular place in the present moment. And, again like involuntary memory, vitality connects us not to a component or object in the world, or even to a combination of objects, but to the world itself, before we move to describe it or analyze it—phenomenologically, psychologically, physiologically, or otherwise.[52]

## 5.2 Remembering hard reality

During much of our sojourn in the world, the inflexible demands of hard reality are well in the background of our experience. Technology allows us to be remarkably sedentary and disconnected from interactions with what Serres calls "hard" reality. This overlooked but essential substratum, travelling under the name "wildness," was also the object of Thoreau's desire:

> Think of our life in nature—daily to be shown matter, to come in contact with it—rocks, trees, wind on our cheeks! the solid earth! the actual world! the common sense! Contact! Contact! Who are we? where are we?[53]

And, elsewhere:

> Let us settle ourselves, and work and wedge our feet downward through the mud and slush of opinion, and prejudice, and tradition, and delusion, and appearance, that alluvion which covers the globe, through Paris and London, through New York and Boston and Concord, through church and state, through poetry and philosophy and religion, till we come to a hard bottom and rocks in place, which we can call *reality*, and say, This is, and no mistake. . . .[54]

Today, however, our remarkable success at bending reality to our will means that we encounter reality to which we must accede and accommodate ourselves less and less often.

Of course, mortality ensures that we are all eventually confronted with the hardness of reality; and events like crop failures, pandemics, and earthquakes occasionally remind us that there are things we cannot control. Nevertheless, at least for those of us in the global north, nature has come more and more under our influence; and it is far too easy to fool ourselves into believing we are the masters of reality. We are largely insulated from hunger; and we can opt to eat almost anything at almost any time, regardless of the season of the year or the bioregion in which we reside. The natural rhythms of summer and winter, day and night, and even youth and age, mean relatively little to us in terms of restricting our activities. Even people of humble means live with comforts far surpassing those enjoyed by kings and emperors of old. With such extravagance, it's not surprising that we find ourselves restless, impatient, and dissatisfied when the world *does* frustrate our desires. I'm not suggesting all these developments are regrettable; but is it any wonder that we've become—in a felicitous turn of phrase given Serres's work—soft?

In contrast, the sort of physical activity that elicits vitality is uncompromising in its honesty; it is a mode of engagement with the world that unfolds without distraction or subterfuge. We can be fooled by many things in the world, and we deceive ourselves about many more. But bend to lift a weight, whether a barbell or a sack of grain, and you will find that "two hundred pounds is always two hundred pounds."[55] There is an unflinching, merciless, direct honesty in the hard. This is the "iron law" of the "thing itself" and what it teaches us; "the thing itself. . . alone, commands [rather than offering an] opinion."[56] But, curiously perhaps, we may come to find that the insistence of the real is something to appreciate, and even desire:

> Here we feel not the penalty of Adam,
> The seasons' difference; as, the icy fang
> And churlish chiding of the winter's wind,
> Which, when it bites and blows upon my body,
> Even till I shrink with cold, I smile and say
> "This is no flattery: these are counsellors
> That feelingly persuade me what I am."
> Sweet are the uses of adversity. . .[57]

This inflexibility forces us to accommodate ourselves to reality rather than the other way around. Take, by way of illustration, the example with which I began this chapter. Traversing the Cathedral cirque I was forced to accept, rather than alter, hard realities. Accept a long day with little food or water, rather than being able to consume anything that struck my fancy, whether or not I was hungry. Forced to accept the weather—bitter cold in the early morning darkness and intense, high-altitude sun with a strong wind in the afternoon—rather than easily adjusting the climate to my liking. And, most strikingly, forced to actually conform my body to hard reality in the act of ascending: a climber ascends rock by inserting fingers, hands, fists, and feet into cracks in the stone, employing a variety of techniques to torque, expand, or otherwise modify the shape of the limb to fit the available space in the fissure. Here, the climber literally reshapes the body in order to accept and adapt to what is given by hard reality, an act of carnal anamorphosis reveals a path upward that is utterly closed, invisible even, to those unwilling or unable to so adapt.[58] Finally, without intending to exaggerate or dramatize the situation, there were the hard realities of gravity and physics that I could not change, along with their potential consequences. And, consequences, Serres notes, are another distinction between the hard and the soft. When dealing with hard reality, we must remember that "minor causes" can have "great effects": "beyond the port: shipwreck for the smallest error; once past the mountain hut: at the slightest mistake you will fall."[59] As a consequence, "you begin to live another way."[60] In everyday life, increasingly characterized by softened forms of reality, things matter in a very different sense: ". . .a thousand things without importance are neither obligatory nor punished here. You do not have to pay for every detail of common life. A hundred spaces beyond the law let you, do, say, or get through as you wish."[61] If one lies about one's experience or abilities at a cocktail party, the consequences of being caught out are relatively minor; but make that same error on a mountain, or out at sea, and the consequences are likely to be immediate and possibly dire. Soft realities compromise, forgive mistakes, and in general cushion the blows of fate; hard reality insists, punishes miscalculations and mistakes. Nevertheless, we often discover that we find this reality beautiful, that its beauty is enhanced, rather than diminished, by its harshness, its uncompromising hardness. Here is something bigger and more permanent and more mysterious than the concerns that characterizes the world of our narrow self-interest.

As C.S. Lewis reminds us, whether we despair of reality has much to do with what we expect of reality, what we think it owes us.[62] When we think we are owed something—health, longer life, success, and so on—we are, as you would expect, deeply wounded if we do not receive it. Unrealistic expectations about the world are a major source of dissatisfaction, and a major cause for despair. But in a world increasingly characterized by abstraction—whether literary, philosophical, scientific, economic, or otherwise—vitality cleaves close to the concrete, the local, the physical, and the fullness of experience. Its metaphysic is elemental, composed of flesh, earth, water, and wind.[63] Vitality puts us in touch with the world and reminds us that in many ways we must accommodate ourselves to it rather than assuming it will accommodate itself to us. This is an important reminder that the world does not revolve around us and our desires; there are other interests at play, forces both beautiful and terrible. And wisdom dictates that we adapt ourselves to this reality.

## 5.3 The thinking body

One of the more provocative insights to arise from careful reflection on vitality is that we must recognize the ways in which the body itself "thinks," "knows," "understands," and, indeed, possesses a kind of "wisdom." Such claims fly in the face of 2500 years of philosophy—at least in the West—which insists that thinking is done with the mind, and done best precisely when freed from the distractions of the body. The body, insists Plato, is a "prison house" for the soul, and is an "obstacle when one associates with it in the search for knowledge"; and Descartes distinguishes between the *res cogitans* of the mind and the *res extensia* of the body, prioritizing the former over the latter.[64] But Chinese and Japanese philosophy have pursued the topic of a thinking or understanding body for thousands of years. And contemporary research in neurobiology and psychology supports this work, articulating the various ways in which the body chooses or acts prior to deliberation, or even conscious attention.[65]

One of the first things vitality teaches us is that the *body* knows and understands the world, and that, at least in some cases, bodily understanding is superior to rational understanding. As Serres suggests: "Go, run, faith will come to you, the body will sort things out."[66] And the body sorts things out best when the mind—analysis and conscious reflection—gets out of its way: "To inhabit your body better, forget it, at least in part. . . ."[67] In certain instances, insight or success hinges, *pace* Plato, on quieting the mind rather than escaping the body. The forgetfulness that Serres speaks of is not an escape from carnality, but rather a manner of being embodied that allows the body to act without the mind second-guessing or micromanaging the situation. True, bodily understanding can err, and it is certainly not appropriate in all circumstances; but when it comes to living, it may be that we overvalue lucidity and, consequently, fail to appreciate the "chiaroscuro" of understanding.[68]

One famous account of insight-in-activity is the story of "Cook Ting" in the *Chuang Tzu*, one of the canonical texts of Taoism. Cook Ting is called on to butcher an ox, and does so with such marvelous skill and grace that all are astonished. Ting confesses that—because he does not actually cut, hack, or otherwise force his will on the carcass, but rather inserts the blade following the natural spaces between the joints—his blades have not required sharpening for over nineteen years. He meets no resistance when performing his work, but "the flesh falls apart like a lump of earth falling to the ground."[69] Here, and in instances documented by Csikszentmihalyi and others, success comes from not overthinking things, but from letting the body act naturally. And such understanding has implications far beyond butchery or sport; as Lord Wen Hui exclaims after watching Cook Ting work, "I have learned how to live life fully."[70]

## 5.4 Experience and reality are trustworthy

Thus, another thing vitality teaches us is that the world is, to a significant degree, trustworthy. Here the foil for vitality is found in overblown instances of the "hermeneutics of suspicion" or in forms of skepticism suggesting that our senses, our bodies, and reality itself are fundamentally untrustworthy and lead us into error. Suspicion has, to be sure, proved enormously productive, whether we look at scientific skepticism and the demand for replicability and experimental proof, or the work of Nietzsche, Marx, and Freud chipping away at accreted dogmatisms masquerading as objective fact. The problem arises when certain strains of hermeneutics take "avoid error," rather than "seek the truth," to be the fundamental epistemological rule.[71] Avoiding error is not the goal, truth is. If all we do is tear down edifices of understanding with the wrecking ball of suspicion, all we are left with is a pile of rubble.

While truth is undoubtedly a moving target in the sense that it is structurally open-ended, and while our grasp of it is conditioned by our finitude and our hermeneutic prejudices, this need not imply that there is no truth, or that we cannot get closer to it. The hermeneutics of suspicion must, as Paul Ricoeur noted, be supplemented by a hermeneutics of affirmation. Taken together, suspicion and affirmation operate to bring us closer to the truth in an ongoing negotiation between critique and conviction. Our beliefs must be subject to critique; but after the critique we must affirm belief again, whether it is the original belief, a modified version of it, or an entirely new belief. This process is open-ended, so that each stage represents a second, or third, or fourth or nth belief or "naiveté."

Because it engages us with hard reality "directly" (i.e., without undue suspicion), and because its actions in this mode are often successful, fulfilling, and beautiful, vitality—a form of carnal hermeneutics—reminds us that we should not entirely repudiate our initial trust in the world. While our senses are limited, our perspectives are finite, and our understanding shaped by hermeneutic biases, reality is intelligible. This naive somatic faith in reality has often been disparaged by philosophy, which has both underestimated the senses and overestimated reason. First, while it is true that our senses can and do deceive us, for every instance of seeing a stick "bend" when inserted in water, there are innumerable instances of our senses operating perfectly well. Moreover, embodied wisdom can, we've seen, grasp truths that reason tends to overlook. After all, reason—often lauded as that which corrects for our supposedly unreliable senses—is also capable of error. In fact, reason can often lead us astray, acting more like a press secretary seeking to justify actions or opinions than a disinterested scientist evaluating phenomena.[72] That our primary sensuous engagement with the world is so regularly accurate, and that rational abstractions about the world are at least sometimes in error, should win for the world and for our bodies at least a measure of our trust.

## 5.5 We belong

When Annie Dillard finally learned to empty herself and to let go, accommodating herself to the second sort of seeing, she found herself "ringing" or resonating with reality: "I had been my whole life a bell, and never known until at that moment I was lifted and struck."[73] In vital action we experience a world to which our bodies are well-adapted, a world for which we were made. This feeling of grateful belonging stands out in stark contrast to the expressions of unease, alienation, and absurdity so characteristic of contemporary philosophy.[74]

In vital action we experience a loss of self, which is the result of being completely engaged or absorbed in the activity. But the "self" that is lost here is the conscious, egoistic, monadic self, the self that makes efforts in order to accomplish things and be productive. What remains when the conscious self, concerned with acting on the world and achieving results, gives way? If the testimony of Laozi, Csikszentmihalyi, Serres, Dillard, and many others is to be believed, we find another self. A self more engaged and participatory, one that acts in and with the world rather than on it, one that delights in the process, the activity itself. The self of vital activity reveals that we are, at some fundamental existential level, a part of this world. It is not merely that we have a home here, but that we belong here in the deepest ontological sense.[75] Not surprisingly, the mood (*Stimmung*) associated with vitality is not *Angst*, but joy.[76] "The world is beautiful," says a fellow traveler to Nikos Kazantzakis, "Even if I were certain I was going to heaven. . . I would pray God to let me go by the longest possible route."[77]

When we are in the grip of vitality, we become detached from both the weight of the past and anxiety over the future, caught up in a moment—however long it may last—that is self-sufficient, fully justified, and profoundly good.[78] People experiencing vitality often speak of the manner in which time is distorted, seeming to slow down or even to stop. They testify to a carnal experience of eternity, in line with experiences described by Woolf as "moments of being" or by Kohák as "eternity" erupting in the everyday. No one reflecting in the wake of such an experience curses the world, even with its cruelty and inexplicable suffering, even with the frustration of our hopes and the inevitability of death. On the contrary, in a moment of vitality, and in its afterglow, the most common and most appropriate response is that of exuberant joy and deep gratitude.

Like moments of joy, moments of vitality triumph over mortality. Not because death is defeated but because, as Proust has it, death becomes a "matter of indifference."[79] This is fundamentally different than Heidegger's analysis of concern (*Sorge*), which submerges us in the world in a way that allows us to avoid or forget of our being-toward-death.[80] The body in vitality is not forgetful of death, nor is it dismissive of death: certain manifestations of vitality presuppose an acute sensitivity to that eventuality, and the possibility of hastening it. Rather, the vital body is indifferent to death, because it experiences and affirms the fundamental and ineradicable goodness of life, of existing, and of being, insights that have been occluded in much contemporary philosophy.

It is all too easy to fixate on the ways in which the world fails to measure up to what we would wish, to lament mortality, finitude, loss, and every other sort of limitation on our hopes and desires. Viewed through the lens of Western hyper-individualism, it seems clear that the world is fundamentally hostile and antagonistic to my being. But the experience of vitality, like related experiences of joy and wonder, tells us a different story. "Heaven," says Thoreau, "is under our feet as well as over our heads."[81] That is to say it is here, in this world, if only we have eyes to see. The glory of being shines forth in all things. We simply need to know how to look, or, in the case of vitality, how to let go and move.[82]

# Chapter 4

# A Twilight Hope

## 1. The logic and the temptation of hopelessness

We've seen that, however dark our circumstances may seem, joy remains an omnipresent possibility. Whether by attending to the extraordinary that percolates within the everyday, or expressing gratitude for the fact that things are rather than are-not, or achieving flow, we can experience joy and gladness even in the "ruthless furnace of this world." But, responds the saturnine philosopher, such moments offer nothing more than a fleeting respite from the doom that will eventually close over us, and emphasizing them or seeking to cultivate them is nothing but a thinly veiled escapism. Our situation, in the end, is hopeless.

Recall the litany of despair we considered in the first chapter: personal experiences of vulnerability, loneliness, anxiety, and depression; pervasive suffering; the looming and inescapable threat of death; the myriad evils that humans inflict upon each other; the erosion of cosmic doom in the expanding and indifferent darkness between the stars. While our situation may admit the possibility of joy—moments of happiness before the curtain falls—it seems to preclude hope, insofar as hope is oriented toward the future and in that future the curtain will, inevitably, fall. Hope depends on a future that is uncertain in many respects but, disturbingly, least uncertain with respect to loss, suffering, death, dissolution, and the other horsemen of despair, which number well more than four.

How can a sanguine disposition—or even a melancholic disposition that finds some relief in moments of glory—be justified in the face of a destiny in which loss seems to have the last word? In such circumstances, isn't hope a flight from reality? The last refuge of minds too weak to accept the world as it is: chaotic, threatening, and utterly indifferent to our desires? A rickety crutch for those who believe—not only without justification, but generally without even an attempt at justification—that "all shall be well"?[1] Surely it is obvious that, in the end, most of our hopes—for justice, for a better life, for more life—are frustrated. Even if we are lucky enough to experience a hope fulfilled, when hope and history rhyme the consonance is only temporary.[2]

Certainly some forms of "hope" are open to such criticism. But a philosophically robust notion of hope reveals something distinct from, and in some cases at odds with, the dispositions or attitudes that are at the root of these critiques: desire, optimism, wish-fulfillment, cheerfulness, confidence, and so forth. If hope is to be compelling, it must be something more than naive optimism that things will work out in the manner we desire, because the most superficial reflection reveals that such a disposition is unwarranted: people don't always recover from illness; injustices multiply; good people suffer; and evil goes unpunished. As Roger Scruton notes, "the belief that human beings can either foresee the future or control it to their own advantage ought not to have survived an attentive reading of the *Iliad*, still less the Old Testament."[3] But, perhaps surprisingly, Scruton avers, in the very course of recommending a salutary dose of pessimism, "I don't go along with Schopenhauer's comprehensive gloom, or with the philosophy of renunciation that he derived from it. I have no doubt that St. Paul was right to recommend faith, hope, and love (*agape*) as the virtues that order life to the greater good."[4] I concur. And I want to suggest that hope, far from delusion or evasion, is the proper response to a reality that seems to counsel, even demand, despair.

How is that possible? How can we hope in the dark?[5]

## 2. The mystery of deep hope

We should begin by distinguishing hope in the sense that interests me here—which I will sometimes call *deep hope*—from various forms of desire, with which hope is often confused.[6] This differentiation builds on a distinction made by Gabriel Marcel, whose account of the problematic and the mysterious we considered in chapter two. Marcel distinguishes hope from desire, and clarifies the nature of each by juxtaposition with its antithesis: the antithesis of desire is fear, and the antithesis of hope is despair. These two pairs—hope and despair, desire and fear—correspond to different spheres of experience; and many of our confusions about hope stem from either confusing hope with desire, or despair with fear.

It will be simplest to begin with fear and desire, which are easily understood because they are concerned with particular objects or events in the world—something that is the object or focus of our concern. To desire something is to want it to arrive; and to fear something is to worry that it will come to pass. I desire that I will get a job or promotion, or a vacation home in the mountains, or a relationship with someone to whom I am attracted. I fear that my job will be lost due to downsizing, or that grizzly bears awakening from hibernation in the spring will come to investigate my campsite, or that the biopsy will come back malignant. In each case, desire and fear have determinate objects; they are clearly anticipatory—they look to the future, either with expectation or with dread. But hope and despair are something altogether different. Hope and despair are not focused on things we might or might not acquire or which might or might not come to pass. Hope and despair are intransitive; they have no determinate object. And, having no determinate object, they are not anticipatory; they do not look to the future for something that is going to arrive. Hope and despair are existential moods that we inhabit, or which inhabit us; they assert something about the meaningfulness or meaninglessness of life, and the goodness or badness of being.

These qualities are often clearest in the case of despair. When a person despairs, truly despairs, she loses faith in existence as such. Properly speaking, a person does not "despair" of the loss of her job, or her home, or even her life (though she may fear any of these). To despair is to come to the belief that, as W.H. Auden puts it in his *Twelve Songs*, "nothing now can ever come to any good."[7] No doubt this can come about as the result of a devastating individual loss—the death of one's child, for example—but such an event is really just a trigger for a more comprehensive desolation. Despair is not the consequence of the loss of any one particular being or object in the world, but rather the loss of one's sense of the world.[8] It leaves a person with nothing in which she can find value, nothing to orient or give meaning to existence. Despair is a loss of faith in reality as a whole, the sense that, ultimately, nothing is valuable.

If despair is the denial of worth, hope is an affirmation that, at least potentially, responds to this denial. Indeed, it is only in the context of the temptation to despair that we can respond with genuine hope. And Marcel claims this is clearly the case in our world: "Despair is possible in any form, at any moment and to any degree, and this betrayal may seem to be counseled, if not forced upon us, by the very structure of the world we live in."[9] William James adds that the "whole army of suicides" stands as a mute testament to the claim that life is not worth living.[10] Nevertheless, it is precisely the omnipresent possibility of despair that can become "the springboard to the loftiest affirmation."[11] Where despair denies that anything is ultimately worthy, hope wagers that reality is worthy of my engagement, perhaps worthy of my complete engagement, even my love (if not, as we will see, my *unqualified* endorsement).

Hope, then, rests on a certain sort of faith; a belief that, despite the apparent lack of worth, the untrustworthiness, the underlying tragedy of reality, there are nevertheless compelling reasons to affirm and endorse it. And this affirmation need not be based on selective optimism that pretends the horror is not there or does not matter, or on resignation to the fact that we have no other world to choose from, or on a Leibnizian theodicy that suggests that this is the "best of all possible worlds." The form of hope I am describing does not deny suffering, loss, and tragedy, which seem, as far as human experience can attest, utterly inescapable. And while some forms of hope may turn on a soteriology of one sort or another, deep hope does not require a trick of transcendent accounting in which goodness will outweigh, pound for pound, evil, and so justify the horror and tragedy. Deep hope is possible even in the face of the finality of death, even in the face of the possibility, on a cosmic scale, of the thermodynamic heat death of the universe itself.

These different foci—the particular object of desire or fear, the existential mood of hope or despair—suggest that the distinction between problem and mystery may again be of use. Desiring something and not yet having it raises the problem of how to go about securing it. Fearing something raises the problem of how to go about avoiding it. Thus, fear and desire operate squarely within the sphere of the problematic; they are difficulties for which we seek a solution that will dissolve the problem, eliminating it. And, as with all problems, the solutions we develop tend toward the impersonal and universal. Although individual people look for particular jobs, many of the steps in "solving" personal unemployment are indifferent to the individuality of the person: networking, polishing one's résumé, preparing for the interview, and so forth. Likewise, while each illness is unique, because each patient is unique, medical treatment follows a more or less universal flowchart: preliminary diagnosis based on the most likely cause, initial treatment or watch-and-wait, follow-ups, referrals to specialists, and so on. The identity of the job applicant or patient, what Ricoeur calls her *ipse* or "whoness," is not really at issue; and the steps in the technical solution vary only in minor details related to her *idem* or "whatness": the precise nature of relevant experience on the résumé, the targeting of a particular macromolecule in immunotherapy.

Hope, however, is not problematic, but mysterious; not tied to technics, but to a specific sort of hermeneutic wager about being and, therefore, to one's way of being in the world. Mysteries, recall, cannot be solved with techniques, because mysteries are issues in which the being of the "questioner" is at stake.

> A problem is something which I meet, which I find completely before me, but which I can therefore lay siege to and reduce. But a mystery is something in which I am myself involved, and it can therefore only be thought of as a sphere where the distinction between what is in me and what is before me loses its meaning and initial validity.[12]

Engaging mystery is a deeply personal and hermeneutic task. Because the being of the questioner is at stake or involved in the mysterious, there is no way to step out of the hermeneutic circle, to take up a "view from nowhere" from which one might judge the situation objectively. How can I separate the question of the meaningfulness and goodness of the world from my experience of meaningfulness and goodness—or the lack of meaning and goodness—in my own life, which takes place in and is part of the world? I cannot. Any pretense to do so misses the mark by interrogating an abstraction.

As mysterious, hope has nothing to do with finding a solution that will dissolve or eliminate potential reasons to despair. That would be to mistake hope for desire, and despair for fear. Mysteries cannot be "solved" or "dissolved"; they are constitutive of a reality that we live and from which we cannot remove ourselves. Therefore, we might say that hope is a way to "deal with" or "conduct oneself with respect to" a reality in which both evil and good seem irreducible.

And here we come up against one of the more challenging aspects of hope. In common usage, in which "hope" is reduced to mere desire, we think of hope as directed toward the future in anticipation of some particular boon or salvation. Such "hope" is at root "hope that . . .," hope that some particular good will be secured or some particular evil avoided. But deep hope—hope that is more than wish-fulfillment—is not fixed on any particular object. Deep hope is not "hope that. . ." but rather "hope in. . . ."[13] To hope in something is akin to having faith in that thing—faith in the broad sense I've articulated, faith that something is of value or has worth, that it is meaningful, that it is good and worthy of my affirmation whatever else might be balanced against that affirmation.

And what does deep hope "hope in . . ."? As the previous chapters have suggested, deep hope is nothing less than hope in the ineradicable goodness of being itself, which is something we can experience at almost any moment and in almost any circumstance. It is not hoping that some future state of affairs will come to pass, but hoping in the goodness of reality, which we experience in the present. Hope is faith in something "more." But the "more" is not something absent in the present that will arrive at some future date; it is the surplus contained in each moment.

## 3. Hoping in the dark

So, deep hope is at its core an expression about and affirmation of the value of being rather than a desire or wish for some particular object or event. As Marcel says: "Hope consists in asserting that there is at the heart of being, beyond all data, beyond all inventories and all calculations, a mysterious principle which is in connivance with me."[14] Although deep hope differs from Marcel's account in important respects, parsing this sentence will help to circumscribe the nature of deep hope. The two accounts share important features including an allergy to conceiving of hope as desire, as well as a recognition that hope is a wager about the value of being and my place in it. With that in mind, Marcel's description of hope emphasizes three things: (1) hope involves an "assertion" that (2) is not based on "calculation," but rather (3) on a belief about the "mysterious relationship" between reality and myself.

## 3.1 Hope is an assertion

First, to say that hope is an assertion indicates that it is both a way of viewing things and a way of being. To hope is not merely to believe certain things about being but to assert, to make active claims about being based on that belief. And, crucially, this assertion is more than rhetorical; it takes form in one's choices, behaviors, and actions. For, as William James notes, "there can be no difference [in viewpoints or beliefs] that does not make a difference somewhere [in the world]."[15] Or, said otherwise, meaningful beliefs have consequences; there is no authentic belief that does not make some difference in one's conduct in the world.

Hope is certainly a type of belief and, therefore, to hope is to adopt a certain way of being in the world. Marcel makes this quite clear when he notes that the affirmation of being is "an affirmation which I *am* rather than an affirmation which I *utter*."[16] And here again we bump up against a kind of faith, insofar as we might say that a willingness to act on the basis of faith is one of the characteristics that distinguishes faith from belief.[17] I can perfectly well desire something without acting on the basis of that desire, as every daydreamer knows. Likewise, I can believe something without acting on the basis of that belief, for mere belief can often be a very thin sort of commitment. But faith suggests something more, a kind of conviction that ought to orient our actions.

Rather than passively awaiting the arrival of something that would justify this affirmation or commitment—some event, some state of affairs—deep hope takes an active role in its own justification, that is, in uncovering a world to which hope is an appropriate response. As James observes in the case of the related question, "is life worth living?":

> . . . often enough our faith beforehand in an uncertified result is *the only thing that makes the result come true*. Suppose, for instance, that you are climbing a mountain, and have worked yourself into a position from which the only escape is by a terrible leap. Have faith

> that you can successfully make it, and your feet are nerved to its accomplishment. But mistrust yourself, and think of all the sweet things you have heard the scientists say of *maybes*, and you will hesitate so long that, at last, all unstrung and trembling, and launching yourself in a moment of despair, you roll into the abyss. In such a case (and it belongs to an enormous class) . . . refuse to believe and you will be right, for you shall irretrievably perish.[18]

James is not suggesting we can imagine up reality whole cloth and tailored to fit our desires—a common misreading of pragmatism. His point is rather that when we "believe that life is worth living" that belief will "help create the fact."[19] Similarly, when we hope in the world—when we believe that the world is worthy of our esteem and appreciation—we help to create the conditions of our experiencing the world as worthy of our hope. Deep hope is, in a certain sense and to a certain degree, self-verifying; it is justified *ante factum*, so to speak.

Thus, when deep hope is actively engaged, a person is evaluating, judging, and acting; she does not meekly accept all aspects of our "broken world," but works to bring about conditions that would justify her aspiration to experience and affirm its goodness.[20] Nevertheless, her hope is not dependent on the arrival or realization of any particular future state of affairs that would justify hope retrospectively. The hopeful person acts in a way that will help to vindicate her faith in the world; but she recognizes that there is no specific state of affairs that will justify her hope, no ideal to which she must be inflexibly committed to be a true believer. Deep hope breeds enthusiasts, but no fanatics. Actions in support of hope are always provisional; they represent our best efforts based on our best current understanding of things. But things change. We grow and evolve. Our situation changes, then changes again. Hope is tested, again and again. And while it must respond determinedly in the face of these challenges, to have any chance of success it must also respond flexibly, adaptively, tactfully.

But that difficult possibility is the best we have. It is not just that there is no specific state of affairs that will magically and unambiguously justify hope, no formula for universal justice or happiness, or for the erasure of evil. The fact is that there is no guarantee that hope will be justified at all, no guarantee that in placing our faith in the world the world will respond in a way that justifies that faith. A person can place her faith in the world, only for the world to spit in her face or turn away in indifference. Philosophers, authors, poets, and artists beyond count have documented the ways in which the human condition is indelibly marked by tragedy. But against that dark background we must also acknowledge that people in truly awful circumstances, people who would be most justified in despairing, are nevertheless able to live in hope and, at least sometimes, the world responds to that faith: Boethius, Václav Havel, Nelson Mandela, Osip and Nadezhda Mandelstam, Dietrich Bonhoeffer, Aleksandr Solzhenitsyn, and many others.[21]

True, we can hope in the world and our hope can fail. We may fail. The world may fail us. Hope is a risk, an uncertain leap in the dark, a wager on which we cast the die of our lives. But if we place the marker of our lives wagering against hope, against meaning, against the goodness of being, we can be sure that we will experience the world in a way that justifies our lack of faith. As James observes, the suicide—that person who most irrevocably wagers on the absence of worth or value in life—completes the bleakness of the picture and makes pessimism "true beyond a doubt." However, in a similar manner, hope can also verify itself; it is a wager I am simultaneously involved in making and justifying.[22] Perhaps, then, we should think of hope in terms of fidelity rather than expectation, desire, or dream. We cannot force the issue, coerce being, make the glory appear to us; the best we can do is to commit ourselves to a way of being that is open to experiencing the present moment as worthy of our fidelity.

## 3.2 Hope is non-calculative

The wager of hope is a risky one. The stakes, one's life, are high; and the odds with respect to many despair- or fear-inducing phenomena are, in fact, not good at all. We can try to hope, try to remain faithful to the world, and the world may not respond in a way that vindicates that hope. A betting person would not lay odds on a favorable experience of things in light of even commonplace examples of suffering and loss, to say nothing of exceptional threats like climate change, population growth, pandemic disease, geo-political instability. The odds are stacked against us. Surveying the inhuman indifference of the world, Robinson Jeffers advises us "not [to be] duped by dreams of universal justice and happiness / these dreams will not be fulfilled."[23]

But we've already seen that the fulfillment of deep hope takes place in the present, not the future; the wager of hope is not tied to some particular outcome, the odds of which one might calculate in advance. That would be to confuse hope and desire. Of course, a person can both hope *and* desire. Even hopeful people think about the future. How could they not? It is only a disingenuous caricature of "living in the present" that equates the poetry of Horace ("seize the day"[24]), Stoicism ("Pass through each day as if it were the last"[25]), Buddhism (embracing "present moments of suchness"[26]), Christianity ("Learn from the way the wild flowers grow. They do not work or spin . . ."[27]), or other expressions of natural spontaneity with absolute blindness to and disregard for the future. One can "live in the moment" and still choose not to smoke, and do so in part out of a desire for a healthier future. Let's not confuse caricature with critique.

However, while all people plan for the future to some degree, *deep hope* is not dependent on that future. Its fulfillment is in the present. So a person of deep hope will be reluctant to trade her forenoons for her afternoons, disregarding the present out of anxiety for an uncertain future.[28] And if she is willing to work or save in the present in order to, potentially, reap a benefit in the future, it will not be to the exclusion of cultivating joy or vitality here and now.

This is why hope is a poor gambler; it's not interested in odds. Václav Havel is one among many advocates of hope who caution us against thinking that hope has to do with a successful calculation:

> Hope, in this deep and powerful sense, is not the same as joy that things are going well, or willingness to invest in enterprises that are obviously headed for early success, but, rather, an ability to work for something because it is good, not just because it stands a chance to succeed. The more unpropitious the situation in which we demonstrate hope, the deeper that hope is. Hope is definitely not the same thing as optimism. It is not the conviction that something will turn out well, but the certainty that something makes sense, regardless of how it turns out.[29]

The uselessness of calculation becomes quite clear if we return to James's formulation of the temptation to despair: is life worth living? Utilitarianism comes up short here. Indeed, it can hardly make a start:

(a) we are incapable of collecting, much less taking into account in a single calculation, the infinitely variegated data points that might bear on the question; (b) even if we could enumerate all such relevant data, we would find—precisely because of the infinite variety—that we are confronted with incommensurable phenomena that cannot be measured in terms of some universal unit for purposes of comparison and calculation; and, (c), much of what matters when it comes to questions like the goodness of being or the value of life cannot be easily measured for quantification and calculation at all. Hope in and perception of "all things shining" are not reducible to facts and data, which certainly bear on, but do not exhaust, the relevant factors in our experience. The wager of deep hope is more like a leap of faith than a carefully calculated bet.

This is not to suggest that hope is a blind leap. While it is not a matter of accumulating statistics or data, hope has its reasons—even if they are reasons that reason, in the sense of disembodied and disinterested calculation, will never know or understand.[30] The wager or assertion of hope is an effort to position and orient oneself—physically, perceptually, intellectually, emotionally, and spiritually—in such a way that the goodness of the world can be experienced. Nor does this mean that hope experiences the world as unblemished or perfect, or that we must endorse it in every detail. Far from it. The world is a vast, multifaceted, beautiful, terrible, confounding, awful/awe-full mystery. It is, rather, to say that the hopeful person seeks—without calculation, even contrary to calculation—to put herself in a position such that experiences of joy, vitality, wonder, and love are possible within a world that is, in a sense, indifferent, and amidst the evil that she cannot ignore, justify, or spirit away.

## 3.3 Hope is bound to the transcendent

Finally, and most provocatively, Marcel suggests that hope includes a feeling that reality is, in some way, in "connivance" with me.[31] Clearly part of what is at stake here is placing hope squarely within the domain of the mysterious: questions, relationships, phenomena, and realities from which I cannot neatly separate myself. Hope and despair are responses to a reality with which I am in intimate communion and from which I cannot extricate myself. Despair experiences reality as fundamentally meaningless and indifferent, whereas hope experiences that same reality in a manner that is shot through with meaning and value, and as something with which I am in relationship. Given the emphasis on "relationship," it should be no surprise that a number of thinkers who have made similar claims express their insights in terms of "personalism."

The diversity of philosophers who travel under the banner of personalism makes any easy definition or slogan hard to come by. When one speaks of reality in "personal" terms, it tends to carry the suggestion of a more or less traditional account of "God," such as one finds in the Judeo-Christian-Islamic tradition, as well as the stark account of human exceptionalism and anthropocentrism that tends to characterize these traditions. And this is certainly the case for a significant number of personalist philosophers, including Marcel. But while deep hope is not allergic to more traditional accounts of divinity, I've made it clear that it does not require such a commitment. For example, while Erazim Kohák's personalist philosophy of nature does not shrink from speaking in terms of God, it's fairly clear in *The Embers and the Stars* that "God" is not limited to formulations conceived of in terms that are "super natural," and that it goes under other names such as "presence," "meaningful reality," and "the goodness of being."[32] Additionally, Kohák's brand of personalism is explicitly committed to the "personal" reality of more-than-human nature, in which human difference is not to be confused with human exceptionalism. Personalist philosophers like Henry Bugbee travel even further afield from any traditional conception of divinity or religious expression. Bugbee's non-anthropocentric personalism experiences reality *tout court* as shot through with value and meaning; and while it recognizes difference—the obvious fact that beings differ from each other, that some differences are significant enough to constitute a difference in kind, and that the human difference means we, like all other beings, have a particular role to play—it does so without suggesting that the fact of human difference constitutes a facile or unproblematic superiority.[33]

In this context we can see that "connivance" is perhaps an unfortunate choice of words, insofar as connivance implies a *uniquely* special relationship with reality, one in which the world works not only with, but in some sense for, me. The word suggests a wink (*nictare*) between co-conspirators, and it is not irrelevant that it often applies to an understanding between people involved in wrongdoing of some sort. Therefore, let's amend Marcel's statement to assert that deep hope experiences reality as a mystery in which I am called to *collaborate*. If connivance implies that reality favors me in some special way in which I have been "let in on the con," collaboration suggests a more participatory relationship and the possibility of working together with reality, a relationship based on what Pierre Hadot calls the "essential co-belonging between myself and the ambient universe."[34]

Hope as such is not an assertion an individual makes in a vacuum, nor is it a choice made simply because lived hope seems preferable to lived despair; hope is a response to a call, to something beyond the individual that we might properly call the transcendent. The transcendence of deep hope cannot be reduced to either a simple case of "vertical transcendence," the classical transcendence of strong theology that takes us to "another world," or to a simple case of "horizontal transcendence," which often comes packaged in a flattened ontology that denies anything particularly special about human beings. Rather, experiences of joy, vitality, hope, and love exhibit aspects of vertical and horizontal transcendence by turn. Václav Havel, a major figure in the audacious non-violent overthrow of the Communist government of Czechoslovakia, recognized and affirmed hope's connection to the transcendent: "[hope's] deepest roots are in the transcendental, just as the roots of human responsibility are" and this is equally true for the theist and "the most convinced materialist and atheist."[35] Here again we must be careful, because while it is related to faith in the expanded sense I've developed here, reference to the transcendent neither avows nor disavows particular religious doctrines. It does not matter that the atheist or agnostic, like Havel, cannot "say anything concrete [i.e., specific] about the transcendental."[36] Deep hope does not require eschatological dogma; it is rooted in the experience of the soul here and now—in this concrete, tragic, wonderful, mysterious world—not in reference to a final *telos* or *eschaton* that is coming sometime in the future. However, deep hope does require reference to something *more*, some excess that escapes totalization in neat epistemic categories, some experience of a "beyond," even if that beyond is understood as a deeper penetration of and immersion in this world rather than an escape to another, utopian world.

This "more" that grounds and justifies deep hope is an excess available in both extraordinary moments and in utterly quotidian experiences. The boundless gratuity of being overflows our ability to experience it, overflows our ability to comprehend or categorize it. And deep hope—faith in the goodness of the world—draws on this wellspring. James observed that "in the deepest heart of all of us there is a corner in which the ultimate mystery of things works out sadly."[37] No doubt. But there is also, in all experience, something more, something that opens a door towards a possible affirmation. There is more in heaven and earth—*more of heaven on earth*—than is dreamt of in our philosophies.

## 4. The 'compensation' of hope: Hoping without a why

That hope has this connection to a transcendent "more" suggests that it is a response to what Marcel calls an "ontological exigence":

> Being is—or should be—necessary. It is impossible that everything should be reduced to a play of successive appearances which are inconsistent with each other . . . or, in the words of Shakespeare, to "a tale told by an idiot [full of sound and fury, *signifying nothing*]." I aspire to participate in this being, in this reality—and perhaps this aspiration is already a degree of participation, however rudimentary.[38]

Ontological exigence is the desire, the *need*, to experience meaning and coherence; it is something like the combination of wonder with an attendant aspiration to understand, if not the entire cosmos, then at least something of one's own place in it.[39] For Marcel, this need is not a "wish" for being or for coherence, which would be nothing more than a "psychological state, mood, or attitude a person *has*; it is rather a movement of the human spirit that is inseparable from being human."[40] Ontological exigence is more than a psychological coping mechanism; it is the result of a fundamental human attunement to reality. Even those who claim to be committed to the notion that there is no meaning in the universe live as if their actions and lives are meaningful, as if some states of affairs are better than others, and as if certain aspects of reality are good and others ruinous. Such people seem, at best, half-hearted nihilists.

This is not to say that we are always aware of, or aligned with, this attunement. Humans can, and do, experience reality as either harmonious or disharmonious, and can feel those experiences in ways that are either shallow or deep. One person looks at reality and sees nothing but indifferent nature, "red of tooth and claw," an *abattoir* in which "ignorant armies clash by night"; another person looks at the same reality, the same experience and sees the cedar tree "buzzing with flame," hears "the faint sound of oars in the silence," feels the "glory."[41] The speculative melancholy to which philosophers are prone—distinct from clinical depression or the sadness of a proximate loss—is the result of seeing reality with only the weary and accusatory eyes of the pessimist, an inability or unwillingness to see reality otherwise, with eyes attuned to wonder and gratitude.

Consider Angelus Silesius's "rose without why," made famous for continental philosophers by Heidegger's treatment in *The Principle of Reason*: "The rose is without why; it blooms because it blooms; It cares not for itself; asks not if it is seen."[42] This celebrated couplet gives voice to a well-established German mystical tradition, one expressed in an archetypal way in the work of Meister Eckhart. Eckhart coined the term "*Gelassenheit*" ("releasement" is the common, if awkward, translation) and also used the phrase "without why," which found its way into Silesius's poem; both the term and the phrase feature prominently in Heidegger's later philosophy.[43] Meister Eckhart used the term *Gelassenheit* to describe the letting-go of egoistic will and subsequent submission to divine will. It is a noun derived from *lassen* (to let), and suggests both a letting-go and a letting-be characterized by calmness, placidity, and equanimity. Heidegger adopted the term to describe twisting free from thinking-as-willing and from the technological worldview that defines the modern epoch, reducing all beings to "standing-reserve" (*Bestand*), a mere well of resources from which to draw for human wants.[44] He claims in his later works that this voluntarism, reaching an apotheosis of sorts in Nietzsche, is a driving force in the descent of the Western tradition into nihilism. Willing has unfolded not simply as purposive action; it is the desire to expand and command, to be master not only of oneself but of the otherness one encounters in the world. For this reason, Heidegger writes, at one point, "the will itself is what is evil."[45]

Willing is at the root of the "enframing" [*Gestell*] of being as technological; and it is not difficult to see here an alternative description of the disenchantment of the world described by Weber and others. *Gelassenheit*, in contrast, is the spirit of an alternative relation to being and to beings. It is not a resistance to or pushing back against technological enframing, willing otherwise or in an alternative key; it is, rather, a step back or a step away, so to speak, from willing itself. Heidegger is famously ambiguous regarding how this is to happen. Does non-willing mean "to willfully renounce willing," or "that which is completely other than willing"? How do we move from the former to the latter? It is difficult not to hear echoes of our earlier consideration of *wu-wei*: action without action, trying not to try. For both *wu-wei* and *Gelassenheit*, what is at stake is a kind of letting-go of the willful self and a letting-be of things; but it is difficult to articulate how this is to happen without our willing it. How do we try not to try? Will not to will? Perhaps Marcel's distinction between activity and passivity is more useful here than willing and non-willing. Letting-go is active, not passive; but its activity is unassertive and receptive rather than willful or potent.[46]

But despite the parallels between *Gelassenheit*, *wu-wei*, vitality, and perhaps even joy, the fact is that when thinkers consider the rose—or person or planet—"without why," they often fixate on the "without why" (the absence of solid foundation or clear purpose, the infinite and indifferent silence that horrified Pascal) and so lose sight of the rose (the beauty and wonder of its presence, irrespective of *arche* or its *telos*).[47] This, in turn, shapes the way in which they conceive of hope. For all his sophistication, Heidegger's own position admits of only a "finite hope," one that is always haunted by the possibility of a final disappointment. For Heidegger there is no "rational basis" for hope, nor can there be hope grounded in love, since Being is impersonal.[48] There is scant comfort in releasement to the inscrutable play of Being. Meister Eckhart, in contrast, can think of hope in "absolute" or "unconditioned" terms and is therefore less troubled by the possibility of a final disappointment.[49] Here, however, I am seeking to unpack a somewhat different perspective on the rose without why, and on what it might mean in terms of hope. With Heidegger, deep hope remains haunted by the possibility of final disappointment; it is a wager and, as such, one that can "fail." But, with Eckhart, deep hope aspires to unconditional expression—without, however, reference to the future—and, we will see, is linked quite closely to love.

What is it to live "without why"? It is to live untroubled by the weight of a past that cannot be changed and a future that cannot be foreseen or controlled. This, in turn, opens up the possibility of fully experiencing and appreciating the present moment, which is in fact the only moment we have. In yet another rumination on roses—perhaps anthophiles have some particular insight into temporality?—Ralph Waldo Emerson wrote:

> These roses under my window make no reference to former roses or to better ones; they are for what they are; they exist with God to-day. There is no time to them. There is simply the rose; it is perfect in every moment of its existence. Before a leaf-bud has burst, its whole life acts; in the full-blown flower there is no more; in the leafless root there is no less. Its nature is satisfied, and it satisfies nature, in all moments alike. But man postpones or remembers; he does not live in the present, but with reverted eye laments the past, or, heedless of the riches that surround him, stands on tiptoe to foresee the future. He cannot be happy and strong until he too lives with nature in the present, above time.[50]

This position aligns neatly with Hadot's retrieval of philosophical practices that train us to see things—things that did not have to be, but are—with new eyes. Such eyes gaze on the stellar interstices and see not only their indifference, but also the gift of their beauty, their glory, and their grace, which, we saw in chapter two, are "eternal." The beauty of the rose-without-why, seen with such eyes, is enhanced rather than betrayed by its contingency—its lack of necessity and its inevitable decay. The rose did not have to be. It might never have been; it could have been otherwise; one day it will not be. Yet here it is. Blooming. *Miraculum*. And I am here to witness it.

Poetry tends to capture this better than philosophy, perhaps because, as poet W.S. Merwin writes, "absolute despair has no art, and I imagine the writing of a poem, in whatever mode, still betrays the existence of hope."[51] It is also because philosophy is so obsessed with interrogating things in order to discover their ultimate foundation—the "what" (*eidos*), the "whence" (*arche*), the "to what end" (*telos*), and so forth—that it often fails to fully experience things as they are. So intent on *examining* life that it forgets to *live* it. Deep hope—like joy and vitality—accepts that there are certain questions that yield no definitive answers; and pursuing such lines of inquiry with an attitude that will only be content when it reaches a clear, comprehensive, unshakeable foundation will inevitably lead to frustration, anger, or despair. This does not mean we should avoid "questions that have no answers," which are the bread-and-butter of philosophy and which St. Exupéry suggests are part of the vocation of a full human being.[52] In some sense the questions without answers are the only ones worth asking. It does suggest, however, that certain realities are "best savored and not interrogated,"[53] experienced rather than dissected, poeticized rather than analyzed. The savoring of life does not ignore the darkness between the stars, but it does allow us to fully appreciate the lights in the darkness: the "starry night" that both inspired Kohák's philosophical reflections and punctuated Van Gogh's sadness, finding its way on to some of his most celebrated canvasses.

## 5. The present of the present

What is required, says Hadot, "is a total transformation of our lives, and one of the principal aspects of this transformation is the *change of our attitude toward time*."[54] We've already seen that there is a crucial connection between the experiences of joy and vitality and the way that we experience and value time, so it should be no surprise that hope has a similarly unorthodox temporality, at least to a contemporary Western sensibility. We must reorient ourselves to live—actually *live*, not merely exist—in the present. As Pascal observes:

> Examine your thoughts, and you will find them wholly occupied with the past or the future. We almost never think of the present, and if we do so, it is only to shed light on our plans for the future. The present is never our end. The past and the present are our means; only the future is our end. So, we never live, but hope to live [*espérons de vivre*], and, as we are always planning to be happy, it is inevitable that we should never be so.[55]

Erazim Kohák makes a similar observation in *The Embers and the Stars*:

> How many autumns since the agonized cry with which humans protest the unacceptability of the inevitable? It is vain to count. Humans must ever make peace with the ending of a life, the parting

> of the loved, with the raccoon wasted on the pavement, struck down by an unheeding motorist. The anguished cry of a child's futile love focuses the helplessness of love in the face of the flow of time no less than the agony of the woman who in vain would enfold with the angel's wings of her love the man plummeting to his death, sixteen stories below, on the refuse-stained concrete of the alley. That aching love is so human—and so vain in the order of time. The fulfillment of life cannot be in its future. That future is always an end. We know that: we ought not to wonder that something perishes. We hurt when we forget that the point of life is not that it should last forever. Its overlooked wonder is that once it was; there once was a man, there once was a raccoon. That is the miracle, that is the point. . . . The fulfillment of time is not where we seek it in vain, in its endless future. It is where we find it, in its perennially present eternity. [56]

To live in the present does not mean that we ignore the past, repeating mistakes for failing to learn from them, nor that we ignore the future, failing to plan reasonably for events we are likely to see. Living in the present is about experiencing and valuing time in a different way.[57] Experiencing the present as it is in itself, rather than in relation to a past to which we are bound by chains of regret or nostalgia, or through the filter of a future we fixate on with desire or fear.

That such a shift in perspective is possible is hardly a novel claim; this insight has been expressed in a variety of different ways. In the *Timeaus*, Plato describes time as the "moving image of eternity."[58] And if time is the moving image or reflection of eternity, what do we get when our experience of time stops in moments of joy, vitality, gratitude, or wonder? Eternity. Goethe claims that such moments are the key to our happiness: "Happiness looks neither forward nor backwards; / And thus the instant becomes eternal."[59] Thoreau exhorts us to "live in the present, launch yourself on every wave, find your eternity in each moment."[60] Kohák insists that "humans, whether they do so or not, are capable of encountering a moment not simply as a transition between a before and an after but as the miracle of eternity ingressing into time."[61] Caputo suggests the possibility of a 'non-dualistic eternity,' that is, an eternity that is not an escape from one world to another. He makes a distinction between the "time of an economy" and the "time of the gift," a distinction that he acknowledges is "poetic, not metaphysical," one based not on "different things" but on "different ways of *regarding* things."[62] Such distinctions should remind us of all the poetical voices that testify to some type of eternity-in-the-moment: William Blake, Walt Whitman, Annie Dillard, Mary Oliver, and many others.[63]

But perhaps one of the more straightforward descriptions is that given by Hadot in the course of his engagement with the "spiritual exercises" of ancient philosophers, particularly Stoics and Epicureans: the secret to living in the present is to experience each moment as if it were both your first and your last.[64] To see the world as if for the last time is to fully value the moment in all its gratuitousness. To experience the pathos arising from the transient beauty of things that did not have to be, but which have been (*mono no aware*, *lacrimae rerum*). It is to look at the world and see that its sorrows, its tragedies, and its savagery take place against a backdrop that is also beautiful, vibrant, and profoundly good, and to be grateful for having had the opportunity to experience it. Irish poet Dennis O'Driscoll captures this well in "Admissions," one of the final poems in the arc of *Dear Life*, a collection that includes a number of compositions—"Last Stand," "Spare Us"—that inveigh against the inadequacies of life and the "silence of God." Yet in "Admissions" O'Driscoll reflects on the "painful route" to the hospital during his terminal illness:

> Before you do down life again,
> badmouth a world that never lives up
> to its billing, recall how glorious it seemed,
> your unwillingness to let go, that evening
> you were driven to Admissions.[65]

O'Driscoll's illness and his impending death awaken him to the profound goodness of being. It is the person living her last day who most fully appreciates the givenness, the giftedness, of the moment, who seeks most conscientiously to "live deep and suck out all the marrow of life."[66] The problem is that we too often forget that we all live under the shadow of impending death.

And yet the appreciation I have in mind is more than that of a sated diner, cracking the bones and sucking the marrow after the meal of her life. It's no doubt true that we should aim to make the most of what poet Mary Oliver calls our "one, wild, precious life," and that, as Nikos

Kazantzakis says, we should aspire to "leave the earth not like scourged, tearful slaves, but like kings who rise from the table with no further wants, after having eaten and drunk to the full."[67] But while a transformed relationship to time includes bracketing the future so as to view the world as if for the last time, it also includes, even emphasizes, the glory of being itself, the gratitude that things are rather than are not. Thus, we must also learn to see the world as if for the first time, with the wonder of a child; we must "get rid of the conventional and routine vision we have of things, [so we can] rediscover a raw, naive vision of reality, [and] take note of the splendor of the world which habitually escapes us."[68] Our perception of time and the way that we see things inform each other. The problem is that we generally only experience the present as either an effect of the past or a cause of the future, never the present as it is in itself. But to see the world "as if for the last time" is to experience it without reference to the future; and to experience the world "as if for the first time" is to experience it without reference to a past. In doing so, we not only experience "eternity," we come to see, and to feel, "the infinite value of the present moment."[69]

Not surprisingly, this has a profound effect on the way one values life. Is life worth living? Is being meaningful? An answer given by a person engaged with an "eternal" moment of "infinite" value will be very different than one given by a person torn between frustration with the past and anxiety about the future. The only moment in which we can be happy or hopeful or joyful or content is right now; there is no other moment. The aim is not merely to value and enjoy happy moments when they occur; it is rather to be able to recognize the value and goodness in every moment.[70] This is theoretically possible at any time; but for a host of reasons we fail to open ourselves to the experience. Caught up in the speed of modern life, covetous of what we do not have, captivated by the belief that we can bend the world to our wants, fascinated by the accomplishments of our technics, and smothered by the accumulated weight of habits, we find ourselves surprised that happiness is always deferred or, like the fruits that tortured Tantalus, just beyond our grasp. But if we can adjust our perception of things and our experience of temporality, we find that there are moments in life that "we simply savor and appreciate and do not interrogate, whose worth we simply affirm but do not feel obliged to justify."[71] This is what it means to live in hope: not the purpose-driven life, but the life without—that is, without the need for—purpose; not life after death, but life before—both "in advance of" and "in the face of"—death.

The present alone is our happiness; there is no other moment. And, viewed rightly and experienced fully, it is enough.[72] But we must be present to the present in order to experience the present as a present.

# Chapter 5
# Amor Mundi

## 1. Only love can save us

Plato argued that love can lead us from the temporal and transitory to the eternal and unchanging, helping to connect us with ultimate truth or reality.[1] Aristotle believed that, even if a person were to possess all the other goods of life in superabundance, without friends to love and be loved by "no one would choose to live."[2] In the Judeo-Christian tradition, the *Song of Songs* tells us that "love is strong as death" and that it is "a flame" of God himself (Song of Songs 8:6). And St. Paul writes that a person with boundless knowledge and power is "nothing" without love, which is the experience closest to godliness, surpassing even hope and faith in importance (1 Corinthians 13).[3] Non-Western cultures and traditions also emphasize the importance of love: the Hindu spirituality of *bhakti yoga* (the path of love); the Confucian concept of *ren* (benevolence), as well as the counter emphasis on *jiān'ài* (universal love) by Mozi and his followers; and the Buddhist quality of *karunā* (compassion). Each of these traditions recognizes in some way the importance of love in human fulfillment.

Given this universal approbation, it should come as no surprise that modern research suggests the sages of these diverse traditions were right. "Happiness is love, full stop." That, at least, is the conclusion of one prominent psychiatrist and researcher who reviewed the data from a seven-decade study.[4] His conclusion is that close, warm, satisfying attachments to other people is a significantly better predictor of happiness than other elements we commonly emphasize: IQ, wealth, social class, years of education, ancestral longevity, and so on. And he is not alone. There is a veritable cottage industry in contemporary psychology, sociology, economics, and popular self-help books that attempts to 'surprise' us with an insight already emphasized by the philosophies, theologies, and poems of the great wisdom traditions: *omnia vincit amor*, love conquers all things.[5]

Thus, we cannot reasonably conclude a book about weathering the storms of life, striking matches in the dark, or finding joy in the extraordinary ordinary without thinking about love. For love is perhaps the single most common and most effective defense against the temptation to despair: our strongest armor against the slings and arrows of fate, our best chance to break the bonds of finitude, and our surest bulwark against the unrelenting erosion of entropy.

Yet love remains a dauntingly vast topic, something that deserves its own book. More, something that deserves—and has generated—volumes of books, vast libraries of thought and reflection and praise: philosophical, theological, psychological, literary, theatrical, poetic, and musical. Novalis wrote that "Love is the final end of the world's history / the Amen of the universe."[6] It is, in the end, perhaps the only topic worthy of our full attention. The *telos* of wisdom, the subject towards which all other subjects should, in their fullness, direct us. Thus, in what follows, I'll need to be circumspect in my goals, limiting my treatment of love, not out of lack of respect for the topic—indeed, precisely the opposite—but rather because of the constraints imposed by the scope of the topic.[7]

What are the essential characteristics of love that mitigate against despair? And, in that context, what else might be said to add to the apparently exhaustive accounts of love already on offer? With respect to the former question, I will propose that it is not the category or type of love that plays the decisive role, but rather the form that love takes or the manner in which it is expressed; for, while all types of love give us reason to turn away from despair, some expressions of love give us stronger and more enduring reasons than others. With respect to the latter question, I will draw our attention to a relatively under-appreciated domain of love: love directed toward the natural world. Commonly, philosophies of love focus on other people, perhaps on God. But if despair signifies a loss of faith in the world itself, it makes sense to reflect on the reasons to love this world, and on what such love might say about us, and do to us, after dark.[8]

## 2. Forms of Love

To begin with the obvious: there is no single, agreed-upon definition of what love *is*. In English, we use the term to indicate things as varied as a fondness for coffee and our willingness to die for a comrade or a lifelong commitment to spouse. True, we have the flexibility to differentiate between "liking" and "loving" absent in some other languages; but often we fail to avail ourselves of this difference. How many people profess to "love" dessert? Or their car? Or the television event of the season? And even when we have a sense of the type of love we are trying to express, we often have a difficult time articulating just what we mean.

Given these ambiguities and difficulties, it should come as no surprise that thinkers treat love in a variety of different ways, even within Western traditions sharing the inheritance of Greek philosophy, Judeo-Christian religion, and the Enlightenment. Thus, perhaps the most obvious way to take up the topic is to begin categorizing different types of love, so that we can get a clear view of what we are talking about; and, indeed, this has been a strategy employed at least since Plato. Some of the relevant Greek terms for love, which still frame most philosophical accounts in the West, include *storge* (affection), *philia* (friendship), *eros* (erotic or intimate love), and *agape* (often translated as charity).

However, while—or perhaps because—a great deal of ink has been spilt in distinguishing between these four types, in what follows I propose to take a different tack. This is not to suggest that the distinctions between *storge*, *philia*, *eros*, and *agape* are irrelevant when considering despair. Far from it. But these classifications have been treated, perhaps exhaustively; moreover, when it comes to the issue of despair—which, after all, is the framework of this project—love seems to work in surprising ways. Different types of love save different people from despair. Consider Henry David Thoreau, a lifelong bachelor who never pursued a romantic relationship with serious interest, certainly nothing like the interest he showed toward his relationship with wildness and nature.[9] Contrast that with a figure like Byron, for whom *eros* was a central concern.

While the traditional strategy of differentiating between classical categories of love has garnered the most attention, there are other relevant distinctions to be made that shed light on how and why love is such an effective bulwark against the darkness. Some of these distinctions can be found in C.S. Lewis's *The Four Loves*.[10] The organization of the book appears to emphasize the classical categories enumerated above, with chapters dedicated to *storge*, *philia*, *eros*, and *agape*. But, for Lewis, particular instances of love are understood not only by identifying the category into which they fall—distinguishing, for example, between friendship and romance—they are also understood in terms of their modes of expression and marked by the experiences or realities to which they are a response, for love is always, in some measure, a response to a call.

Despite his popularity, drawing on Lewis's account of love might be polarizing for some readers. Why turn to perhaps the most popular Christian apologist of the 20th century in the context of reflections in which I have—while suggesting that hope cannot be disentangled from a certain kind of faith—insisted on bracketing commitments to any *particular* form of faith or refusal-of-faith? In this context, Lewis may well appear too doctrinaire, too committed to a particular tradition; he values the various forms of love he studies either in terms of making us more like God or in terms of bringing us nearer to God, with God conceived in distinctly Christian terms. One response to that concern might be that Christianity, for better or worse, has framed thinking in "the West," including thinking about love, in a way that we can embrace or reject, but which we cannot escape.[11] But another, more attentive defense would note that Lewis's insights into human behavior, for all their Oxford donnishness—hilariously, he speaks of companionability, a kind of proto-friendship, in terms of "clubbableness"—and Christian specificity, are both penetrating and familiar. Despite the evident diversity of the ways in which people experience and express love, it would, I think, be difficult to dismiss many of his keen observations about affection (*storge*), friendship (*philia*), and *eros*, even for those who object to his particular goals and biases.[12] In this context, what does Lewis have to say about love?

He begins his treatment by distinguishing between "need love" and "gift love": "The typical example of gift-love would be that love which moves a man to work and plan and save for the future well-being of his family which he will die without sharing or seeing; [and an example of need-love], that which sends a lonely or frightened child to its mother's arms."[13] In the most general sense, need-love is the love we feel for something we receive, something that satisfies some lack on our part, such as water when we are thirsty or food when we are hungry. Gift-love, in contrast, is something disinterested, something that we give to others without reference to, or at least with markedly less emphasis on, our own well-being. Gift-love does not satisfy a lack; its object is not loved because it is needed, but for the sake of the object loved. It is gratuitous. Thus, roughly speaking, we might say that need-love is the love we feel in receiving, gift-love is the love we feel in giving.

That is not to suggest that need-loves are irredeemably selfish or gift-loves are invariably saintly. While need-love can become vicious—selfish, greedy, insatiable—it would be ridiculous to criticize every child seeking shelter in her parent's arms, or every hungry person tucked into a meal. Speaking from his own Christian commitments, Lewis observes that need-love "either coincides with or at least makes a main ingredient in man's highest, healthiest, and most realistic spiritual condition."[14] And the same observation could well be made from alternative hermeneutic frames. For example, a broadly secular and ecological humanism might well recognize need-love as a fitting expression of our fundamental animality, in which we are connected to a complex and interdependent web of life. We are finite beings, and therefore needs are part of our constitution; satisfying those needs is not necessarily a bad thing, and in many cases is in fact a very good thing. Appropriate need-love recognizes our dependence on others, whether we frame that in terms of our creatureliness, our animality, our social and emotional nature, or otherwise. It is *good* that we have needs, and that others—people, non-human animals, ecosystems, places—can help us to satisfy them. Of course, need-love can and does become perverted if people grasp beyond what is appropriate, when we consume more than we need for our own well-being, harming ourselves through overconsumption and others by deprivation, or when the relationship of dependence on others becomes parasitic rather than symbiotic.

But gift-loves are subject to their own particular perversion: a form of idolatry that sets up the love and the beloved as a *sine qua non*, not merely for our happiness in the present, but for the worth or meaningfulness of being itself. The danger of such illiberal gift-love is susceptibility to, even the inevitability of, the bleakest, most profound form of despair: despair that snuffs out all the matches in the dark, and which forecloses the possibility of ever striking another. Thus, when Augustine's unnamed adolescent friend dies, he writes:

> My heart was made dark by sorrow, and whatever I looked upon was death. My native place was a torment to me, and my father's house was a strange unhappiness. Whatsoever I had done together with him was, apart from him, turned into a cruel torture . . . I hated all things, because they no longer held him.[15]

When we love someone or something perishable—a lover, a friend, a child, a place, a time in life—as if it were imperishable, something we will be able to love and enjoy forever, we have set it up as a god and it is inevitable that when it perishes we will conclude that "nothing now can ever come to any good."[16]

Thus, both need-love and gift-love have appropriate and inappropriate forms. And the perversion of gift-love mirrors that of need-love. In each case, the perversion is a result of loving in a manner that is inappropriate to the kinds of beings that we are: dependent, vulnerable, finite, mortal. In perverted need-love we love as if we are gods and the world exists to serve us; and in perverted gift-love we love as if the things we love are gods, eternal and imperishable.

Lewis further observes that love is generally tied to pleasure. We use the term in all sorts of cases to express a strong liking for something, and liking something means, among other things, that we take some pleasure in it. When I say that I love coffee, or wine, or maple syrup, I am clearly speaking about the sensuous pleasure I get from consuming them, and perhaps as well some more abstract pleasures I get from associations or memories connected to them. Likewise, when I say that I love the Sierra Nevada, I am indicating, in part, the aesthetic pleasure experiencing, viewing, or contemplating it gives me; and when I say I love climbing, or skiing, or sailing, I mean that these activities bring me certain pleasures.

But pleasure, like love, comes in various forms, two of which strike Lewis as particularly significant: "need pleasures" and "pleasures of appreciation."[17] Need-pleasures, like need-loves, are preceded by a lack of which we are more or less conscious and by a desire to satisfy that lack. For example, people on long treks or climbs often find themselves relishing even the simple foods that are staples on such trips; and, after satisfying their hunger at the end of a long day, they frequently comment enthusiastically about the quality of food that would, in other circumstances, seem plain or even unpalatable. Hunger, it is widely agreed, is the most flavorful spice. The pleasures of appreciation, however, are something else altogether. They do not come about as a consequence of satisfying a need; rather, they arise spontaneously when we experience something good and when we recognize its goodness. Pleasures of appreciation tend to come upon us unanticipated and unbidden; even when we try to look for them, they are always something of a surprise, like Serres's "pleroma of exultation" in the mountains or Dillard's experience of the cedar tree "transfigured, each cell buzzing with flame." Not surprisingly, just as we often find different forms of love mixed together, so too we can find these two pleasures mingled. For example, when we are hungry and are also lucky enough to have access to good food, we get the need-pleasure of satisfying hunger along with appreciative-pleasure for the quality of the food.

Reflecting on these two forms of pleasure raises the issue of our relationship to time yet again: "when Need-pleasures are in question we tend to make statements about *ourselves* in the *past tense*," as when I assert, after slaking my thirst, that *I* really *wanted* that; but "when appreciative pleasures are in question we tend to make statements about *the object* in the *present tense*."[18]

It might seem odd that need-pleasure is somehow at odds with the present, since needs like hunger are always experienced in the present. But, consider, need-pleasure and need-love disappear completely once the need in question is satisfied, so it makes perfect sense that we speak about them primarily in the past tense. In fact, even the act of satisfying the need is not really attentive to the present moment. True, eating when one is hungry does give pleasure; but the hungry climber down from the mountain tends to wolf down food indiscriminately rather than savoring the meal, which is the source of many a post-climb bellyache. In addition, and paradoxically, the insufficiency at the root of need-pleasure and need-love also means that they are obsessed with the future. When a person has a terrible thirst, all she can think about is how to find a drink to satisfy it; she is not attending to the present moment, but obsessing about a future in which her thirst will, she hopes, be satisfied. Thus, when it comes to need-pleasures, the desire that precedes them causes us to obsess about the future, pulling us away from the present moment; and the fact that they vanish utterly once we are sated means that we are left with a memory that is nothing other than a desiccated shell, lacking any of the substance of the actual experience.

The pleasures of appreciation, in contrast, are rooted in and experienced most intensely in the present. These are not pleasures of *having* (having some thing, having been satisfied) but pleasures of *being* (being in the presence of beauty or goodness, being grateful). Rooted so deeply in an experience of the present, it is no surprise that love—like joy, vitality, and hope—"stops time." As one of Pearl Buck's characters muses, "each experience of love . . . is a life in itself. Each has nothing to do with what has taken place before or will take place again. Love is born, it pursues its separate way, world without end . . ."[19] Because these moments almost invariably come upon us as a surprise, they are pleasures that we cannot anticipate in the same way that we anticipate pleasures that satisfy our needs. Thus, pleasures of appreciation are not fixated on the future. True, I can leave on a hike or go for a surf looking to put myself in the path of the glory of "all things shining," but one can never quite be sure where, when, or how the doors of perception will swing open.[20]

The pleasures of appreciation have a similarly special relationship to the past, because they are not so tightly linked to the proximity, spatial or temporal, of the loved object. Because appreciation is not a response to a lack, it cannot become sated in the way that need or lack can; and, thus, it does not disappear in the way need does once it has been satisfied. Moreover, appreciation can be authentically "made present" in a way that is obviously impossible with need. My thirst and hunger cannot be satisfied by water and food existing somewhere else, or by a poem about water or food; but my appreciation for some particular person or place is possible even when they are not immediately present to me. Or, put another way, objects of appreciation can be "present" to me despite spatial or temporal distance from me. Of course, everyone knows there is a difference between, on the one hand, being in the presence of the object of one's appreciation and, on the other, experiencing that appreciation when the object is distant in time or space. Nevertheless, we do seem to be able to appreciate at a distance, and take genuine pleasure in doing so, in a way that we cannot in cases of need (i.e., we cannot become sated at a distance). And we can enhance our appreciation of an absent object through the use of aids like rich images, virtuosic poetry, and even Proustian sense-triggered recollection.

Lewis's comments about the temporality of pleasure also make note of a second type of orientation. Need-pleasures are quite naturally self-centered; they are related to the satisfaction of desires arising from a lack *I* experience: my thirst, my hunger, my fatigue, my loneliness. The *sine qua non* of need-pleasure is me, experienced primarily as a bundle of wants and needs. But while I am obviously the locus of appreciative-pleasure as well, the focus of that pleasure is very different: the quality, beauty, or goodness of the thing that elicits my appreciation. In appreciative-pleasure we acknowledge something that is good in itself, independent of the pleasure its goodness gives us. There is an unselfish, even disinterested, quality to this pleasure; and we would want the source of our pleasure to endure, even if we ourselves could not partake of it. For example, through his writing, John Muir induced thousands of Americans to love and value natural places that they had never heard of and which most of them would never visit.

In need-pleasure we want the object that will appease our desire, and only insofar as it will appease our desire; but in appreciative pleasure we feel that it is we who owe something to the object in question, that appreciation of it is right and just.[21] We lay claim to the objects of need-pleasure, but the objects of appreciative-pleasure make a claim on us. This awareness is the root of the lament expressed by both Malick's Mr. O'Brien and Dostoevsky's Markel, born of a recognition that they failed to respond to reality with that which is, so to speak, its due: "I alone dishonored everything, and did not notice the beauty and glory of it all." Reflecting on appreciative pleasure leads Lewis to identify a third expression of love: "In the Appreciative pleasures, even at their lowest, and more as they grow into the full appreciation of all beauty [and goodness], we get something that we can hardly help calling *love* and hardly help calling *disinterested*, towards the object itself."[22] In need-love we express our reliance on others, and in gift-love we offer ourselves to others; but in appreciative-love we express our gratitude that some thing simply is.

Each expression of love can, in its own way, help to ward off despair. Even the most basic need-love gives us, in both the anticipation and the pleasure of satisfaction, a reason to go on. However, on its own this seems a very thin kind of purpose or meaning, both egoistic and shallow, and not a very strong reason to resist despair. On the other hand, the mystery of gift-love—in which we live for the selfless pleasure of giving to those we love—seems to provide a very substantial reason to resist despair. Such gift-loves give purpose and meaning to many lives: the parent who sacrifices to provide for a family; the husband or wife who faithfully cares for an ailing spouse; the activist who commits herself to a cause bigger than herself; and the craftsman or artist who feels that his or her work contributes to and sustains a culture. In each case, to give (of oneself) is to receive (a meaningful life, a purpose, a reason to go on).

However, it is appreciative-love that provides perhaps the most powerful antidote to the disease of despair. For in this kind of love we find ourselves in the presence of something that is mysteriously, but also ineluctably, good. Such things call us to admiration, even reverence. The natural response to this is gratitude, gratitude for goodness and for our chance to experience it. And gratitude is one of the most certain ways to resist despair. If to despair is to give in to the belief that "nothing now will ever come to any good," appreciative-love is, at its core, the recognition that "something is—and, whatever may come, will have been—good."[23]

## 3. Nature as teacher

One refreshing aspect of Lewis's account is that he recognizes the need to speak of "likings and loves for the sub-human" in his treatment of love.[24] It seems obvious that certain types of love extend to our relationship with non-human nature, the most obvious being *storge* (affection). But nature has more to offer us than the affection we feel for the old dog that sleeps by the fire at the local pub. In nature we often find ourselves confronted with phenomena that draw us to a form of adoration. Lewis goes so far as to point out that for many people, including himself, nature provides a kind of context, even content, for the terms they use to describe their ultimate commitments:

> Nature never taught me that there exists a God of glory and infinite majesty. I had to learn that in other ways. But nature gave the word glory meaning for me. I still do not know where else I could have found one. . . . And if nature had never awakened certain longings in me, huge areas of what I can now mean by the "love" of God would never, so far as I can see, have existed.[25]

But if Lewis recognizes, with the Psalmist, that "The heavens declare the glory of God; the skies proclaim the work of his hands" (Psalm 19:1), his admiration extends only so far. While he appreciates that the glory in nature calls us to something like love, he is nevertheless deeply concerned about what meaning we might find there; and he is highly skeptical that nature can ultimately teach us anything about the most fundamental and important things.[26] For Lewis, the value of nature lies in how it points beyond itself.

Lewis's objection seems to stem from a concern that one might take nature as an instructor concerning "ultimate" goods: moral instruction, the human *telos*, what and how we ought to love, and similar things. He is wary that people might lapse into something like a "nature religion." Nature, he insists, is not a reliable teacher of such subjects. Notwithstanding its glory, in the schoolroom of nature we will find either that nature teaches us things we ought not accept as normative—violent competition for example—or, with a bit more reflection, that nature actually does not teach at all.

Speaking to the former possibility, Lewis claims that attending to nature we will find that "sex and hunger and sheer power there operate without pity or shame."[27] And if we take that as instructive it will incline us to, at best, a kind of egoistic hedonism and, at worst, an unabashed Nietzschean will to power. If nature is a schoolroom, its first and last lesson is to "look out for number one" with all the tools at our disposal, from tooth and claw to lucre and *logos*. The schoolroom of nature is, in fact, a charnel house, a vast Colosseum littered with the corpses of the impotent and uncompetitive. No doubt such a characterization will strike many readers as a selective and biased distortion. And, indeed, merciless combat was not Lewis's own predominant experience of nature. Many people look to nature and find other, more virtuous lessons: St. Francis, Thoreau, Dillard, Snyder, and many others.

To this, Lewis responds that plurivocity of nature—the fact that it "speaks" in many voices, some savage and others soothing—is consequence of the fact that nature's speech is really only an echo of our own, and so nature does not actually instruct at all. We find nature brutal and beautiful in turn, its apparent lessons alternatively competitive and compassionate, precisely because nature does not teach us anything that we do not "put" there ourselves: "If you take nature as a teacher she will teach you exactly the lessons you had already decided to learn; this is only another way of saying that nature does not teach."[28] Nature is not normative; it does not dictate rules for behavior. We cannot, as Hume would say, derive an "ought" (how we ought to be) from an "is" (how we are or how nature is).[29] When we take nature to be a teacher, we fall into a vicious hermeneutic circle in which we see only those parts of nature that reinforce the view we were already hoping to confirm. That, in any case, is Lewis's concern; but this objection is too easy by half.

First, the danger of motivated reasoning—accepting as "facts" only those phenomena that reinforce one's preexisting assumptions—is characteristic of reason itself, not reasoning-about-nature. The consequence of this tendency is not to abandon reason, but rather to exercise reason carefully, which surely applies to reasoning about God or morality or any other subject as much as it does to reasoning about nature. Indeed, one could well argue that motivated reasoning is, if not more characteristic, at least more *influential* when we reason about abstract issues such as the essence of justice, the first principles of morality, or the existence and nature of God. The denominational bickering about what the Bible teaches—a situation close to Lewis's own heart, and the inspiration for his own attempts to champion "mere Christianity"—are evidence enough that reason does not operate in a vacuum, insulated from culture, history, language, and experience. Different sects of Christianity—to say nothing of other thoughtful and intelligent non-Christians (Jews, Muslims, Buddhists, and so on)—find very different kinds of instruction and meaning in the Gospels. In contrast, hard reality, the reality often associated with nature, is highly resistant to distortion or manipulation. We can bring our desire for prosperity to our theology and, as a consequence, find in the Bible justifications for the so-called prosperity gospel: we hope that God wants us to be rich and, *miraculum bonum*, we find that God wants us to be rich. But whatever expectations or hopes or desires you bring to hard reality, two-hundred pounds remains, inflexibly, two-hundred pounds. Nature is what it is.[30]

Second, while Lewis is right to point out that we do encounter nature through the particulars of our hermeneutic lens, there is nature and then there is nature. It may well be the case that we find in nature only what we bring to it if we do our reflecting while pottering about in Lewis's garden at the Kilns or tramping from cozy pub to cozy pub in the

Cotswolds, but venture beyond the garden gate and into the wilderness and you will find that nature imposes itself on us much more frequently and forcefully than the other way round.[31] In such environments it is nature that does the demanding and dictating; and it is the role of wisdom to listen and obey, as nature imposes direct inflexible consequences when we fail to do so.[32] Of course, some of these lessons are available in the garden and the city as well as in wilderness, and those who are attentive will hear them there; but, not surprisingly, the number of "filters" between us and phenomena changes the experience. As Kohák reminds us, under the starry sky, far from urban development or pastoral domestication, the voice of hard reality is unmistakable. When God wants Job to listen, he speaks from the whirlwind, not the hearth by the couch.

# 4. *Amor feri*

Traditional accounts of love tend to overlook or diminish the significance of the ways in which we can and do come to love the natural world, and therefore the role that love of nature and wildness can play in resisting despair. Although there is a rich poetic and literary tradition testifying to the deep connections people have with particular natural places, when it comes to philosophical treatments of love, accounts of nature are notably scarce. Perhaps this is because philosophy has focused on *philia*, *eros*, *agape*, and similar categories, which fit best when describing personal relationships, and we tend to think of nature as an impersonal reality.[33] But if we put aside the classical categories of love and focus instead on the distinctions between expressions of love (need-love, gift-love, and appreciative-love), it becomes clear that nature can, and perhaps *ought to*, have quite a prominent place in our experience of love.

## 4.1 Love and nature

At the outset we encounter an obvious problem: an increasing number of people no longer have significant experience with nature, at least not in the sense of "nature as independent of us," or "nature indifferent to us," or "nature as an immense and mysterious whole of which we are an impossibly small part."[34] The day-to-day experience of the average person, at least in the global north, is of an environment that is designed rather than wild, constructed rather than evolved, inanimate rather than organic, homogeneous rather than distinctive. Such people no longer experience what Jack Turner calls "gross contact" with wildness, or what Henry Bugbee calls "immersion" in nature; they are alienated in obvious and indisputable ways from the more-than-human world.[35] So perhaps it should not be surprising that our experience of loving nature has atrophied; it is difficult to love what you have not experienced.

This alienation is unfortunate and, if you will pardon the pun, quite unnatural. The primordial experience of nature is one of belonging. The notion of a fundamental disconnect between humans and nature is curious and radically counter-intuitive, which is evident from considering either the experiences of children or the experiences of myriad non-Western cultures that do not predicate their worldviews on a nature-culture dualism. Being at home in the world, not alienation from it, is the primordial given.[36] We evolved on this particular planet, alongside the creatures with whom we share it; and although we can distance ourselves from it, our affinity for this world is, as it were, "baked in" to our being. We would not be at home on Mars. Language reveals the historical experience of intimate connection and kinship with the earth. In the Judeo-Christian-Islamic tradition, the myth of creation has the first person formed from the clay of the Earth. "Human" is traceable to the proto-Indo-European root **(dh)ghomon-*, "earthling" or "earthly being"; and *humus*, soil, is related to *homo*, human. Unsurprising then that Adam takes his name from the Hebrew *adamah* (ground, earth), and Eve is related to *chavah* (to breathe) and *chayah* (to live, to give life). Other mythologies have similar "made from earth" structures. Dust we are, and to dust we will return.

Precisely because our connection to and belonging in the world is so fundamental, our relationship with the rest of nature can never be wholly severed. British nature writer Robert Macfarlane notes that the keen observer will find countless testimonies from quite ordinary people—poems, photographs, postcards, paintings, plaques, paths—to the enduring power of the relationship between individuals and particular natural places.

> [Such] markers . . . [reveal] a process . . . continuously at work throughout these islands, and presumably throughout the world: the drawing of happiness from landscapes both large and small.

> Happiness, and the emotions that go by the collective noun of 'happiness': hope, joy, wonder, grace, tranquility and others. Every day, millions of people found themselves deepened and dignified by their encounters with particular places . . . Daily, people were brought to sudden states of awe by encounters such as these: encounters whose power to move us was beyond expression but also beyond denial. . . . Little is said publicly about these encounters. This is partly because it is hard to put language to such experiences. And partly, I guessed, because those who experience them feel no strong need to broadcast their feelings.[37]

But, despite testimonies both prosaic and poetic, it would be hard to deny that contemporary society is profoundly alienated from nature. Macfarlane's journey in search of wildness in the United Kingdom—a place with a rich tradition of pastoral odes to nature, but smaller and more isolated pockets of wildness—begins with the recognition that, because of a more and more distant relationship with wildness, "we are, as a species, finding it increasingly hard to imagine that we are part of something which is larger than our own capacity."[38] Thoreau diagnosed a similar problem in his own time:

> . . . we know not what it is to live in the open air, and our lives are domestic in more senses than we think. From the hearth to the field is a great distance. It would be well, perhaps, if we were to spend more of our days and nights without any obstruction between us and the celestial bodies.[39]

Without strong experiences of and connections to the natural world, the scope of our imagination is restricted. When man is the measure of all things, the world becomes the mere echo of humanity that Lewis warns us about.[40]

Indeed, alienation from nature is increasingly recognized as an actual disorder with both physical and psychological consequences.[41] The treatment for this ailment is straightforward; and in this particular case the prevention and the cure are one and the same: the tonic of nature. And although one might be inclined to seek this tonic in a local park or home garden, in many cases, given the extremity of our condition, stronger medicine is required. This is because the active ingredient in the cure is not mere sunshine or chlorophyll, but wildness. We need, Thoreau observes, "an infusion of hemlock, spruce or arbor vitae in our tea."[42] Wildness—free nature, hard reality, unbent to human ends—reminds us what it is to be alive and how good life itself is; it elicits in us feelings of appreciation and gratitude that are powerful antidotes to despair.

## 4.2 Seeing nature

We should begin, then, by reacquainting ourselves with the natural places around us, for we cannot love what we do not know. When we do so, we frequently find that particular places do offer particular lessons: "the landscape is . . . not a static diorama against which human action plays itself out, but rather . . . an active and shaping force in our imagination, our ethics, and our relations with each other and with the world. . . ."[43] Take, as merely one example of the way that nature directs us, the influence of topography. If we are attentive, we notice that reality itself "leans"; its actual incline (the physical gradient of its topography and terrain) inclines us (predisposes, influences us) toward experiencing the world in certain ways. Topography—steep hills, river valleys, open plains, and so on—directs those who dwell in or move through it to do so in particular ways. That influence shapes what we experience, which, in turn, shapes what we understand, value, and love. If we don't experience something or don't know about it, it's hard to care about it. Thus, it turns out, the teaching of nature can be quite significant; it informs our view of things, both literally and metaphorically.[44]

Unfortunately, although the physical presence of topography is somewhat resistant to levelling, in the increasingly homogenized world of the global north the particularity of place is largely lost: villages, towns, and cities laid out to cater to cars rather than people; the ubiquity of familiar forms of urban life; a standardized, smartphone-mediated way of relating to the environment and others within it. Serres suggests that this detachment from place began when monotheisms of a certain sort put an end to pagan spiritualities, which were often rooted quite explicitly in the distinctiveness and sacredness of particular places.

> A sudden thunderclap. The holy land is no longer here/there but elsewhere . . . What an enormous anthropological revolution the

> conversion of paganisms to Christianity triggered: the land on which we lived, the soil that we worked and defended lost the sacred and became profane, secularized. From then on, we were born from elsewhere. In its turn, the entire country found itself like every one of us, delocalized. Indifferent, therefore, objectifiable. An objective science and technological intervention in life and the Earth then became possible and permissible. Separate, independent, from then on subjects, we faced objects, thrown there. All of us, children of Eve, are exiles.[45]

The degree to which the desacralization of the world is an artifact of a certain type of monotheism, or of modernity, or of capitalist consumerism is up for debate.[46] The relevant distinction is between a way of being in the world that experiences it as sacred—shot through with meaning, and worthy of our respect—and a way of treating the world as if it were profane, meaningless, interchangeable, a mere object for our (ab)use. For those with a "pagan" sensibility, certain landscapes and places are "capable of bestowing grace upon those who pass through them or live within them."[47] In contrast, when place is desacralized, landscape is just space. We become mere renters or tenants, and nature becomes mere object, its value reduced to utility, no longer the focus of reverence or love.

How, then, can we recapture this pagan experience—whatever our metaphysical commitments—and receive the grace of the world? Mere exposure to nature or wildness is not sufficient. We must "listen" to nature; and listening, as with communication between persons, first requires silence.[48] No one can really hear someone else unless and until they stop speaking themselves; and, so, with respect to nature we must become more silent and receptive. Next, because genuine communication requires that we must give up anticipating what the other person will say and hold back from imposing our own interpretation of things, we must become better students and observers of nature, on alert for what shows itself and what it might mean.

This requires a substantially different way of being in the world than that to which we are accustomed. The language of the world is not expressed in words; it is expressed in bodies (i.e., materially) and understood in bodies (i.e., carnally, sensuously).[49] Fortunately, as our reflection on vitality revealed, the body communicates with the world and the world with the body. Thus, we must do more than look and listen, which are certainly challenging enough on their own; we must touch, taste, and smell, act and interact, explore and experience. We must get the feel of a place in a global sense, come to know its rhythms and seasons and moods. Live with it and experience it over time. It takes time to develop "new eyes," which is the only way to see otherwise; but the best way to begin is with a dose of solitude (to escape the din and distraction of society), a habit of silence (to quiet our egocentric narrator and, more generally, to minimize the soft mediation of language), and a commitment to observation (to attend to what is present).

And, when we attend to it, when we expose ourselves to raw, untamed nature, and do so with an eye to what it shows us and an ear to what it tells us, what do we find? We find, just as Lewis says, that nature is both beautiful and brutal. But not, as Lewis asserts, merely because we bring to it in turn an eye for the beautiful or an eye for the brutal; it is rather because both brutality and beauty really are there. Because despite our desire for the clarity of a black or white answer, nature is both an obscene and amoral *abattoir* and, at the same time, a grace, a beautiful and profoundly good gift. *Mysterium tremendum et fascinans*. It's another mystery with no bottom. "The paradox is exquisite."[50]

As with all mysteries and paradoxes, we distort things if we try to force a resolution that is not true to the contradictory particulars of the experience. It is true that the shadow of death and suffering hovers over each experience of beauty, glory, and grace; it is also true that the light of being, beauty, life, and goodness sparkles even against the backdrop of nature's indifference and brutality. As poet Gary Snyder puts it,

> I have a friend who feels sometimes that the world is hostile to human life—he says it chills us and kills us. But how could we be were it not for this planet that provided our very shape? Two conditions—gravity and a livable temperature range between freezing and boiling—have given us fluids and flesh. The trees we climb and the ground we walk on have given us five fingers and toes. The "place" (from the root *plat*, broad, spreading, flat) gave us far-seeing eyes, the streams and breezes gave us versatile tongues and whorly ears. The land gave us a stride, and the lake a dive. The amazement gave us our kind of mind. We should be thankful for that, and take nature's stricter lessons with some grace.[51]

Nature terrifies and harms as well as consoles and heals. And exposing oneself to wildness is no guarantee that one will see the glory. As Lewis observes, when we go to nature hoping to be overwhelmed by the glory, "nine times out of ten nothing will happen."[52] However, if we practice listening and observing well, we may catch a glimpse of something quite outside the ken of everyday experience. "Beauty and grace are performed whether or not we will or sense them. The least we can do is try to be there."[53]

One of the ways in which nature manifests beauty is through its unwavering fidelity to and expression of the real. Lewis's admonition that "nature does not teach" seems difficult to square with his own love of nature—donnish, domesticated, and English as it was—as well as some reflections that seem to suggest that the experience of nature could, if not serve as an example, at least provide useful instruction. In a letter to his former student turned Benedictine monk and yogi, Bede Griffiths, Lewis opines on the subject of obedience: "I think that this is one of the causes of our love of inanimate nature, that in it we see things which unswervingly carry out the will of their Creator, and are therefore wholly beautiful . . ."[54] The same observation, made outside the correspondence between a Christian apologist and a Catholic monk, might note that we perceive beauty and goodness in nature because there *things are themselves*, they are what they are rather than pretending to be something else. And so, Nan Shepherd writes of nature expressing itself in the "elemental mysteries" of her beloved Cairngorms: "it does nothing, absolutely nothing, but be itself."[55] Lewis and Shepherd are far from alone in admiring this feature of nature. It seems not so different from Serres's appreciation for the honesty of hard reality, which presents itself to us forthrightly and without dissimulation, or Shaftsbury's concern with the connection between beauty and honesty.

Moreover, nature, being honest with us about itself, is equally forthright about us; it asks of us nothing other than that we express ourselves with similar integrity: "everything in nature invites us constantly to be what we are."[56] That is, nature accepts us for who and what we are, asks nothing other than that we behave as good creatures. What does it mean to be a good human creature? Many things assuredly; but one thing in particular is worth noting in the context of despair and love. Recall Erazim Kohák's contention that goodness—which, for Kohák and others, is manifest in an exemplary way in the vibrancy and wildness of the natural world—is of an order other than (i.e., 'outside' of) time. Although it is true that beauty and grace are present whether or not we experience them, our perception, experience, and appreciation of them adds something to the world, completes a certain circuit, catalyzes an ontological reaction. When we experience the goodness of the world, something comes to be in a way that would not be the case without our perception, experience, and appreciation. And as far as we know, we are the only beings who do this; we are the only beings who, in addition to experiencing the world, in addition to desiring and using things in the world, can also give thanks for it and love it in the sense of appreciative-love.

*This is the human vocation*: to love and celebrate and give thanks for the world, the miracle that things are rather than are-not, and the incomparable gift that we are here to witness it.

It cannot be repeated often enough that this does not require that we explain away, ignore, or minimize confusion, loneliness, injustice, suffering, loss, finitude, death, or any other manifestation of evil. Indeed, in some sense love makes things even more terrible. The person who loves the most is most harmed by the loss of the beloved: "There is no safe investment. To love at all is to be vulnerable. Love anything, and your heart will certainly be wrung and possibly be broken."[57] And so the person who loves the world will also, naturally, lament its passing. But what else shall we do? Deny goodness because it does not last forever in the temporal order? Refuse the world because it is fraught with brutality as well as beauty? Because love, like all desire, causes suffering? Shall we "love" tepidly, holding the world at a distance rather than embracing it? Will we go even further out of a desire to protect ourselves? Despair of the world, disparage it as unworthy of love, a composite of meaningless matter, and all-too-temporary at that? Comfort our loveless security with the assurance that it never could have lasted anyway? "Would you rather love the more, and suffer the more; or love the less, and suffer the less? That is, I think, finally, the only real question."[58]

What shall rule us: the fear of being hurt or the conviction, the faith, that love is worth it all? Perhaps we should not be so quick to remove ourselves from the world in order to avoid the heartache that comes with loving it.

> Standing at the brink with his calm, venomous smile . . . the great prestidigitator . . . blows and makes the world disappear. But we do

> not want the world to disappear, nor do we want Christ to load it on his shoulders and transfer it to heaven. We want it to live and struggle here with us. We love it just as the potter loves and desires his clay. We have no other material to work with, no other solid field over chaos to sow and reap.[59]

But if the beauty and goodness in the world are small flames, points of light in the darkness, we have other options than sitting by passively while they are extinguished by the winds of entropy or, worse, helping to blow them out.

> It has seemed to me sometimes as though the Lord breathes on this poor gray ember of Creation and it turns to radiance—for a moment or a year or the span of a life. And then it sinks back into itself again, and to look at it no one would know it had anything to do with fire, or light. . . . But the Lord is more constant and far more extravagant than [this] seems to imply. Wherever you turn your eyes the world can shine like transfiguration. You don't have to bring a thing to it except a little willingness to see. . . . that is, to acknowledge that there is more beauty than our eyes can bear, that precious things have been put into our hands and to do nothing to honor them is to do great harm.[60]

This is no sentimental bromide; it is a recognition of love's role in a distinctively human vocation. Nan Shepherd has the same insight, born of a lifetime living in and loving a particular natural place:

> A certain kind of consciousness interacts with the mountain-forms to create this sense of beauty. . . . It is something snatched from non-being, that shadow which creeps in on us continuously and can be held off by continuous creative act. So, simply to look on anything, such as a mountain, with the love that penetrates to its essence, is to widen the domain of being in the vastness of non-being. *Man has no other reason for his existence*.[61]

# Chapter 6
# Melancholic Joy

Something is wrong with either your eyes or your heart if you do not experience, *profoundly*, both the joy and the sorrow of this world. On the one hand, it would take monstrous egotism, cold indifference, or willful and cowardly ignorance not to have your heart broken and your soul wrung by the obscene suffering woven into the fabric of being, and magnified by human vice; and, on the other hand, it would take appalling insensitivity or cultivated shallowness not to be moved to tears by the overflowing, gratuitous, miraculous beauty of it all. The consolations of glory and the desolations of catastrophe are the warp and weft of our lives, and each makes irresistible demands on the attentive soul. It's an intractable but ineluctable mystery, at once tragic and salvific.[1]

How should we respond?

## 1. Naiveté

The clearest example of joy is the happy child, ecstatic with delight over an ordinary tree or simple game and utterly ignorant of any number of sorrowful facts weighing on the scales of reality: the political unrest that grips her community, perhaps based on forms of bigotry to which she herself will be subjected, perhaps heralding broader civil unrest; or the economic pressures that undermine the stability of her home and the security of her daily bread; or the furious divorce about to rip her family apart; or the deteriorating health of her parents; or perhaps even, harkening back to our encounter with Ivan Karamazov and Dr. Harte, her own recent diagnosis of a terminal illness. The existence of such evils, or of countless others just like them, will eventually bring an end to her childish joy. She will learn, inevitably and all-too-soon, the irresistible and harsh truths of the world. Each of us will eventually awake to the darkness, which, like the Gate of Hell in Dante's *Inferno*, is a passage on the other side of which hope is lost.

It is common, of course, to feel joy (or, at least, to resist despair) when one is in the bloom of youth, health, or love, when one enjoys the security of stable community, a safe home, and a full belly. But a great many people do not enjoy these advantages; and, in any case, the longer one lives, the less secure the citadel defending such fragile assets. No matter how privileged or fortunate one is, evil finds a way to penetrate the fortress, burrowing under defenses, sneaking through gaps, murdering sentries in the night. It is implacable and it can afford to be patient, for once naive joy is wounded by evil it can never fully recover. Like the cut of a poisoned blade, the wound created by the experience of evil festers and spreads; it will never fully heal, no matter what salves we apply. Time is against us. Eventually we all suffer the loss of someone we love. Or our health fails. Or our most cherished projects and aspirations are frustrated. Or perhaps we just awaken one night to suspicion that, really, none of it matters.[2] In the end, nothing lasts. After that realization, we can never return. The gates of Eden close behind us.

That's not to say we don't try. Quite the opposite in fact. Joy is a powerful intoxicant, and people are generally disposed to try to recapture happiness in some form. However, the joy that we've lost, the naive joy of a child, is rooted in innocence and inexperience; and for an adult who has some experience and who is no longer innocent, capturing something like naive joy comes at a price. Perhaps one attempts to maintain a kind of willful ignorance, trying to minimize knowledge about sorrow and suffering of the world. Or, perhaps, one seeks to conjure away or otherwise minimize that suffering via a deft trick of metaphysical or theological accounting. Or, again, perhaps one simply embraces some form of egotism that seeks to revel in joy carelessly, that is to say without concern for entropy tearing at the edges of the world elsewhere. But whatever attempts we make, we find that we can never quite recapture that naive, innocent, childlike joy. Experience changes us, and we can never undo its effects.[3] This is especially true for anyone who is philosophical, or poetic, or indeed who possesses even an ounce of introspection.

But the past several chapters have enumerated, at length, the ways in which vitality, hope, and love do allow us to experience a world with all things shining. How is this possible after the rupture of evil, after our exile from innocence? In a world that seems to counsel despair, how can we be naive enough to embrace joy? The answer, it turns out, depends on what kind of naiveté we are talking about.

The model I have in mind takes its cue from the work of Paul Ricoeur, who employed it in a rather different context. Ricoeur argues that ancient myths, in which we certainly no longer harbor naive belief, can still teach us and have meaning for us. Moreover, we can live out this meaning as part of a "second naiveté," a voluntarily chosen, post-critical belief that takes up, rather than overcomes, the doubt or critique that undid our initial, naive perspective.[4] Such a naiveté includes or takes into account both the naive belief and the critique of that undoes that naive belief. In a similar way, I want to say that we can recapture joy as part of a voluntarily chosen second naiveté, one that takes account of both the post-critical truth that *reality counsels despair* and the pre-critical truth that *reality calls us to joy*.

Once our pre-critical, naive joy has been disrupted, our options are either despair, evasion, or some new way of living in the wake of that disruption. True despair leads us to the pistol or the bottle, and so is not really sustainable.[5] Thus, the first option is relatively rare, although it remains a temptation. The vast majority of people choose to try to avoid despair-inducing thoughts and live as happily as they can, as if they had not glimpsed the truth of "borrowed time and borrowed world and borrowed eyes with which to sorrow it."[6] However, while those attempts can be effective for a time, in the end each is a dissimulation, an attempt to ignore the truth; and, therefore, each is dissatisfying because harsh reality is ultimately unavoidable.

This leaves us with the last option, which, like the first, is rarely pursued. Second naiveté requires something of us, and the joy it wins is a wiser, more experienced, ripened joy, not the innocent joy we lost. I'll call this "*melancholic joy*," a joy that is chosen and won again after the loss of naive joy, a joy lived in the shadow of the legitimate—and inescapable—reasons to despair. As I wagered in the first chapter, it is possible, standing at the edge of the abyss, after looking nihilism and pessimism straight in the face, after acknowledging the persistence of irredeemable and inexplicable suffering, after accepting the long, dark, inhuman indifference of deep time, and without trying to dismiss or minimize any of it, to turn again to the world and say: "yes, I will take you / I will love you, again."[7] This is a love, a joy, that is faithful to both the child's eyes of innocence and the adult's eyes of experience. It is a hermeneutic wager, a leap of faith. But it is not a faith that turns its back on or betrays the world; it is, precisely, a faith that—answering Ivan Karamazov's demand—remains true to the facts.

## 2. Coming to grips with reality

On first glance, it might seem that the facts do not favor joy, even a melancholic joy. We enumerated them in detail in the first chapter: loneliness, isolation, and alienation; the stifling drudgery of securing our daily bread, along with the reality, for many people, of being unable to do so; diverse forms of economic injustice; our impotence with respect to many of our goals; the fragility of all our accomplishments and projects; the stubborn persistence of myriad bigotries and sectarian divisions, and the brutal manifestations of violence to which they all-too-often lead; diverse and unavoidable forms of physical and psychological suffering; predation and parasitism; the inevitability of death, for us and for everyone we love; and stalking all this, just out of sight, the dark and silent menace of an utterly indifferent universe. These facts and others like them are precisely what suggest that reality actually counsels despair.

But what do we mean when we say something is "real"? Our first instinct is likely to rely on elementary definitions like "something actually existing"; but that turns out to be not very helpful, since we still need to clarify what it means to "actually exist." Perhaps another common definition, "something in fact occurring," will be more helpful, insofar as a fact is "something indisputable." But here C.S. Lewis confounds us again by pointing out a significant confusion with the way we talk about what is real.[8] When Serres experiences a "pleroma of exultation" while climbing, or Dillard sees her cedar tree "transfigured, each cell buzzing with flame," people are inclined to say "actually, all that '*really*' happened was that Serres climbed a mountain and saw the sunrise, and Dillard went for a walk and observed a tree." In this case, 'real' means "the bare physical facts, separate from the other elements in the experience."[9]

But if a person expresses optimism about a difficult or challenging task, people will say "just wait until you see what it is 'really' like, then you will change your tune." Here 'real' means "not the physical facts . . . but the emotional effect those facts . . . have on a human consciousness."[10] In one type of instance, we use 'real' to name physical features and in another to name subjective effects, and almost always with an eye to denying the mysterious or personal in favor of the reductively material. In a world captivated by forms of reductive materialism, disenchantment is a *sine qua non*. Anything that is not demonstrable, measurable, quantifiable, and, ideally, commodifiable is disparaged—"subjective" (i.e., *merely* subjective), "emotion" (i.e., *only* emotion), "wishful thinking" (i.e., delusion), "romanticism" (i.e., poetic flight), and so on.

When people deny inconvenient facts about the world, they are often accused of wanting to have their cake and eat it too; but Lewis points out that our confusion about reality puts us in real danger of "paying for the cake and not eating it," which in this case means spending one's life enduring the harsh aspects of reality while denying, and thus failing to experience, the glory of reality.[11] However, if reality is what in fact occurs, and if a fact is something indisputable, it is not immediately clear why Serres's exultation is less real than the mountain on which he climbs, or why the sorrow of those who have died on that mountain (Mont Blanc), and the sorrow of those who loved them, is more real than Serres's joy. Some people might suggest that this is because the physical reality of the mountain is demonstrable in a way that Serres's joy is not. But Saint Exupéry reminds us that truth "is not that which is demonstrable, but that which is ineluctable."[12] This is not to suggest that demonstration is unrelated to truth, or to suggest we should not try to demonstrate where demonstration is possible. It is, rather, to say that the ultimate criterion of truth is ineluctability, not demonstration. We value demonstration because it makes evident one type of ineluctability; but it is not the only type. All truth is ineluctable; only some truth is demonstrable.

Taken more broadly, why should we think that the joy of living or glory of being are less real than the inescapability of death or the intractability of evil? I've argued throughout this work that both are ineluctable. We don't want to ignore, dismiss, or conjure away the evil; but neither do we want to overlook, minimize, or explain away the glory: "beauty is real. I would never deny it; the appalling thing is that [we] forget it."[13] And that forgetting, which afflicts everyone to one degree or another, has real consequences for how we evaluate reality and the case for despair or joy. Perhaps part of the problem is that we confuse our often-clumsy attempts to remember experiences with the experiences themselves, confuse life recollected with life lived. Proust wrote that "the reason why life may be judged to be trivial although at certain moments it seems to us so beautiful is that we form our judgment, ordinarily, on the evidence not of life itself but of those quite different images which preserve nothing of life—and therefore we judge it despairingly."[14]

To judge well we need to take into account the fullness of reality, to consider both the glory of all things shining and the tragedy of all things perishing; and to do that, we need to improve our vision.

## 3. New eyes

We need to experience reality in all its mysterious diversity and to take the fullness of that experience seriously. This requires—as several of the preceding chapters have suggested—that we learn "to see with new eyes." As Kazantzakis advises, since "we cannot change reality, let us change the eyes which see reality."[15] Not in order to deny or dismiss the sorrowful aspects of reality, nor out of a desire to deceive ourselves and escape into an unreal fantasy, but rather to make ourselves attentive to the fullness of reality. Obviously, this is not just about seeing in a narrow, literal sense. After all, sight itself is merely an abstraction from a more global and comprehensive experience. So, to develop new "eyes" that will help us to "see" better, we are really talking about developing new eyes, new tongues, new skin, new powers of attention and appreciation—an entire new way of being in the world that can help us perceive and appreciate those aspects of reality that reductively-minded people tend to dismiss as "mere feeling," "purely subjective," or "fantastical." However, for ease of expression I'll retain the metonym of new "eyes."

Experiencing the world through the lens of our normal vision, we are all too apt to focus on the ways in which reality resists us and fails to satisfy our desires, to overlook or to forget the gratuitousness of being, the glory of all things shining. And, taking the frustrating and sorrowful *aspects* of reality with which we daily grapple to be reality *tout court*, we understandably despair. This is what is real, we say; and, of course, the sorrowful aspects of reality are real. We must take them into account. But just as fear of a difficult passage above can blind a climber to the beauty of the world spread below her feet, the sorrowful aspects of reality can induce a sort of tunnel vision that causes us to miss the glory twinkling in our peripheral vision.

As we've seen, developing new vision is not so simple as just deciding to experience things differently or willing something to reveal itself. When we try to force ourselves to see things differently or to compel reality to reveal itself to us, we generally fail to get what we are after. That failure only increases our frustration, which often leads people to dismiss the possibility of seeing "all things shining" as nonsense, and to mock the "glory" as make-believe. Alternatively, our inability to coerce reality into revealing its glory can lead us to settle for mere simulacra, inauthentically affirming a splendor and beauty that our experience does not validate. But like the person who pretends to be in love, and who goes through the motions of being in love, rather than admit she has not yet found genuine love, such a nostrum does little to actually alter our perception of the world; it is nothing more than a make-believe, and it will crumble to dust at the first touch of resistance from the hard and sorrowful aspects of reality.

Which comes first, the experience of glory that causes the scales to fall from our eyes, or the development of the eyes that will allow them to perceive the glory? We cannot get what we are after by aiming at it directly. Acquiring new eyes for reality requires that we let go of desire to control everything, that we cultivate a habit of openness to what reality is revealing, and that we commit ourselves to salubrious doses of silence and solitude. This, to be sure, is challenging. "The hardest thing of all is to see what is really there."[16] For most of us, developing new eyes will require a cultivated practice, an *ascesis* even. And thus the paradox of "trying not to try," a strange discipline in which we make an effort to give up making an effort, exert our power to relinquish power, develop self-mastery in order to give up mastery over things, and practice self-discipline so that we can renounce the self as the center of concern. More than just seeing otherwise, it requires that we change our fundamental way of being in the world so that we are more open, more patient, more attentive, and more appreciative. And, still, there remains an element of chance at play. We make ourselves receptive to the world; but the world reveals itself in unanticipatable ways. We can cultivate new eyes, but the world gives itself impartially, independent of whether our eyes are open or closed.

The eyes that will attune us to these hidden aspects of reality combine the innocence of a child's sight and the experienced perspective of an elder or veteran. The eyes of youth allow us to see the world with wonder, "as if for the first time." When we can do this, the world becomes new again, a world, as Wallace Stegner writes of Norman Mclean's childhood in the American West, "with dew still on it," one "younger, fresher, and more touched with wonder and possibility."[17] These experiences are often associated with literal youth; but we can, with practice, learn to see the world through youthful eyes again. Naturally, as we are no longer actually young, when we go to the world with youthful eyes we will no doubt experience our share of "undistinguished" days; but "now and then, unpredictable and unforgettable, come the hours when heaven and earth fall away and one sees a new creation . . . and one can read at last the word that has been from the beginning . . ."[18] This is certainly why "morning" is perhaps the most repeated trope and image in *Walden*; and why Thoreau, exhorting us to a new way of being in the world, reminds us of the need to see otherwise: "There is just as much beauty visible in the landscape as we are prepared to appreciate,—not a grain more."[19] The youthful quality of new eyes allows us to see the reality of the contingent, ephemeral, gratuitous, wonder of the world.

But the eyes of second naiveté are not only those of innocence; they are also eyes of experience, and this in at least two senses. First, the eyes of second naiveté have already lost their naive innocence: they have seen evil; they have experienced loss; they know suffering; but they nevertheless choose not to be mesmerized by it to the occlusion of the rest of reality. As Flannery O'Conner reports, using an appropriately ocular metaphor to speak of her own difficult struggle with Lupus: "I can with one eye squinted take it all as a blessing."[20] Note that to squint is not to close one eye, as if we could block out the suffering on one side of things to focus on the good on the other; it is, rather, to focus better, as when a nearsighted person squints—O'Connor herself wore glasses—not to look away from things, but precisely to make them clearer.

The eyes of second naiveté are experienced in another important sense: they view the world "as if for the last time," with eyes made wise by the weight of the knowledge that this—this experience, this life, this world—will be gone, and all too soon. Certainly there will be a melancholic or bittersweet aspect to such vision, about which I'll say more in a moment. But despite the heartache that accompanies the acute awareness of ephemerality, to see reality as if for the last time can, in second naiveté, result in more gratitude than sorrow. It is the vision of a person who has been given one last, unexpected day with a lover before shipping off to war, of someone with a terminal disease given six months of remission by an experimental treatment.[21] For such people, attention to every detail of the world is enhanced. On his deathbed, Thoreau was visited by his friend Parker Pillsbury. Seeing Thoreau was very weak, Pillsbury said, "You seem so near the brink of the dark river that I almost wonder how the opposite shore may appear to you." To which Thoreau, who loved this world, replied: "One world at a time."[22] That appreciation of and fidelity to this world not only gave Thoreau a good life, it gave him a good death as well. As Hannah Arendt argues, "what ultimately stills the fear of death is not hope or desire [for another world], but remembrance and gratitude [for this one]."[23]

The eyes of second naiveté—both innocent and experienced, marked by joyful wonder and bittersweet gratitude—transform our experience of not only the world, but time itself. The eruption of the "eternal" in the everyday is something we've touched on in describing joy, vitality, hope, and love. These experiences, which are related to the gratitude of which Arendt speaks, allay the anxiety rooted in our being-toward-death and allow us to dwell fully in the goodness of the present moment and the adventure of death-not-yet.

> A minute freed from the order of time has re-created in us, to feel it, the man freed from the order of time. And one can understand that this man should have confidence in his joy, even if the simple taste of a madeleine does not seem logically to contain within it the reasons for this joy, one can understand that the word "death" should have no meaning for him; situated outside time, why should he fear the future?[24]

It is not the case that we make a decision, employ the appropriate techniques and exert the appropriate effort, and thereby free ourselves from the order of time, which then allows us to see the world otherwise. It is rather that, if we open ourselves to the world, there will be occasions in which experiences like this come upon us like an unexpected gift and, as a consequence, we are freed—for a moment, but an 'eternal' moment—from the ravages of time. Like a man before the firing squad savoring a last cigarette, or good friends enjoying a fine wine before parting for the last time, in these moments we live, in a sense, forever: "There is a whole lifetime in a glass of Margaux," write Serres, which can no doubt be true; but if we have cultivated not just new eyes, but new fingers, noses, and mouths as well, we may find this to be true of "even a simple cob loaf."[25] Nikos Kazantzakis's Zorba is fond of saying that men like him should "live a thousand years" because they love life more than other people.[26] And if loving life is tied to the human vocation of witnessing and appreciating the glory of the world, which opens us to the experience of eternity in the everyday, perhaps they do.

## 4. Melancholic joy

In the previous chapters, I've described manifestations of melancholic joy in some detail; but what can we say about it in more general terms? Obviously, as a form of joy, it delights in the world; and, therefore, while it certainly experiences sorrow, disappointment, regret, and the like, it will not give in to despair. Despair, we've seen, is associated with a loss of faith in the world itself, the state of coming to believe that "it's not worth it." Thus, it should come as no surprise that genuine despair rarely lasts long. Its fullest and most uncompromising expressions are generally destructive, and often self-destructive. Despair is the state-of-being of the suicide, whether she chooses the abrupt end of a pistol shot or the drawn-out resolution of the bottle.[27] For this reason, it is perhaps more common to find people who succumb to some degree of pessimistic miserabilism, a gloomy perspective or disposition that has eyes only for the negative: betrayal, injustice, loss, pain, sorrow, death, decay. Often such people will claim to be "realists"; but we've seen that a full and fair accounting suggests that miserabilism and pessimistic realism are, more often than not, the result of a very selective attention to the real. Nevertheless, we must remember that the experience of evil that leads people to miserabilism is real, which is precisely why the joy of second naiveté is, and must remain, melancholic.

But if genuine despair is unsustainable and miserabilism is, to say the least, unpleasant, there are other ways in which people have sought to navigate the challenges of the human condition.

## 4.1 Escape and evasion

The most common way to deal with the threat of despair is to try to recapture the state of mind that preceded it: the naive joy of innocence. This can take a variety of forms, various ways to try to distract oneself from what experience has revealed about the world: that it is full of suffering, frustration, sorrow, and loss; that the loves and joys we experience are, in the order of time, few, fragile, and bound to pass; and that many of our most important existential questions have no clear, complete, final answers. These are harsh truths, and hard to accept. So, people seek to forget themselves in a shopping mall, or lose themselves in work (whether or not they find it meaningful), or validate themselves and their activities with social approbation. They focus on happiness and, if they spare a thought for beauty, they try to avoid the fact that it is ephemeral. They do not think about the vast and silent darkness between the stars, and turn away from experiencing or contemplating mystery. "Oh Larry," sighs an exasperated Isabel in Somerset Maugham's *The Razor's Edge*, frustrated with her fiancé for turning down a lucrative position in finance to "loaf" in Paris on a kind of spiritual quest, seeking, among other things, an answer to the problem of evil. "It all sounds so adolescent to me. Those are the sort of things sophomores get excited about and then when they leave college they forget about them. They have to earn a living."[28]

But distraction and evasion can only ever be partially successful in turning us from the "big questions" or hiding the sobering aspects of reality. And they often lead us, as Thoreau says, to "lives of quiet desperation": futile and unfulfilling attempts to ignore the emptiness of modern life and the specter of our common doom. We may outrun fate for a time—a day, a year, a period of life—but entropy is an implacable hunter that will, in the end, run us to ground.

People want to forget their mortality; but, in so doing, they often deny or forget their humanity, and this in two senses. First, they deny implicitly what they are: creatures. That is to say, evolved, finite, wild, embodied, mortal animals. Insignificant in their ordinariness, the brevity of their lives, and the restricted scope of their experience and vision. Rather than asserting the *imago Dei* separates us from other creatures, we act as though Bloomingdale's, corner offices, Netflix subscriptions, and regular social media postings do the same. But to lose oneself in these trivial distractions is to forget one's humanity in a second sense. It is to forget what we might become: full human beings—rational, emotional, imaginative animals that can contemplate the melancholic, wonderous splendor of it all, and who take up the human vocation of bearing witness to it in appreciative-love, which is anything but insignificant.[29]

## 4.2 Job: Theodicy

Other, more sophisticated ways to deal with the temptation of despair can be found in various philosophies. We've seen that one common way to try to do this is captured in the logic of theodicy, which I've treated at length in chapter two. Theodicy has a long history in various cultures, but it remains a bitter, bitter draught. It is contaminated by the "but . . ." that so offends Ivan Karamazov. It asks us to accept the horror of a lifetime of locked-in syndrome for the child in Dr. Harte's story; it tells us Alzheimer's disease, *naegleria fowleri*, COVID-19, and countless other horrors are part of a perfectly good world. Theodicy takes these horrors and asks us to accept that our experience of them as "evil" is merely an error caused by self-centered perception or judgment, that they are actually part of some larger, incomprehensibly perfect arrangement or plan. It asks us to accept that the unbearable suffering of an innocent child is justifiable because it purchases some future good.

Melancholic joy will not be bought off with such an exchange. It is no longer innocent; it is marked, scarred even, by experience. It has felt the prick of the thorns on the rose-without-why. It hears the wailing of innocent children, smells the charnel house of history, tastes the funerary ashes in its mouth, and knows that entropy is constantly eroding the edges of reality, playing the patient, long game. So melancholic joy is no longer willing to confidently affirm, whether through optimism in progress or faith in theodicy, that "all will be well, all manner of things shall be well."[30] The joy of second naiveté is not simple naive joy; it is a complicated—even conflicted—melancholic joy. It knows and appreciates that reasons for joy, experiences of vitality, and occasions for appreciative-love exist alongside powerful reasons for sorrow, despair, and aversion or even hostility toward the world.

## 4.3 Epicurus: *Ataraxia*

Another way of dealing with the mystery of evil is through some form of acceptance or resignation—Epicurean, Stoic, or otherwise—with which melancholic joy has apparent similarities. After all, I've acknowledged that we will have to recognize and accept evil as part of the mystery of being; not only is it beyond our power to eradicate, it is beyond our ability to comprehend or understand. A wise person will appreciate the difference between those things she can control or change and those she cannot; and she will focus her attention on the former rather than the latter. We may overcome particular instances of evil, and should strive to do so; but evil itself is in no danger of being eliminated from the world. It seems the better part of wisdom to accept what we cannot change.

Nevertheless, melancholic joy rejects Epicureanism and other forms of detachment from the world, which demand that we desensitize ourselves to its sorrows or diminish our joy in its beauties. The happiness aimed at by such philosophies is the happiness of *ataraxia*, the absence of pain or distress, whether physical or mental; and that happiness is purchased at the price detachment. But while there is much to learn from these traditions, especially Stoicism, mere *ataraxia* is at best a consolation prize, and a meager one at that. It is a safe happiness, a secure happiness; but it is a feeble one. It is less than we are capable of, and we should not settle for it.

The thinkers referenced in the preceding chapters—Kazantzakis, Aragon, Dillard, Bass, Shepherd, and others—remind us to love the world, passionately, despite its complicated, mysterious complicity in tragedy. They would want to linger here, joyfully and appreciatively, even if we were bound for another world. Not so the Epicurean, whose goal is not "joy," but rather "less sorrow." Resignation, detachment, and denial restrict our experience of joy and come at the cost of living and loving fully. To love more is to suffer more, even when we love appropriately, loving mortal things as mortal; and so, philosophies of detachment tell us that to suffer less we must love less.[31] But melancholic joy is not willing to purchase tranquility at the price of joy, physical safety at the price of vital living, or emotional security at the price of love. The person living melancholic joy is never going to kiss her child and remind herself 'I am kissing a corpse.'[32]

## 4.4 Camus: Sisyphean revolt and resignation

Resignation and detachment bleed into additional forms of life that suggest the way to deal with the world is simply to "go on." This sentiment comes up in a variety of places, but perhaps its most well-known expression is in Albert Camus's absurd hero Sisyphus. Readers familiar with Camus will note the similarity between his account of Sisyphus and that of melancholic joy, insofar as both seek to sort out how to live happily in a world that is in some way fundamentally disappointing to our desires. After all, the most famous line of *The Myth of Sisyphus*—too often the only line cited—is: "One must imagine Sisyphus happy."[33] But here everything hinges on just how the world is disappointing, how we go about finding happiness in it, and what that happiness looks like.

For Camus, the fundamental disappointment of reality is that it is not fully comprehensible: "I want everything explained to me or nothing."[34] Absurdity results from the inability of human reason to understand everything, not only the particulars of the world, but the universals which govern them: "understanding is, above all, to unify . . . it is an insistence upon familiarity, an appetite for clarity . . . [u]nderstanding the world for a man is reducing it to the human, stamping it with his seal."[35] The world is absurd because we cannot reduce it to the human without remainder. Camus's world is absurd merely, and merely absurd, because Camus is not omniscient; he is not God. There is, we should note, precious little room for appreciative joy in such a perspective.

But Camus is not interested in appreciating mystery. He critiques a number of "humiliated"—others might say "humble"—thinkers who accept in some way the unreasonableness of the world, some aspect of the world that is resistant to or beyond complete and clear comprehension. Such thinkers, he says, suggest that "reason is useless but there is something beyond reason" while "[t]o an absurd mind reason is useless and there is nothing beyond reason."[36] He seems to think that any concession to mystery amounts to an actual valorization of unreason over reason. This is not the place to defend any of the "humiliated" thinkers Camus critiques, but it should be obvious that his claim that "*nothing* is clear, *all* is chaos"[37] would be a ridiculous caricature if applied to second naiveté's acknowledgement that there are *some* things that are mysterious.

To acknowledge mystery does not mean that reason is useless, or that nothing is clear, or that all we have is chaos. Some aspects of reality are quite clear to reason, and others are in the process of becoming clearer. In such spheres, we might hope, with Charles Sanders Peirce, that a clear understanding of reality is something we approach asymptotically. Nevertheless, there are aspects of reality—love, evil, and the meaningfulness or meaninglessness of life are prime examples—that remain, and will remain, mysterious. In these spheres, rational, analytic interrogation proves sterile; it will never find the clear answers it demands, and consequently—one might say, "in retaliation"—it dismisses such questions as mystical obfuscation, and answers rooted elsewhere than reason as meaningless gibberish.

A philosophy of mystery or second naiveté does not assert that there is something "beyond" reason in the sense of "better than reason" but rather in the sense of "other than reason." Mystery does not demean reason. Reason is a very good thing, and heaven knows we need more of it. Nor does it suggest that emotion or intuition or faith is better than reason *tout court*. However, reason does have limits, which are most obvious when it is used indiscriminately and applied identically to every sphere of inquiry or experience. Reason is not an all-purpose solvent for philosophical or existential problems, and certainly not for mysteries.[38] Try, for example, giving a full, clear, rational, analytic explanation of your love of some particular person.

In addition to differences in the diagnosis—absurdity versus mystery—Camus's prescription for life diverges from that of melancholic joy. What does Camus's hero do in response to absurdity, the incomplete correspondence between human understanding and reality? Revolt. Seize awareness of the whole of experience and existence—without hope of reconciling absurdity and without resignation. Be defiant to the bitter end. Drain life, deplete oneself. All this might seem quite close to certain aspects of melancholic joy, but the devil is in the details and significant differences remain. For Camus, the appropriate mode is not celebration and appreciation of the goodness of being, nor scandal at the persistence of evil and some kind of benevolent attempt to ameliorate it, but defiance and scorn at the absurdity of it all: "[t]here is no fate that cannot be surmounted by scorn."[39] It is true that Camus speaks of joy and happiness; but, in the end, defiance is little more than stubborn endurance, choosing to put one foot in front of the other as we each trudge up our own particular Sisyphean slope, pushing our own particular boulder. Life is reduced to a "dull resonance" in which there is no mention of the glory of things shining, and "heroism" to a listless refusal of suicide in a meaningless, indifferent, grey world.[40]

There are others who see a certain significance in the simple act of trudging on: Samuel Beckett's "I can't go on. I'll go on"; William James's observation that struggle itself gives us a reason, however thin, to live; and Simon Critchley's "There is only my dying and your dying and nothing beyond . . . Until then, we carry on."[41] However, the dull resonance of Sisyphus's labor brings to mind neither these thinkers or any of the absurd heroes Camus mentions (Don Juan, the dramatist, the conqueror, etc.), but rather the unnamed man and boy in Cormac McCarthy's apocalyptic *The Road*.[42] The man and the boy trudge meaninglessly and hopelessly in the wake of a nameless event that has destroyed civilization and laid waste to the environment, leaving little more than roving bands of cannibalistic rapists living off other survivors. The journey on the road combines the drudgery of Sisyphus's labor with the horror of Dante's vision of hell. Although the man and the boy attempt to project meaning on to their lives beyond mere animal survival—their journey toward the coast, their struggle to keep "the fire" within—the senselessness of their existence is complete, overwhelming, absolute. When they encounter an old man on the road, one of the few people they have met who is not out to enslave, rape, or eat them—they ask: "How do you live?" And the man replies simply, but senselessly, "I just keep going."[43]

For Camus, the struggle is enough to fill a person's heart with a kind of happiness, and even with the conclusion that "all is well."[44] Melancholic joy takes exception to both claims. First, while Camus is, with William James, correct to point out that stubborn struggle can be enough to motivate us to resist suicide, melancholic joy is disinclined to accept such scraps, not when a banquet is on offer. Simply enduring existence is not life, which is why the "uncounted and uncalendared" days in *The Road*—with "No list of things to be done. The day providential to itself.

The hour. There is no later. This is later"—are not the same as the uncounted, uncalendared, providential days of melancholic joy.[45] The eternity of the road is eternal duration as existence grinds on, relentlessly and remorselessly and indifferently, day after meaningless day. The eternity of melancholic joy is the eternity of the present moment in which time stops, uniquely and irreplaceably and gloriously. In addition, melancholic joy will not accept that "all is well." All is *not* well. Of course, there are different forms of evil in the world. Some forms of evil can be addressed, and others may be addressable in the future; but evil itself seems part of the warp and weft of reality. But while wisdom dictates that we accept the latter, at least in the sense of accommodating ourselves to it, the former should arouse our complaint and our active resistance.

In the end, revolt is but another term for steadfastly plowing on, with little emphasis on the quality of the days through which we plow and the experiences that fill them. Camus, for example, is obsessed with the quantity of life with a surprising disregard for the quality: "what counts is not the best living but the most living"[46] and "no depth, no emotion, no passion, and no sacrifice could render equal in the eyes of the absurd man . . . a conscious life of forty years and a lucidity spread over sixty years."[47] But this seems difficult to square with a full and honest appraisal of the diversity of life paths. Which shall we prefer: seventy-five years of scornful, defiant resistance in a life characterized by meaningless drudgery, in which we fret obsessively about our inability to comprehend every last mote of reality, and in which our greatest accomplishment is to resist the siren's song of suicide and endure another day, or a life of only fifty or sixty years characterized, certainly, by moments of profound pain, sorrow, confusion, and loneliness, but also by glorious, transcendent experiences, moments in which time stops and the world unfolds to reveal something more—eternity in a moment, heaven on earth?[48]

## 4.5 Nietzsche and Dionysian pessimism

The attentive reader will no doubt have observed that melancholic joy bears more than passing similarity to Nietzsche's commitment to a form of pessimism that is nevertheless "a Dionysian yes-saying to the world as it is.'"[49] Nietzsche may be a kind of 'pessimist,' but his is a joyful, dancing pessimism. However, here again there remain significant differences that distinguish the two positions. Nietzsche is, needless to say, a challenging thinker; and there are nearly as many interpretations of his work as there are readers of it. Nevertheless, it is clear that Dionysian pessimism is closely linked to additional commitments with which melancholic joy would have trouble reconciling itself: first, the derisive rejection of faith and religion, at least on the common reading of Nietzsche, and, second, the doctrine of the eternal return of the same.

Most readers will assume that Nietzsche's attack on religion represents the most significant gap between Dionysian pessimism and melancholic joy; after all, it has become clear that the latter is rooted in a kind of faith. Joy and deep hope rest on faith in the world, a faith that finds expression in appreciative-love. I've endeavored to describe that faith in terms that remain a live option for a wide variety of people, people with commitments ranging from traditional theisms to secular humanism. But is it compatible with Nietzsche's highly polemical attacks?

It is true that Nietzsche is highly critical of Christianity, but to some extent the outsized nature of that target is a function of his particular history and the history of the culture in which he was embedded. The fundamental dispute, made evident by his parallel critique of Platonism, is with any religion, philosophy, or system of belief that locates value and meaning in some world other than this one. That objection, however, does not seem to apply to the threshold faith necessary for melancholic joy, which explicitly brackets debate about forms of transcendence advocating escape from this world in favor of forms of transcendence emphasizing the ways in which we can experience this world more deeply. Thus, on a fundamental level Nietzsche's most biting critiques do not really apply to the faith associated with melancholic joy.

Moreover, it is not at all clear that Nietzsche's criticisms apply to "faith" as distinct from "religion" in the way those terms have come to be understood by contemporary philosophy.[50] Again, speaking only for melancholic joy, what is at issue in faith is a commitment to first principles that we argue from rather than argue for, which lay the foundation for our beliefs about meaning and which structure our way of life: how one ought to live, what constitutes a good life, whether or not the world is meaningful in some sense, and so forth. Nietzsche's work seems far from antagonistic to faith in that basic sense.

Indeed, speculation about a "faithful" or "mystical" side to Nietzsche and his work came to the fore as early as 1894—when Nietzsche was still living, though incapacitated by his mental breakdown—in the work of his friend, former traveling companion, and unrequited love Lou Salomé. On the basis of both a close association with the man and a close reading of his books, Salomé insists that "All of Nietzsche's knowledge arose from a powerful religious mood . . ."[51] and, further, that "Of all his great intellectual dispositions, none is bound more profoundly and unremittingly to his whole intellectual being than his religious genius."[52]

Surprising words, perhaps, to many of Nietzsche's casual readers. But Nietzsche was raised a pastor's son in the context of fervent Lutheran Pietism, and this early inculturation remained influential in his intellectual itinerary. His mature philosophy is clearly a reaction to and rejection of the other-worldly focus of Pietism; nevertheless, a number of commentators argue that his later work remained connected to the spirit of that early Pietism in complex ways. Salomé characterizes Nietzsche's most famous book, *Thus Spoke Zarathustra*, as a "mystical" work. This is evident not only in the substitution of the *Übermensch*—a self-projection of sorts and, according to Salomé's analysis, a "creature of religious mysticism"—for God; it is also evident in the Nietzschean-Dionysian emphasis on the ecstatic expression (*Rausch*: intoxication, rush, exhilaration) of the will to power.[53] On this account, Nietzsche remains captivated, as one modern idiom would have it, by a kind of "religion without religion," and remains a person of (a certain kind of) faith.[54] Graham Parkes suggests that *Zarathustra* ends with a "new kind of religion . . . aptly called 'Dionysian pantheism'"[55] Bruce Benson goes even further, suggesting not only that Nietzsche remained a philosopher of faith, but also that in many ways this faith retained the odor of Christianity.[56]

However, in order to reconcile Dionysian pessimism with melancholic joy we do not need to make these latter, stronger claims, only the former, weaker one. We don't need to imply that Nietzsche was a crypto-theist or that he was religious in the sense we normally use that term. The faith that invests us in the world, giving us "new eyes" that allow us to see otherwise, only requires, I've argued, a minimal commitment to the meaningfulness of reality and the goodness of being. It does not require dogma or church or even community, although it is not allergic to any of them construed in a certain way; and it is far from clear that faith of this sort is incompatible with Nietzsche's criticism of religion. It is much more likely that melancholic joy has more than enough room for Dionysians, and that Dionysians would feel quite at home in the faith of melancholic joy.

The larger problem with Dionysian pessimism is its connection to the doctrine of the eternal return of the same, which Nietzsche himself asserts is the "fundamental conception" of his *Thus Spoke Zarathustra*.[57] It is the *telos* of his work, the pole-star of his thinking.

> Zarathustra [is one who] . . . has the hardest, most terrible insight into reality, that has thought the "most abysmal idea," [and] nevertheless does not consider it an objection to existence, not even to its eternal recurrence—but rather one reason more for being himself the eternal Yes to all things, "the tremendous, unbounded saying Yes and Amen."[58]

What is this fundamental thought? Perhaps the most succinct expression is found in *The Gay Science*:

> What, if some day or night a demon were to steal after you into your loneliest loneliness and say to you: "This life as you now live it and have lived it, you will have to live once more and innumerable times more; and there will be nothing new in it, but every pain and every joy and every thought and sigh and everything unutterably small or great in your life will have to return to you, all in the same succession and sequence – even this spider and this moonlight between the trees, and even this moment and I myself. The eternal hourglass of existence is turned upside down again and again, and you with it, speck of dust!" Would you not throw yourself down and gnash your teeth and curse the demon who spoke thus? . . . Or how well disposed would you have to become to yourself and to life *to crave nothing more fervently* than this ultimate eternal confirmation and seal?[59]

This point, eternal return, is particularly tricky. Although Nietzsche calls it the "fundamental conception" of his work, he does not provide a clear account of it and, in fact, does not speak about it either as directly or as often as one would expect. Nevertheless, we can distinguish between three possible interpretations of this wish for the "eternal return of the same": metaphysical, normative, and existential.

The metaphysical claim would be that eternal return is in fact the order of the universe. This would seem to follow from the account in *The Will to Power*, in which Nietzsche asserts that in a mechanistic world that is materially finite and temporally infinite, every possible concatenation of matter would, eventually, repeat itself. But melancholic joy does not have much to say for or against the metaphysical claim; and in truth does not have much time for speculation about it. Like the heat death of the universe in some incomprehensibly distant future, the metaphysical truth or falsity of eternal return over infinite time is so remote as to be practically unrelated to life here and now. Obsessing over it would be nothing than another form of the escapism Nietzsche derides in theologies focused on life-after-death.[60]

The existential claim, in contrast, asks us to imagine how we would change if eternal return were true and our actions would repeat themselves forever. How would you live? What would you change about your way of life? Your actions? Your priorities? Many other thinkers endorse similar ways to appraise one's life. The existential import of eternal return is more of a thought experiment designed to help us keep focused on living maximally fulfilling lives, and it is wholly unobjectionable to melancholic joy, even welcome. A person confronted with the idea that her choices and actions might echo into eternity would, one supposes, be that much more likely to strive to experience life miraculously.

But if melancholic joy finds the metaphysical claim unimportant and the existential claim unobjectionable, the same cannot be said for the normative claim; and this is problematic because many people read Nietzsche in this normative sense. The normative claim goes further than the existential claim. The latter asks us to imagine a future in which our actions would repeat themselves, and to act accordingly. The normative claim, however, insists that we ought to positively endorse repetition, the eternal return of everything about reality—past, present, and future—down to the most minute detail imaginable. "Every thought and sigh." "Every pain." "*Nothing* new." On the normative reading of eternal return, any hesitancy to endorse and embrace any aspect of reality is a failure to accept reality, a betrayal of it. The only real "yes" to reality is one that has no room for any "no."[61] For a melancholic joy sensitive to evils in the world, this is intolerable.

On the normative reading, the eternal return of the same is theodicy without the *theos*; it demands that we positively endorse every detail of the world, wish for it to occur again and again and again. Every joy and celebration, yes; but also every rape, every murder, and every wasting, diseased, lonely death. It implies that our objections to the latter are somehow the consequence of an insufficiently objective view of the world, an artifact of wishful thinking based in a self-centered and self-interested view of things, or an attempt to flee from this (the only) reality for some transcendental fairyland. It demands that we love the world indiscriminately and implies that any reservation is ultimately a failure of love. But that is not how real love works. It is entirely possible, appropriate even, to love people and simultaneously desire for them to be the best version of themselves they can be, which means recognizing they are not yet the best version of themselves. One can love someone unreservedly and, simultaneously, wish for that person to overcome an alcohol or drug addiction. And it is possible to love the world in all its awful/awe-full mystery and still regret that specific evils afflict specific people. Recall that melancholic joy is willing to accept that evil *per se* is not going to be vanquished; but it also recognizes that individual evils—as least some of them—can be ameliorated.

It might be useful to think of the undesirable aspects of the world in terms of "fundamentals," "contingencies," and "individuals" or "cases." This world, and our human experience of it, is structured by certain fundamental facts, some of which are troubling to us: finitude, entropy, and so forth. There are, in addition, contingent facts about the ways in which those more fundamental structures are made manifest: that an individual is born at one time and in one culture rather than another, that human life is counted in decades rather than centuries, and other similar facts. And, finally, there are specific individual cases in which those fundamental and contingent facts unfold: *this* orphan, *this* victim, *this* invalid. Melancholic joy can bring itself to accept—and even to appreciate with a kind of tragic wisdom—the fundamental and contingent elements: the ephemeral nature of beauty in things subject to entropy, the inevitability of death, the finitude that constrains all human projects. But melancholic joy recoils at specific cases of evil: not human fallibility and the inevitability of accidents, but *this* accident (e.g., Harte's locked-in child); not human finitude and mortality, but the painful, wasting death of *this* young cancer victim; not the ephemerality of temporal things, but the passing of *this* moment of peace and security. Melancholic joy will not try to erase the scandal of these individual evils with the "but . . ." that enrages Ivan Karamazov, and it will not endorse their recurrence as part of some misguided "overcoming" of judgment about good and evil. And this unwillingness to endorse specific cases of evil is a manifestation of its love of the world, not a defect of it.

When Nietzsche comes to these particular evils, I suspect he is too willing to look away: "I do not want to wage war against what is ugly. I do not want to accuse; I do not even want to accuse those who accuse. Looking away shall be my only negation."[62] He rightly refuses to conceal the ugliness of evil by sleight of hand or philosophical trickery, but he wrongly refuses to confront it. Turning a blind eye to ugliness or instances of evil in order to enjoy the world is wrong, whether the goal is bourgeoise happiness or the "creation of new values." It is precisely the negation of looking away that allows the otherwise unconditional Nietzschean affirmation of fate. Out of sight, out of mind. "My formula for greatness in a human being is *amor fati*: that one wants nothing to be different, not forward, not backward, not in all eternity. Not merely bear what is necessary, still less conceal it . . . but love it."[63] Nietzsche's affirmation requires that we love and affirm everything that has happened and will happen: the Holocaust and the Enlightenment; the polio vaccine and COVID-19; compassion and care for others as well as rape, murder, and torture. Melancholic joy, in contrast, asserts that we can be genuinely life-affirming without requiring that we positively endorse evil, tragedy, injustice, and the like. We can have unconditional *amor mundi* without requiring unqualified *amor fati*.

Philosophers sometimes claim that pessimism gets a bad rap because optimists distort the position, and in some sense that is no doubt true.[64] But philosophical pessimists are equally to blame when it comes to non-standard use of terms to make their arguments. Pessimism, from *pessimus*: the *worst*. To be a pessimist is to see the worst in things, or to believe that the worst will happen. This is why we so often associate pessimism with a kind of miserabilism, and even with despair. Of course, in this sense, Nietzsche is no pessimist. His 'pessimism,' like many others, is really just a rejection of optimism—hopefulness or confidence about the future—especially optimism rooted in a world other than this one. And, says melancholic joy, that's fair enough. This world is not optimal, and it would be foolish to believe that it is. But neither is this world the worst; and that is the case even if the fate of the universe lies in the heat death of thermodynamic equilibrium. For it is better that things are than are not; and it is, and will have been, better that things were than that they never were. And although this is not the best of all possible worlds, it is the world that we've got and, importantly, "it is enough."[65]

Melancholic joy reminds us that both optimism and pessimism are distortions of reality. It asks us to recognize both the evil and the good in the world and to accept their irreducibility, to experience the mystery. It rejects despair, and rejects common forms of dealing with despair. Theodicy—whether classically formulated by strong theology, or in the non-theistic guises of deep ecology or eternal return—attempts to explain away evil, asks us to accept or even endorse it. But melancholic joy does not believe we can explain away evil, and is unwilling to endorse it.[66] Detachment, *apatheia*, and *ataraxia* limit certain kinds of suffering, but in so doing limit our experience of love and joy. Melancholic joy asserts that appreciative-love for the world is part of the human vocation, and worth the price of suffering that comes with it. Diverse forms of "endurance"—in Camus, McCarthy, and others—insist that the best we can do is put our heads down and plow aimlessly ahead, denying any meaning and reducing life to bare existence. Melancholic joy finds life and the world shot through with meaning, mysterious to be sure, but saturated with value and significance. Melancholic joy is unwilling to compromise on reality. It acknowledges, fully, both the reasons for joy and the reasons for sorrow, without minimizing or disparaging either—a bittersweet appreciation of the mystery of being.

## 5. Thus passes the glory of the world

Where, then, does this leave us? Well, right where we started: here and now, in the midst of life and things. In one sense, nothing has changed. We perish, each alone. We are born into a world that quickly shows us its indifference. Our journey through life is marked by confusion and anxiety, punctuated by pain and fear. We are powerless to eradicate evil, our projects fail, and we experience the frustration of impossible dreams that will not be fulfilled. And, as we struggle along this harrowing journey, each day brings us closer to our inevitable death. All true.

However, to inventory this catalog of woe is to see only half the facts, and to understand less than half the truth. It's a problem as old as history. *The Epic of Gilgamesh*, one of humanity's oldest surviving literary expressions, tells the story of a hero and demi-god who, despite his power and wealth, falls into despair under the weight of mortality, and embarks on a frenzied quest to achieve eternal life. During his journey, he encounters the alewife Siduri in the Garden of the Gods. Learning of Gilgamesh's quest, she admonishes him:

> Gilgamesh, where are you hurrying to? You will never find that life for which you are looking. When the gods created man they allotted to him death, but life they retained for their own keeping. As for you, Gilgamesh, fill your belly with good things; day and night, night and day, dance and be merry, feast and rejoice. Let your clothes be fresh, bathe yourself in water, cherish the little child that holds your hand, and make your wife happy in your embrace; for this too is the lot of man.[67]

It has been said that humans "cannot bear very much reality"; but sometimes what drives us to despair is precisely *not enough* reality, in the sense that we often allow one aspect of reality (i.e., that which we experience as a burden) to occlude another (i.e., that which we experience as a gift or a grace).[68]

Despair is a vice, and a recipe for suicide. But, for a responsible adult, innocent joy is unsustainable in a world governed by entropy, a history burdened by barbarism, and a life riddled with privation and doomed to extinction. To seek innocent joy as an adult is unseemly at best and more often vicious: the mark of extreme (frequently willful) ignorance and bourgeois self-absorption, or of a cloistered affluence that is indifferent to the suffering of others, or of philosophical justification bordering on sociopathy. We might go so far as to modify Mr. Ramsey's claim from chapter one: to be in a state of innocent joy in a world of misery is, for an honest person, a despicable crime. However, this does not mean we should despair. Human beings are made for joy;[69] but it must be an enlightened joy, a joy that neither takes goodness for granted nor hides from the reality of evil. Such a joy will, inevitably, retain the mark of melancholy. How could it not?

No doubt certain natures need a salutary dose of pessimism—that is, anti-optimism, a curbing of unqualified faith in meliorism—while others need to be reminded that, despite it all, there are reasons to celebrate. But whether an individual person would benefit from contemplating the reasons for melancholy or the reasons for joy, the goal is the same. Insofar as this is an "invitation to look and see," as I promised in chapter one, it is an invitation to look and see the whole of reality, as honestly and completely as we can. To see the predation and parasitism of nature "red of tooth and claw." To feel the loneliness of those who have been abandoned, the agony of the young mother wracked by pain in the oncology ward, or the terror of the child cowering as an "active shooter" stalks the halls of a school. To hear the cries of the desperately poor and of victims of injustice. And to sense, in the background of all that suffering, the jaws of entropy gnawing incessantly at the fabric of reality.[70] But at the same time, alongside and amidst those realities, to be able to see the glory of all things shining. To feel our bodies alive for another day in the world for which they were made. To experience a sense of appreciation and gratitude that things are rather than are not and, for those things that have passed away, that they were rather than were not. If, as Ricoeur says, "Man is the joy of yes in the sadness of the finite,"[71] it is not the Nietzschean "yes" of *amor fati* and eternal return; it is the "yes I said yes I will Yes" of Molly Bloom, the "yes" of Ms. Ramsey's "it is enough," the "yes" of Ellen Bass's "I will love you again," and the "yes" of Thoreau's desire to "live deep and suck out all the marrow of life."

This, then, is the wager of this book: that the proper response to the fullness of reality is melancholic joy. To assert that, despite it all, life is worth it; and to do so with full attention to both the desolation ("*despite* it all") and the consolations ("it *is* worth it").[72] The joy toward which I am pointing—the joy of watching Kohák's "children by the river" or hearing Gilbert's "faint sound of oars in the silence"—is not the joy of innocence, but the joy of experience. It is a joy that appreciates the goodness of being in the present moment, aware that that moment, as temporal, will pass. Aware that, ultimately, all temporal things will pass. *Sic transit gloria mundi* . . . "Thus passes the glory of the world." Nevertheless, *dum vivimus vivamus*: "while we live, let us live."[73] Taken together, these classical phrases give voice to the tension in melancholic joy: the *pathos* of *sic transit gloria* alongside the *ethos* of *dum vivimus vivamus*.

# Notes

## Chapter 1 Sadness Will Last Forever

**1** According to his brother Theo, Vincent Van Gogh's last words were: "*La tristesse durera toujours*" ("Letter from Theo van Gogh to Elisabeth van Gogh, Paris, 5 August 1890." From *Van Gogh's Letters: Unabridged and Annotated*. Accessed, January 27, 2020. http://www.webexhibits.org/vangogh/letter/21/etc-Theo-Lies.htm. Note that the French admits of alternate translations (e.g., "sadness will last forever," "the sadness will last forever," etc.).

**2** A phrase uttered by Mr. Ramsey in the last section of Virginia Woolf's *To the Lighthouse* (Dublin: Roads Publishing, 1927), 177. Ramsey himself is quoting William Cowper's 1799 poem "The Castaway," the final stanza of which reads: "No voice divine the storm allayed / No light propitious shone, / When, snatched from all effectual aid, / We perished, each alone: / But I beneath a rougher sea, / And whelmed in deeper gulfs than he" (William Cowper, "The Castaway" in *The Complete Poetical Works of William Cowper* [University of California Libraries, 1905], 45).

**3** Seneca, *Moral Essays II* (Cambridge, MA: Loeb Classical Library, 1990), 289.

**4** This in response to a jibe that Marcel was overly-concerned with death. See Emmanuel Levinas, "The Diary of Léon Brunschvicg," in his *Difficult Freedom*, trans. Sean Hand (Baltimore: The Johns Hopkins University Press, 1990), 39–45 and Gabriel Marcel, *Tragic Wisdom and Beyond* (Evanston. IL: Northwestern University Press, 1973), 131.

**5** Jim Moore, "It is Not the Fact that I Will Die That I Mind," in *Lightning at Dinner* (Minneapolis, MN: Greywolf Press, 2005). On the significance of precisely this sort of love, see chapter five below.

**6** Gerard Manley Hopkins, "Pied Beauty" in *The Selected Poetry of Gerard Manley Hopkins* (New York: Dover, 2011), 24.

**7** Jim Moore, "It is Not the Fact that I Will Die That I Mind," in *Lightning at Dinner* (Minneapolis, MN: Greywolf Press, 2005). A similar sentiment is expressed by Roy Baty in Ridley Scott's *Blade Runner* (*Blade Runner.* Directed by Ridley Scott. Screenplay by Hampton Fancher and David Peoples. [Warner Bros., 1982]), who, when dying, reflects that "all these moments [his experiences] will be lost in time. . . like tears in rain."

**8** At the moment, in late March 2020, estimates of the case fatality rate of COVID-19 are commonly cited as near one percent, although there is a very high degree of uncertainty in such early estimates, with first-wave case fatality rates ranging from something close to one percent in places like South Korea to over ten percent in Italy. Due to inadequate testing and record keeping, we may never know the true infection fatality rate. Nevertheless, however devastating COVID-19 will have been, consider that other potential pandemics—one of which we may still have to face—have a much, much higher case fatality rate. For example, case fatality rate for H5N1 flu is about sixty percent.

**9** Gabriel Marcel, "On the Ontological Mystery" in *The Philosophy of Existentialism*, trans. Manya Harari (New York: Citadel Press, 1995), 26. Emphasis mine.

**10** William James, "Is Life Worth Living?" in *The Will to Believe* (New York: Dover, 1956), 32. As will become clear, my interest in despair is not focused on clinical pathologies, but rather on those who fall prey to what we might think of as "speculative melancholy" or *tedium vitae*—although I do believe that in certain cases this distinction is one of degree rather than kind.

**11** "At this very moment, I am suffering—as we say in French, *J'ai mal*. This event, crucial for me, is non existent, even inconceivable for anyone else, for everyone else" (E. M. Cioran, *The Trouble with Being Born*, trans. Richard Howard [New York: Arcade Publishing, 2012], 11).

**12** "A zoologist who observed gorillas in their native habitat was amazed by the uniformity of their life and their vast idleness. Hours and hours without doing anything. . . Was boredom unknown to them? That is indeed a question raised by a *human*, a busy ape. . . . Inaction is divine; yet it is against inaction that man has rebelled (Cioran, *The Trouble with Being Born*, 193). Think here of Thoreau's comments about the desperate busyness of even our leisure: "A stereotyped but unconscious despair is concealed even under what are called the games and amusements of mankind" (Henry David Thoreau, *Walden* [Princeton, NJ: Princeton University Press, 1971], 8). This is also reminiscent of Kundera, who writes: "No one can give anyone else the gift of idyll; only an animal can do so, because only animals were not expelled from Paradise. . . . Therein lies the whole of man's plight. Human time [unlike the time of Karenin, the dog] does not turn in a circle; it runs ahead in a straight line. This is why man cannot be happy: happiness is the longing for repetition" (Milan Kundera, *The Unbearable Lightness of Being*, trans. Michael Henry Heim [New York:

Harper Perennial, 1984], 298). I will have more to say below on the issue of time and repetition, for while Kundera's point is well taken—and suggests not only the importance of reconnecting with our animality but also the necessity of dialogue with traditions that retain a circular view of time—there are vicious forms of repetition or return as well.

**13** Eugene Thacker, *Cosmic Pessimism* (Minneapolis, MN: Univocal, 2015), 5.

**14** Oscar Wilde, *De Profundis and Other Writings* (London: Penguin, 1954), 161.

**15** The wonderful turn of phrase "viciously interlocking teleologies" comes to me by way of my colleague Virgil Martin Nemoianu, in reference to the idea of interlocking telelogies and the problem in evil in Peter Geach, *Providence and Evil* (Cambridge: Cambridge University Press, 1977).

**16** Although estimates vary, some suggest that *over half* of the forms of life on Earth are parasitical. See Andy Dobson, et al. "Homage to Linnaeus: How many parasites? How many hosts?" *Proceedings of the National Academy of the Sciences of the United States of America*. Accessed November 9, 2019. http://www.pnas.org/content/105/Supplement_1/11482.full.pdf. When Annie Dillard reads an estimate that parasitism may account for just ten percent of life forms, she calls it, darkly, "the Devil's tithe" (Annie Dillard, *Pilgrim at Tinker Creek* [New York: Harper Perennial, 1974], 236), and rages "what happened to manna?" (Ibid., 242). What then will we call an arrangement in which parasitism constitutes the *majority* of life, to say nothing of the wages of predation? Or, consider COVID-19 and other pandemics. Depending on how one defines "life," viruses may not even be living; so here we have a microscopic entity that preys on life, but which may do so without even the comfort that the detriment of one life is to the benefit of another (as is the case, for example, in predation).

**17** As Tennyson would have it in his famous "In Memoriam A.H.H.," in *Tennyson: Poems* (New York: Everyman's Library, 2004), 205.

**18** Author Matthew White gives the estimate of 203 million in the "Necrometrics" of his "Historical Atlas of the 20th Century" (Accessed September 17, 2019. http://necrometrics.com/all20c.htm). Other estimates are not that far off from White's number. Zbigniew Brzezinski, National Security Advisor to President Jimmy Carter, estimates something in the neighborhood of 175,000,000 from politically motivated violence (see Zbigniew Brzezinski, *Out of Control, Global Turmoil on the Eve of the 21st Century* [New York: Touchstone, 1995]). And the intensely debated *Black Book of Communism* (Cambridge, MA: Harvard University Press, 1999)—critiqued by Noam Chomsky and others—suggest nearly 100 million may have perished in wars and oppression related to communist movements. A similar point could be made with other, very contemporary examples. In June of 2019, the BBC reported on UNHCR statistics concluding that "The number of people fleeing war, persecution and conflict exceeded 70 million globally last year—the highest number in the

UN refugee agency's almost 70 years of operations" ("More than 70 million displaced worldwide, says UNHCR." BBC News. Accessed November 21, 2019. https://www.bbc.com/news/world-48682783). These displacements are largely the result of conflict, oppression, manmade economic crises, anthropogenic climate change, and similar causes—that is, the result of human failures. And seventy million, like two hundred million, is a number that, in a real sense, surpasses comprehension.

**19** Shakespeare, *King Lear*, Act 4, Scene 6.

**20** Anthropogenic climate change is a threat of a fundamentally different order, presenting us with a challenge, and a despair, that is unique. Climate change is: (1) a slowly-unfolding catastrophe that is, therefore, less instinctively alarming; (2) a potentially existential threat, capable of major disruptions to civilization and to life on earth; (3) caused by the collective actions of humans who, for the most part, are (4) simply going about their everyday business without malicious intent; (5) a crisis that we know, with certainty, how to avert but which (6) we suspect, with growing alarm, that we will not avoid, in part because (7) addressing climate change is a now-or-never proposition (i.e., every degree of warming is "locked in" for all intents and purposes for any humanly-relevant timescale). Other important issues share some of these characteristics; but climate change alone exhibits all of them. What kind of planet will my daughters know? Their daughters? How much more impoverished will it be in terms of diversity and beauty than the planet I've experienced, or the planet that nurtured Thoreau, Muir, Leopold, and Dillard?

**21** Cormac McCarthy, *The Road* (New York: Vintage, 2006), 110. For a haunting poetic example of a similar realization, see Philip Larkin, "Aubade" in *Collected Poems* (New York: Farrar, Straus and Giroux, 2003).

**22** *Philosophy and Truth: Selections from Nietzsche's Notebooks of the Early 1870's*, ed. and trans. Daniel Breazeale (Atlantic Highlands, NJ: Humanities Press, 1979), 79.

**23** We experience the pressure of entropy as one manifestation of the "arrow of time." See Stephen Hawking, *A Brief History of Time* (New York: Bantam, 1990), 145. Interestingly, Hawking also wrestles with the possibility that "the second law of thermodynamics has a rather different status than that of other laws of science, such as Newton's law of gravity, for example, because it does not hold always, just in the majority of cases. The probability [of entropic reversal]. . . is many millions of millions to one, but it can happen" (Ibid., 103).

**24** Here, the famous conclusion of *Moby Dick* is apt: "all collapsed, and the great shroud of the sea rolled on as it rolled five thousand years ago" (Herman Melville, *Moby Dick* [Oxford: Oxford World Classics, 1998], 582). Only, in this case, the sea is cosmic rather than terrestrial. There are, however, other extant theories. And the final heat death of thermodynamic equilibrium is not certain. There may be new things to discover that undermine our current understanding of cosmic inflation and deflation. There may, for example, be multiverses. For a useful, if popular, account see Adam Becker, "How will the universe end, and could anything survive?" BBC News. Accessed May 30, 2018. http://www.bbc.com/earth/story/20150602-how-will-the-universe-end.

**25** John D. Caputo, *Against Ethics* (Bloomington, IN: Indiana University Press, 1993), 17.

**26** It's a difficult puzzle to work out just where continental philosophy begins. But the term passed into common and contemporary usage in the mid- to late-20th century, just as the "widening gyre" of nihilism—political, economic, cultural, and ideological chaos—swallowed Europe. Simon Critchley notes that the problem of nihilism is one of the themes that distinguishes continental philosophy from other forms of inquiry (Simon Critchley, *Continental Philosophy: A Very Short Introduction* [Oxford: Oxford University Press, 2001], especially chapter 5).

**27** Note, to conclude this list, that among analytic philosophers the case is no more heartwarming. Some people point out that the worth or worthlessness, meaning or meaninglessness of life has historically generated little interest in analytic philosophy relative to its prominence in continental philosophy (Joshua Seachris, "The Meaning of Life: Contemporary Analytic Perspectives" in *The Internet Encyclopedia of Philosophy*. Accessed September 1, 2014. http://www.iep.utm.edu/mean-ana/). However, recent work by Thaddeus Metz and others has gone some way to address that lacuna. See, for example, Thaddeus Metz, *Meaning in Life: An Analytic Study* (Oxford: Oxford University Press, 2013) and Joshua W. Seachris, ed., *Exploring the Meaning of Life: An Anthology and Guide* (London: Wiley-Blackwell, 2013). But, while Metz concludes that there is, or can be, meaning in life, others working in analytic philosophy share common cause with their gloomy continental counterparts. Take, for example, "anti-natalists" who argue anew that birth itself is a harm, and that it is "better never to have been," (David Benatar, *Better Never to Have Been* [Oxford: Oxford University Press, 2009]), or even that it is "better no longer to be" (Rafe MacGregor and Emma Sullivan-Bissett, "Better No Longer to Be" in *The South African Journal of Philosophy*, vol. 31, no. 1 [2012]: 55–68). Or again, take John Gray's work, which embraces both nihilism and misanthropy (John Gray, *Straw Dogs* [New York: Farrar, Straus and Giroux, 2007] and *Black Mass* [New York: Penguin, 2009]).

**28** Cioran, *The Trouble with Being Born*, 11. A sample: "We are reluctant, of course, to treat birth as a scourge: has it not been inculcated as the sovereign good—have we not been told that the worst came at the end, not at the outset of our lives? Yet evil, the real evil, is *behind*, not ahead of us. What escaped Jesus did not escape the Buddha: 'If three things did not exist in the world, O disciples, the Perfect One would not appear in the world. . .' And ahead of old age and death he places the fact of birth, the source of every infirmity, every disaster" (Ibid., 4). On the idea that coming-into-being is always a harm, see David Benatar *Better Never to Have Been* (Oxford: Oxford University Press, 2009).

**29** Although, amusingly, Cioran also claims that suicide is not really worth it: "It is not worth the bother of killing yourself, since you always kill yourself too late," that is, too late to avoid being born (Cioran, *The Trouble with Being Born*, 32). And again: "Only optimists commit suicide, the optimists who can no longer be. . . optimists. The others, having no reason to live, why would they have any to die?" (E.M. Cioran, *All Gall is Divided*, trans. Richard Howard [New York: Arcade, 2019], 87).

**30** Cioran, *The Trouble With Being Born*, 85. This critique anticipates, in a way, my claim in chapter six that Nietzsche remains committed to a certain kind of faith.

**31** Ibid., 110.

**32** Thacker, *Cosmic Pessimism*, 53.

**33** Cioran, *The Trouble With Being Born*, 127 and 130. Accordingly, he sees pregnant women as "corpse bearers" (Ibid., 130).

**34** Ibid., 130.

**35** Ibid., 14.

**36** W.H. Auden, "Twelve Songs" in *W.H. Auden: Collected Poems* (New York: Vintage, 1991), 141.

**37** Cioran, *The Trouble With Being Born*, 210. This claim is directly to the point of an issue that will come up in the following chapters: our seeming inability to free ourselves from regret over the past and anxiety over the future. Shall we take "the entirety of cosmic time" as our frame, or "the eternity of the present moment"? That is the question.

**38** Blaise Pascal, *Pensées*, trans. Rager Ariew (Cambridge: Hackett, 2004), 64: "The eternal silence of these infinite spaces frightens me."

**39** James, "Is Life Worth Living?", 41–2.

**40** Joshua Foa Dienstag commenting on Leopardi's *Operette Morali* (219/489) in his *Pessimism: Philosophy, Ethic, Spirit* (Princeton: Princeton University Press, 2009), 49. Dienstag points out that "pessimism might well be the more realistic response to the experience of temporality" (ibid., 53). I am indebted to Dienstag's lucid and compelling defense of pessimism, even if our projects disagree as to the nature of "pessimism" vis-à-vis "anti-optimism."

**41** Shakespeare, *Macbeth*, Act V, Scene V.

**42** Plato, *Theaetetus* in *Plato: Collected Dialogues*, eds. Edith Hamilton and Huntington Cairns [Princeton, NJ: Princeton University Press], 845–919

(155d) and Simon Critchley, *Very Little. . . Almost Nothing: Death, Philosophy,* Literature (London: Routledge, 1997), 2.

**43** Woolf, *To the Lighthouse*, 52. Note that the distraction which shamefully interrupts Ramsey's metaphysical ruminations is not thoughtless gluttony, or petty ambition, or the frivolous amusement of games; it is nothing less than the consolation of his wife's love and care for their son, and his own inexpressible love and need for his family. "Trifles" indeed. Perhaps one might argue that the melancholic focus of philosophy is the proper response to our everyday tendency to overlook, ignore, or gloss over finitude, tragedy, and death. We hide from the ultimate truth of our being-toward-death in our everydayness. But surely this is equally true of wonder, joy, and vitality, which we miss, pass over, and do not appreciate because of the very same everydayness: routinized habits, narrowly pragmatic concerns, and the blind delusional belief that we've all the time in the world.

**44** Martin Heidegger, *Being and Time*, trans. John Macquarrie and Edward Robinson (San Francisco: Harper San Francisco, 1962), Division II *passim*, especially part I.

**45** Percy Bysshe Shelley's famous "Ozymandias" *The Poems of Shelley*, vol.2, 1817–9 (London: Routledge, 2000), 307. Horace Smith's "Ozymandias," written in competition with Shelley, makes the same point with an even more stark emphasis that this fate—decay, destruction, and disappearance in the sands of time—awaits the greatest modern figures and achievements as well.

**46** James, "Is Life Worth Living?", 42.

**47** Precisely because despair is a mood that can characterize an age, and which can take different forms—resignation, distraction, and so on—different generations experience despair differently, and more or less acutely. Some potential manifestations of despair are recognizable: melancholy, pessimism, despair, anomie, ennui, resignation, indifference, a lack of passion. But other forms are counterintuitive. Perhaps analogous to the manner in which a person can be experiencing a high degree of stress, in a medical sense, while simultaneously not consciously "feeling" stressed at all, the mood of despair is perfectly compatible with a variety of ways of being that do not obviously appear to be despairing. It is for this reason that Thoreau can claim:

> The mass of men lead lives of quiet desperation. What is called resignation is confirmed desperation. From the desperate city you go into the desperate country, and have to console yourself with the bravery of minks and muskrats. A stereotyped but unconscious despair is concealed even under what are called the games and amusements of mankind. There is no play in them, for this comes after work (Thoreau, *Walden*, 8).

**48** Henry David Thoreau, *Journal*, vol. X, ed. Bradford Torrey (Boston and New York: Houghton Mifflin and Co., 1906), 143.

**49** To this we could add the effects of a European culture that focused on Greek tragedy as a paradigm for art. Consider the work of Hegel, Nietzsche, Heidegger, and others in this regard. For generations the intellectually gifted students in Europe were taught to think of Greek tragedy as a repository of enduring wisdom; and, given that foundation, when philosophers from this tradition wanted to think about art in particular and about aesthetics more broadly, they turned to tragedy, the paradigm of ancient Greek artistic expression. My thanks to Chris Lauer for making this observation and discussing it with me.

**50** Albert Camus, "Pessimism and Courage" in *Resistance, Rebellion, and Death*, trans. Justin O'Brien (New York: Vintage, 1988), 59. Emphasis mine.

**51** The way to correct for the lacunae and blind spots in our own perspective is by working to see the world differently or otherwise. Not because we might eventually achieve some comprehensive, God's-eye perspective that would be without blind spots; but, rather, because the best way to correct for the blind spots of one contingent and limited perspective is to try to see things from another perspective that, if also contingent and limited, is contingent and limited differently.

**52** Robert Browning, *The Poetical Works* (London: Smith Elder and Co., 1897), 202.

**53** David Moreau, "Borrowed Time" in *Sex, Death, and Baseball* (Portland, ME: Moon Pie Press, 2004). It must be noted, however, that Moreau's "Borrowed Time" is not itself a miserabilist expression; it expresses, rather, precisely the kind of appreciative gratitude for the world associated with "melancholic joy" below. For another account of our journey down that "old path not marked on any map," consider George Saunder's *Lincoln in the Bardo*: "all pleasures should be tainted by [the] knowledge" that we are strolling through a slaughterhouse, an inescapable trap sprung at birth, and are "able to laugh and dream and hope" only because horror has not yet closed over us or our children, although it will inevitably do so (George Saunders, *Lincoln in the Bardo* [New York: Random House, 2017], 155–6).

**54** Paul Ricoeur expresses this in terms of first naiveté, doubt, and second naiveté (Paul Ricoeur, *The Symbolism of Evil*, trans. Emerson Buchanan [Boston, MA: Beacon Press, 1967]). When the first naiveté of childhood belief is shipwrecked on the shoals of doubt, or evil, or philosophical reason, or science, this may lead to the end of (that particular expression of) belief. Nevertheless, the possibility remains of a freely chosen second naiveté, which reembraces belief not in the manner of first naiveté, but precisely in shadow of doubt. Or, to illustrate with an example from outside typical descriptions of "faith," consider the way in which the dewy-eyed romance of one's youth might be challenged by any number of misfortunes—the banal routine of paying the mortgage and washing the clothes, infidelity, disease, or age—only to reemerge as a different, more mature love of the same person.

**55** Ellen Bass, "The Thing Is" in *Mules of Love* (Rochester, NY: BOA Editions, 2002). "Naiveté" is perhaps a misleading term in this context, because the wager I have in mind is open-eyed; it recognizes and acknowledges the darkness but remains attentive to, and even cultivates, the simultaneous presence of light or goodness "after dark."

**56** James, "Is Life Worth Living?", 43. We might, playing on C.S. Lewis's famous attempt to articulate a "mere Christianity"—an account of the core Christianity that is shared among historical schisms and points of disagreements—think of faith in the present work in terms of "mere faith," that is to say the bare commitment to *meaningfulness* that is, I contend, shared among all persons—atheist, agnostic, theist, or otherwise inclined. All of us have beliefs about things that have not been demonstrated to us or things we have not yet verified personally. For example, the belief that Abraham Lincoln delivered the Gettysburg Address on November 19, 1863 or the belief, for someone who has never been there, that Vladivostok exists. But there are important differences between such trivial beliefs and something we might call faith. For our purposes here, let's say faith is the affirmation of first principles that are taken as given rather than logically proven—particularly first principles about meaning, first principles that orient one's actions and way of life. There may be reasons of various sorts that enhance the plausibility of any given first principle to the person who holds it or potentially holds it (and, therefore, we are not committed to a narrow or strict fideism); but, in general, we argue *from* rather than *for* such first principles, and that constitutes faith.

**57** In the "lonely emergencies of life"—and whether or not to despair certainly constitutes a fundamental crisis for each of us—"maxims fail and we fall back on our gods" (William James, "The Sentiment of Rationality" in *The Will to Believe* [New York: Dover Publications, 1956], 105). Simon Critchley writes, citing Oscar Wilde, "Everything to become true must become a religion" (Simon Critchley, *The Faith of the Faithless* [London: Verso, 2012], 3). Wilde here means truth in terms of *troth*, in terms of fidelity to something, religion as commitment to first principles in which one has faith and which shape one's way of life. Such principles can be immanent and tangible as well as transcendent and intangible. Take, for example, James Joyce's leap of faith when he left Ireland and the Catholic Church for art, expressed in the voice of his surrogate Stephen Dedalus: "You made me confess the fears that I have. But I will tell you also what I do not fear. I do not fear to be alone or to be spurned for another or to leave whatever I have to leave. And I am not afraid to make a mistake, even a great mistake, a lifelong mistake and perhaps as long as eternity too" (James Joyce, *A Portrait of the Artist as a Young Man* [New York: Signet, 1991], 248).

**58** James, "Is Life Worth Living?", 39. Religious people are sometimes ridiculed for an easy optimism rooted in salvation-to-come; but Alain de Botton, a self-described atheist, notes that non-religious people have their own equally incredible faith in salvation:

> The secular are at this moment in history a great deal more optimistic than the religious—something of an irony, given the frequency with which the latter have been derided by the former for their apparent naivety and credulousness. It is the secular whose longing for perfection has grown so intense as to lead them to imagine that paradise might be realized on this earth after just a few more years of financial growth and medical research. With no evident awareness of the contradiction they may, in the same breath, gruffly dismiss a belief in angels while sincerely trusting that the combined powers of the IMF, the medical research establishment, Silicon Valley and democratic politics could together cure the ills of mankind (Alain de Botton, *Religion for Atheists: A Non-believer's Guide to the Uses of Religion* [New York: Pantheon Books, 2012,] 184).

It is, Botton claims, religious people who often see the warts and wounds of the world more clearly; and he calls for a salutary dose of pessimism in cases—theistic or atheistic—in which people are drunk on, or simply misled by, immoderate hope and optimism.

**59** Thacker, *Cosmic Pessimism*, 4.

**60** Ralph Waldo Emerson, journal entry, May 20, 1831 (Ralph Waldo Emerson, *Emerson in his Journals* [Cambridge, MA: Belknap Press, 1984], 77).

**61** See, in particular, John D. Caputo, *The Prayers and Tears of Jacques Derrida* (Bloomington, IN: Indiana University Press, 1997), John D. Caputo, *The Insistence of God* (Bloomington, IN: Indiana University Press, 2013), Richard Kearney, *Anatheism* (New York: Columbia University Press, 2010), and Simon Critchley, *The Faith of the Faithless* (London: Verso, 2010). Critchley, the most outspoken atheist among them, nevertheless points out that his atheism does not exclude faith per se: "Faith is not necessarily theistic" (ibid., 18).

**62** Erazim Kohák, *The Embers and the Stars* (Chicago: University of Chicago Press, 1984), xiii. Given some of my previous work it should come as no surprise that I feel that metaphor and argument should not be so sharply distinguished. See, for example, *Emplotting Virtue* (Albany, NY: SUNY Press, 2014).

# Chapter 2 Joy and the Myopia of Finitude

1 *Calvary*. Directed by John Michael McDonagh. Screenplay by John Michael McDonagh. Fox Searchlight (2014). Spin out Harte's story in your mind. What would the little boy think? How long before he started to wonder, as children do, whether it was something *he* did that caused his parents to abandon him? Was he being punished? How long before he called out—sobbing, begging—that he was sorry, whatever it was that he did? Please come get me and I'll be a good boy! Please, please, please! How long before that little boy spirals into madness alone in the dark, like some innocent version of one of Beckett's effaced narrators? See, for example, Samuel Beckett, *The Unnameable* in *Three Novels: Malloy, Malone Dies, The Unnameable* (New York: Grove Press, 1958), or "Not I" (London: Faber and Faber, 1973).

2 Dennis O'Driscoll, "Last Stand" in *Dear Life* (Port Townsend, WA: Copper Canyon Press, 2013), 18.

3 Dennis O'Driscoll, "Admissions" in *Dear Life* (Port Townsend, WA: Copper Canyon Press, 2013), 99.

4 Susan Neiman, *Evil in Modern Thought: An Alternative History of Philosophy* (Princeton, NJ: Princeton University Press, 2015), 5. And, regarding the necessity of accounting for evil, no matter what one's metaphysics might be, she adds: "Were we offered an account [of the world] that showed Auschwitz to part of the order of things, most of us would reject it. Yet any account of the world that ignores it will be worth very little" (ibid., 324). Here Neiman anticipates some of my concerns with theodicy, eternal return, and similar doctrines below.

5 Neiman, *Evil in Modern Thought*, 317. This is to say that we don't begin with an omnipotent God and, from that starting point, spin out a theory of evil. Rather, we begin put to the pins, beset by evils and, from there, posit God as one way to explain evil.

6 See Emmanuel Levinas, "Transcendence and Evil" in *Job and the Excess of Evil*, trans. Michael Kigel (Pittsburgh, PA: Duquesne University Press, 1998), 182.

7 Fyodor Dostoevsky, *The Brothers Karamazov*, trans. Richard Pevear and Larissa Volokhonsky (New York: Vintage Books, 1990), 244. Ivan's response to this injustice is, famously, ". . .they have put too high a price on harmony; we can't afford to pay for such admission. And therefore I hasten to return my ticket" (Ibid., 245). By "returning his ticket" Ivan does no less than to reject God. He does not deny God's existence—the conclusion of many undergraduate misreadings of *The Brothers Karamazov*. No. What Ivan does is far more radical. He rejects God, wants

nothing to do with a God that would allow the horrific suffering of children as part of some greater, "more perfect" plan. Another expression can be found in Maugham's *The Razor's Edge*, in which Larry says: "[I]t is easy enough to bear our own evils, all we need for that is a little manliness; what's intolerable is the evil, often so unmerited in appearance, that befalls others" (Somerset Maugham, *The Razor's Edge* [New York: Penguin, 1978], 265).

**8** Paul Valéry, *Mauvaises Pensées et Autres* (Paris: Gallimard, 1942).

**9** Or, to give another example, Camus's fictional Meursault lives as a kind of nihilist (Albert Camus, *The Stranger*, trans. Matthew Ward [New York: Vintage, 1989]). However, Camus himself—member of the Resistance, leftist activist who was also opposed to the Soviet expression of communism-as-totalitarianism, critic of French colonialism in North Africa, and supporter of European integration—certainly did not. There are, of course, other possible explanations for this. Perhaps nihilism is true, but no one is really courageous enough to live as a nihilist, so we pretend things are meaningful. Or perhaps nihilism is true, but no one is really psychologically equipped to believe it, so we attach meaning to things that are actually meaningless. But, as chapters one and six argue, those claims about nihilism are tenets of their own kind of faith, first principles from which someone argues rather than principles for which someone argues. And there is another equally plausible explanation for why, when put to the pins, no one really lives as a nihilist: that, in addition to meaning and value that we create, there is meaning and value that we discover in the world, independent of our creation, meaning in "*the thing itself* before it has been *made* anything" (Virginia Woolf, *To the Lighthouse* [Dublin: Roads, 2013], 205, emphases mine).

**10** In the United States this manifests itself in our shared faith in techo-capitalism. Our church is at the local shopping mall or on the internet; our liturgy is consumerism. Life may well be meaningless, which is troubling and frightening; so, best not to think about it too much, and accumulating rubbish is our preferred way of distracting ourselves.

**11** Shakespeare, *King Lear*, Act IV, Scene I.

**12** Augustine, *Confessions*, trans, John K. Ryan (New York: Image Books), 85 (Book III, 12).

**13** Boethius, *The Consolation of Philosophy*, trans. P.G. Walsh (Oxford: Oxford University Press, 2000), 68.

**14** Dostoevsky, *The Brothers Karamazov*, 245.

**15** John D. Caputo, *The Weakness of God* (Bloomington, IN: Indiana University Press, 2006). In what follows, I do not intend to make strong claims about God, heaven, eschatological justice, and the like. My claim here is narrower: that life, life here and now, life full of suffering, loss, tragedy, and death, is nevertheless still fundamentally good and still fundamentally worthwhile. I also bracket, at least for the moment, the worst cases of truly unbearable pain or torment, cases in which any talk of joy would be an obscenity. I do this not because these cases are philosophically insignificant (they are not), and not because we do not have to deal with them (we do), but rather because while such limit cases demand an account of some sort they do not change the fact that suffering that is *literally* overwhelming or unbearable is not the experience of the vast majority of people, even people who live in truly dire situations or who experience substantial pain. As I will argue below, there is glory, or the possibility of glory, even in very desperate circumstances (not only in the lives of the wealthy or healthy). And, as we will see, while the glory does not justify or make up for the evil we experience, neither can that evil ever fully occlude the good.

**16** John D. Caputo, *The Insistence of God* (Bloomington, IN: Indiana University Press, 2013), 11.

**17** Ibid., 9. In analytic philosophy, a related strategy seems to reimagine what we mean when we say God is "omnipotent." See, for example, Alvin Plantinga, *God, Freedom, and Evil* (Grand Rapids, MI: Erdmans, 1977).

**18** Richard Kearney, *Anatheism: Returning to God after God* (New York: Columbia University Press, 2010), 58. Thus, in what follows, I do not reject the existence of God, nor do I reject the belief that God cares for Creation in some sense. The argument here is entirely agnostic on such questions—as we see below, the experience in question is common to atheists (Woolf) and theists (Kohák). I am, however, critiquing the notion that God micromanages reality in some reliable way such that a person could depend on God to insure the propitious outcome of individual (e.g., health) or social (e.g., climate change) challenges. I am also critiquing traditional theodicies that would call into question our ability to discern something like the just and reliable organization of the world by suggesting even the most excessive horrors of existence are part of an obscure and perfect plan.

**19** The traditional response—that death and suffering come about as a result of the rebellion of Adam and Eve in the Garden of Eden and the consequent fallenness of Creation as a whole—only raises more problematic issues related to the hereditary nature of punishment. If one finds the notion of theodicy philosophically problematic, one will hardly be comforted by doctrines of original sin.

**20** John D. Caputo, *The Insistence of God* (Bloomington, IN: Indiana University Press, 2013).

**21** Ibid., 49.

**22** Richard Kearney, *The God Who May Be* (Bloomington, IN: Indiana University Press, 2001) and *Anatheism: Returning to God after God* (New York: Columbia University Press, 2010).

**23** Kearney, *Anatheism*, 58. "God" can only change the world if we act as God's hands. Thus, Kearney suggests that, "To God's 'I may be' each of us is invited to reply 'I can"' (Kearney, *The God Who May Be*, 108).

**24** See John D. Caputo, *The Weakness of God* (Bloomington, IN: Indiana University Press, 2006) and Richard Kearney, *The God Who May Be* (Bloomington, IN: Indiana University Press, 2001).

**25** Gabriel Marcel, "On the Ontological Mystery" in *The Philosophy of Existentialism*, trans. Manya Harari (New York: Carol Publishing, 1995). Some of the following characterizations of Marcel's work draw on chapter three of my *Aspects of Alterity* (New York: Fordham University Press, 2006), chapter six of *Emplotting Virtue* (Albany, NY: SUNY Press, 2014), and on "Constellations: Gabriel Marcel's Philosophy of Relative Otherness" in *American Catholic Philosophical Quarterly*, vol. 80, no. 3, 2006.

**26** Gabriel Marcel, *The Mystery of Being*, vol. 1 (London: The Harvill Press, 1950), 213.

**27** Marcel, *Being and Having*, 118. Problems are solvable, at least theoretically. For example, the feasibility of economically viable, production-scale fusion reactors is a problem, with a technical solution, whether or not a technical solution is ever discovered. In contrast, the question of love or of the goodness of being is not something I successfully solve, after which I can turn my attention to other problems. No. A mystery like love is something one must live, day-by-day, in a series of creative acts that help to make the reality of love. Leonard Lawlor addresses the open-ended nature of certain "problems"—albeit in a very different register and context—in his *Thinking Through French Philosophy*: *The Being of the Question* (Bloomington, IN: Indiana University Press, 2003).

**28** This is not to endorse some form of neo-Manicheanism, to assert that there are incompatible powers or substances in reality, one good and another evil. It is rather a recognition that evil and good, joy and sorrow, life and death are all tied together in the experience of being, and in a way that is mysterious rather than problematic. Of course, we still suffer (and, all too often, perpetuate) evil, but the meaning of that evil changes entirely in the transition from strong to weak theology. In this vein Caputo rereads the story of Job (in dialogue with Katherine Keller): "The effect of this retelling is to concede, on the one hand, that life is rent with tragic loss, but to sustain the faith, on the other hand, that the world is nonetheless a place of majesty and beauty. All things are knotted together, the good and the bad, and life goes on, so don't let hope die" (Caputo, *The Weakness of God*, 78).

**29** Dostoevsky, *The Brothers Karamazov*, 243. We must come to grips with the mystery of evil, because, as Neiman says: "If you cannot understand why children are tortured [or why infants develop leukemia or suffer strokes] nothing else you understand really matters" (Neiman, *Evil in Modern Thought*, 325).

**30** Marilynne Robinson, *Gilead* (New York: Farrar, Strauss and Giroux, 2014), 243.

**31** Here "cope" carries the modern sense of "to manage" or "come to grips with" as well as the etymological sense of "resisting" (the Middle English "cope" meaning "to meet in battle," associated with the French *colp*, from which we get *coup*, "a blow," via Latin from the Greek *kolaphos*, "a blow with a fist").

**32** Annie Dillard, *Pilgrim at Tinker Creek* (New York: Harper Perennial, 1974), 9. Or, as Thoreau puts it while reflecting on the nature of predation: if we persevere in experiencing reality, we may "at length, perhaps, detect the secret innocence of these incessant tragedies which Heaven allows" (Henry David Thoreau, *A Week on the Concord and Merrimack Rivers* [Princeton: Princeton University Press, 1980], 223).

**33** Erazim Kohák, *The Embers and the Stars* (Chicago: The University of Chicago Press, 1984), 182. Kohák says "the presence of God" is utterly basic; however, in the context of the entire argument, it is clear that "God" is more or less equivalent to personal being, and that personal being is more or less equivalent to meaningful being, the goodness of being. This is not to diminish Kohák's own experience of goodness as God, but to emphasize that his description can be valid for those who do not share his experience of God (ibid., 194).

**34** Marcel, "On the Ontological Mystery," 15. *Pace* Heidegger, this is a world in which we fit, one in which we have a natural place, even if we do not understand it fully. This is true whether one characterizes our fittedness to this world in metaphysical (i.e., religious) or physical (i.e., evolutionary) terms. We have been made for *this* world, which is precisely why we feel out of place to the degree in which we alienate ourselves from it.

**35** Kohák, *The Embers and the Stars,* 82.

**36** Adam Potkay, *The Story of Joy* (Cambridge, UK: Cambridge University Press, 2011), 10. Although my own use of "joy" is not entirely congruent with the history outlined by Potkay, his work offers an illuminating and welcome account of the sense of joy in the Western tradition. Much of Ciskszentmihalyi's work on "flow," which we take up in the next chapter, also serves to circumscribe the meaning I ascribe to joy.

**37** Martin Heidegger, *Being and Time*, trans. John Macquarrie and Edward Robinson (San Francisco, CA: Harper San Francisco, 1962), and "The Letter on Humanism" in *Basic Writings*, trans. David Farrell Krell (San Francisco, CA: Harper Collins, 1997).

**38** Nikos Kazantzakis, *Report to Greco* (New York: Touchstone, 1975). Psychologist Abraham Maslow reminds us that these experiences do not last, at least in the order of time: "Man can be perfect, but for five minutes, in a peak experience, in some great moment; it is possible. But we just can't stay perfect. You must give up the notion of a permanent heaven. We can get into heaven, but for five minutes. Then you have to come back to the world again" (Audio of Maslow recorded at a retreat in 1966 from *The T.E.D. Radio Hour*. "Maslow's Human Needs" Accessed April 19, 2015. https://www.npr.org/programs/ted-radio-hour/399796647/maslows-human-needs). For a fuller account of such peak experiences, see Mihaly Csikszentmihalyi, *Flow* (New York: Harper Perennial, 1990).

**39** Robert Frost "Nothing Gold Can Stay" in *The Poetry of Robert Frost* (New York: Henry Holt, 1969), 222–3.

**40** Note that "moral," following Kohák's usage, has to do with the meaningfulness of being and the correspondence between the being and human being, rather than the narrower sense in which it is commonly used. It is interesting, however, to play hermeneutically with the polysemy of the terms of this dichotomy. "Temporal" carries the primary meaning of being bound by time, but it also used in juxtaposition with "spiritual" or "eternal" things. "Moral" has the aforementioned ethical sense, of being concerned with right and wrong conduct, but also serves as an adjective denoting psychological states (e.g., offering "moral support"), and like "morale" comes to English from the Old French *moral*. The two loanwords came into use at different times, hence the different meanings between moral and morale. Modern French distinguishes between *la morale* and *le moral*.

**41** Kohák, *The Embers and the Stars*, 162. Emphasis mine. This paragraph and some of the related points are drawn from my essay "Hope in the Anthropocene" in *Ecology, Ethics, and Hope*, ed. Andrew Brei (Lanham, MD: Rowman and Littlefield, 2015).

**42** Martin Luther King, Jr., *Sermon at Temple Israel of Hollywood*, delivered February 26, 1965.

**43** On this count—although I address the issue in chapter one and elsewhere, because it seems to trouble some people—I confess I am not much worried about the cosmic implications of the second law of thermodynamics, which fuels certain forms of nihilism (see, for example, Ray Brassier, *Nihil Unbound: Enlightenment and Extinction* [London: Palgrave Macmillan, 2010]). When it comes to the meaningfulness of life, we rightly apply something like an "existential discount rate" that suggests proximal factors influencing our judgment will always weigh more heavily than remote ones (see chapter four, note 57). The suffering likely to be caused by climate change over the next several decades weighs more heavily on my evaluation of life's worth than the eventual extinction of cultures I value, which, while remote, weigh more heavily than the destruction of the Earth when our sun expands to become a red giant in five to six billion years. Against such concerns, the possibility of the eventual heat death of the universe in some incomprehensibly remote future matters, at least for me, very little, something approaching insignificance. Yes, we are constituted by our being-toward-death; and, yes, entropy will eventually claim every thing that we care about. But we who are here now are "dead-not-yet"; and, without denying death or positively endorsing it, we can accept it as part of the fullest celebration and assumption of our creatureliness.

> Oh me! Oh life! of the questions of these recurring,
> Of the endless trains of the faithless, of cities fill'd with the foolish,
> Of myself forever reproaching myself, (for who more foolish than I, and who more faithless?)
> Of eyes that vainly crave the light, of the objects mean, of the struggle ever renew'd,
> Of the poor results of all, of the plodding and sordid crowds I see around me,
> Of the empty and useless years of the rest, with the rest me intertwined,
> The question, O me! so sad, recurring—What good amid these, O me, O life?
>
> *Answer.*
>
> That you are here—that life exists and identity,
> That the powerful play goes on, and you may contribute a verse.

Walt Whitman, "O Me! O Life!" in *Leaves of Grass* (Boston: Small, Maynard & Company, 1904), 215.

**44** *The Tree of Life*. Directed by Terrence Malick. Screenplay by Terrence Malick. Cottonwood Pictures (2011). Thomas à Kempis, *The Imitation of Christ*, ed. Harold C. Gardiner, S.J. (New York: Image Books, 1955), 186–9. I confess a resistance to referring to the selfish and negative pole of this dichotomy as the "way of nature," insofar as what "nature" is, and does, and offers is richer and more variegated than suggested by this simple distinction. See chapter five below. Moreover, while a number of Ms. O'Brien's reflections and observations are close paraphrases of Thomas, the stark dichotomy between grace and nature does not seem to be Malick's view as expressed in *Tree of Life*, *The Thin Red Line*, *To the Wonder*, *A Hidden Life*, and other films. It is Thomas, not Malick, for whom grace "renounces all created things." Malick's adaptation of Thomas seems directed precisely at loving all things in this world, which Thomas ascribes to Nature, not Grace; his films seem to suggest that we can love the eternal (grace) in the beauty and goodness of this world (nature). He does not make the same sharp distinction between "love of earthly things" and "love of heavenly things," because he does not make such a sharp distinction between earth and heaven.

**45** Dostoevsky, *The Brothers Karamazov*, 289. Markel is Father Zosima's younger brother.

**46** *The Thin Red Line.* Directed by Terrence Malick. Screenplay by Terrence Malick. Fox 2000 (1998).

**47** Malick, *The Thin Red Line* (1998).

**48** The closest thing to an answer to the question, "how can we experience the glory," comes not from Train, but from Bell, another soldier: *love*. Not coincidentally, this is also how Ms. O'Brien characterizes the core imperative of the "way of grace." On this subject, see below, chapter five. Note that there is often debate as to whether some of the more "philosophical" musings in the voiceovers belong to Private Witt or by Private Train. Most people assume the voice is Witt's, as he is the closest thing to a protagonist in the ensemble cast. However, while it is often difficult to distinguish between their similar Southern drawls, the subtitles of the film attribute a number of voiceovers to Train.

**49** A turn of phrase borrowed from Kearney, *Anatheism*, 102.

**50** Woolf is said to have written of T.S. Eliot: "I have had a most shameful and distressing interview with dear Tom Eliot, who may be called dead to us all from this day forward. He has become an Anglo-Catholic believer in God and immortality, and goes to church. I was shocked. A corpse would seem to me more credible than he is. I mean, there's something obscene in a living person sitting by the fire and believing in God" (Walter Hooper, *C.S. Lewis: A Companion and Guide* [Fount, 1997], 25). Kohák explicitly references God in *The Embers and the Stars* and identifies himself as a lifelong Christian believer (see, for example, *Czech Radio*. "Erazim Kohák: Grateful to be Home, Grateful to be Alive." Accessed April 11, 2015. http://www.radio.cz/en/section/one-on-one/professor-erazim-kohak-grateful-to-be-home-grateful-to-be-alive). Malick was raised by Assyrian Christian parents, and his movies all have a distinctly "spiritual" quality, but his famously private and reclusive life precludes insight into his own religious beliefs, if any. Jack Gilbert, treated below, seems to have no specific position on these matters that I am aware of.

**51** Woolf, *To the Lighthouse*, 114. Emphasis mine.

**52** Ibid.

**53** Ms. Ramsey's internal life seems not so different from Ms. O'Brien's: "Help each other. Love everyone. Every leaf. Every ray of light" (Malick, *The Tree of Life* [2011]).

**54** "The sound of the bell of Jetavana echoes the impermanence of all things" (*Hieke Monogatari*, trans. A.L. Sandler [Tokyo: Charles E. Tuttle Company, 1972], 22). Here we might note one source of the challenges that face a Western approach to questions of mortality and entropy: our relationship with the idea of nothingness. Eugene Thacker goes so far as to write: "the great lie of Western culture—the preference for existence over non-existence" (Eugene Thacker, *Cosmic Pessimism* [Minneapolis, MN: Univocal, 2015]). That statement may well be too sweeping, but insofar as "Eastern" philosophies and religious traditions have a very different relationship to the concept of nothingness than that found in Judaism,

Christianity, or Islam, their experience of and reflection on suffering and finitude takes a rather different approach. This is not to suggest that either set of traditions has the "correct" approach to the experience of nothingness and mortality, but rather that ongoing dialogue is likely to expand our understanding of the same. For Virgil's *lacrimae rerum*, see *The Aeneid*, trans. Allen Mandelbaum (New York: Bantam, 1981), 17 (Book I, 655).

**55** Dillard, *Pilgrim at Tinker Creek*, 84. Or, again, with poet Denise Levertov, we must keep in mind that each experience of wonder and joy is unique, occurring only once; there may be others, but each of those will also be unique—unrepeatable and irreplaceable (Denise Levertov, "Once Only" in *This Great Unknowing: Last Poems* [New York: New Directions, 1999], 46). Perhaps, as Nicolas Bouvier muses, "our feeble hearts could not stand more" (Nicolas Bouvier, *The Way of the World*, trans. Robyn Marsack [New York: New York Review Books, 1992], 95).

**56** Cf. Virginia Woolf, *Moments of Being* (New York: Mariner Books, 1985).

**57** Woolf, *To the Lighthouse*, 121.

**58** Ibid., 172.

**59** Ibid. These little daily miracles are intertwined with what Dillard calls the "extravagance of the minutiae" (Dillard, *Pilgrim at Tinker Creek*, 130).

**60** Ralph Waldo Emerson, *Nature* in *Ralph Waldo Emerson: Essays and Lectures* (New York: The Library of America, 1983), 47. Thus, "to the wise. . . a fact is true poetry" (ibid.).

**61** Woolf, *To the Lighthouse*, 172.

**62** Ibid., 73. An affirmation aligned with the commitment to immanence implied in Stephen Daedalus's assertion that God is "a shout in the streets" and which echoes Molly Bloom's "Yes!" in Joyce's *Ulysses* (New York: Vintage International, 1990), 34 and 783 respectively. Here we have what I take to be an unambiguous affirmation of life, but without the Nietzschean error that suggests such an affirmation must also include endorsing tragedy, loss, suffering, and death. We can affirm life, full-throatedly, while recognizing and even accepting its finitude; but this does not require that we positively affirm and endorse the negation of life. See below, chapter six.

**63** Jack Gilbert, "A Brief for the Defense" in *Refusing Heaven* (New York: Knopf, 2007), 3.

**64** Jean-Luc Nancy writes that "Nihilism is perhaps the absence of joy before anything else" (Jean-Luc Nancy, *The Possibility of a World*, trans. Travis Holloway and Flor Méchain [New York: Fordham University Press, 2017], 129).

**65** Paul Ricoeur, *Fallible Man*, trans. Charles A. Kelbley (New York: Fordham University Press, 1986), 140. E.M. Forester makes a similar remark: "By the side of the everlasting Why there is a Yes—a transitory Yes if you like, but a Yes" (E.M. Forester, *A Room with a View* [New York: Bantam, 1988], 22).

**66** Gilbert, "A Brief for the Defense," 3.

**67** On my reading this is (a) not a theodicy and (b) not universalizable. It is not a theodicy because it has little to do with God (*theos*); the "compensation" here is existential, aesthetic, particular, and immediate, rather than theological, economic, or eschatological. It is not universalizable because while evil may be understandable in my life, even in terms of a quasi-theodicy (if we must use that term) or a "brief for the defense," it remains an unconscionable offense applied to the lives of others. The faint sound of the oars in *my* ears does not make the suffering of homeless people in Bangladesh worth it. Rather, the experiences of joy that each of us has makes, or can make, life worth it. Thus, while the current study does not focus on it, a full life of what I will call "melancholic joy" in chapter six would also be concerned in some way with justice and alleviating the suffering of others. In seeking to remain attentive to the joy in our lives—whatever our particular circumstances—we must remember those who are not currently experiencing joy. As Shakespeare's King Lear shouts on the heath: "Poor naked wretches, whereso'er you are, / That bide the pelting of this pitiless storm, / How shall your houseless heads and unfed sides, / Your looped and windowed raggedness, defend you / From seasons such as these? O, I have ta'en / Too little care of this! Take physic, pomp. / Expose thyself to feel what wretches feel, / That thou mayst shake the superflux to them / And show the heavens more just" (Shakespeare, *King Lear*, Act 3, Scene 4).

**68** The final sentences of this essay draw the conclusion of my "Hope in the Age of the Anthropocene" in *Ecology, Ethics, and Hope*, ed. Andrew Brei (Lanham, MD: Rowman and Littlefield, 2015).

**69** These moments of glory and grace may not even outnumber or outweigh suffering in my own relatively fortunate life. See, for example, David Benatar, *Better Never to Have Been: The Harm of Coming Into Existence* (Oxford: Oxford University Press, 2008).

**70** Dillard, *Pilgrim at Tinker Creek*, 80–1.

**71** Kohák, *The Embers and the Stars*, 82–5, 95–103, etc. See the account of appreciative-love in chapter five below.

**72** It would be easy, all too easy, to dismiss this wager as naive or fantastical. Or as the frivolous and unjustified privilege of someone lucky enough to be born into dominant power narratives—white, male, heterosexual, and so on—in the United States during the affluence of the latter half of the 20th century. But such criticism is too easy by half. First, the fact that it is, supposedly, "easy" to say that life includes wonder and joy as an ever-present possibility from the perspective of privilege does not make it any less true. James is correct to suggest there are temperamental inclinations toward optimism or pessimism. But I cannot see why we should accord obvious epistemic privilege to despair and melancholy, despite their allure (to myself and others) and their prevalence in literature and philosophy. Both optimism and pessimism can be psychologized and subjectivized. If we work to convince ourselves that life is meaningless, we should not be surprised that we find it so. Likewise, if we work to convince ourselves that life has meaning, we may hope to experience a meaningful life. Second, it is all-too-clear that while privilege may protect a person from certain forms of suffering, such protection is at best partial and temporary. It is, moreover, often radically overstated. Everyone suffers, and everyone dies. In addition, some forms of privilege come with their own sets of blinders, which also work to obscure the glory. Finally, dismissing the significance of joy ignores the testimony of some people in desperate circumstances, such as crushing poverty or terminal illness. No one is suggesting that evil, suffering, and tragedy are insignificant, or that they can be bought off by moments of joy. Nor am I suggesting that everyone suffers equally. The point is rather that, even in the wreckage of a life, goodness shines out, eternally, from all things. This glory is available to both the "poor women at the fountain" and the melancholic continental philosopher.

# Chapter 3 From Mortality to Vitality

**1** John Donne, Sermon II, Preached in the Evening of Christmas Day, 1624. See *The Sermons of John Donne* in the BYU Library Digital Collections. Accessed February 15, 2016. http://contentdm.lib.byu.edu/cdm/compoundobject/collection/JohnDonne/id/3210/rec/2.

**2** In such cases, we do not see the world as one looks at an exterior object; rather, we live the world from the inside, immersed in it rather than observing it placed in front of us. See Maurice Merleau-Ponty, "Eye and Mind" in *The Primacy of Perception* (Evanston, IL: Northwestern University Press, 1964), 178.

**3** Aldous Huxley, *The Doors of Perception and Heaven and Hell* (New York: Harper Perennial, 2009), 76. Or, as Michel Serres put it: "Garden or boarding school? A fork in the road of child-rearing. . . If you wish to train an army of statues socially dedicated to the struggle for dominance, give them a poor, dry lexicon, as hard as wood and as cold as iron, studded with technical jargon like an endless refrain, form their senses through these words, give them access to the given through this language. . . As they begin their existence, children will shield their eyes when they raise them towards the patch of sky visible at the top of the well shaft which is their school-prison. . . If [rather] you form their words through the senses, amidst the hawthorn and primrose, if rose, in all its declensions, can be related to the exploding, fragrant bouquet of shapes and hues, if you build their language through the given, then anything can happen. Even a poet. Even a happy adult; even a wise one. . . ." (Michel Serres, *The Five Senses: A Philosophy of Mingled Bodies*, trans. Margaret Sankey and Peter Cowley [London: Continuum, 2008], 192).

**4** "Epicurean" in the modern/pejorative rather than the classical/philosophical sense. On the body as a prison for the soul, see Plato, "Phaedo" in *Five Dialogues*, trans. G.M.A. Grube (Indianapolis, IN: Hackett, 1981), 98, Bekker 62b.

**5** See John D. Caputo, *Hoping Against Hope* (Minneapolis, MN: Fortress Press, 2015), 157ff. Odd how many people lament not having enough time to live well, when even the time they *do* have is not spent well. As Henry Miller wrote from his home in Big Sur: "I have known cripples and invalids who were radiant sources of joy and inspiration. And I have known 'successful' men and women who were like running sores. Had we the power to resurrect the dead, what could we offer that life itself has not already offered, and continues to offer, in full measure?" (Henry Miller, *Big Sur and the Oranges of Hieronymus Bosch* [New York: New Directions, 1957], 168).

**6** Abraham Maslow, *Religions, Values, and Peak Experiences* (London: Penguin Books Limited, 1964). Mihaly Csikszentmihalyi, *Flow: The Psychology of Optimal Experience* (New York: Harper Perennial, 1990). Laozi, *Daodejing*, trans. Edmund Ryden (Oxford: Oxford University Press, 2008).

**7** Csikszentmihalyi, *Flow*, 3.

**8** Ibid., 48ff.

**9** Ibid., 67.

**10** Ibid., 83.

**11** Edward Slingerland, *Trying Not to Try* (New York: Broadway Books, 2014), 44.

**12** See Edward Slingerland, *Trying Not to Try* (New York: Broadway Books, 2014).

**13** Confucius, *The Analects*, Internet Classics Archive. Accessed June 22, 2019. http://classics.mit.edu/Confucius/analects.1.1.html

**14** See, for example, the account of exhibiting the Tao in butchery in *The Book of Chuang Tzu*, trans. Martin Palmer, with Elizabeth Breuilly, Chang Wai Ming, and Jay Ramsey (New York: Penguin Books, 1996), 23; and *Chuang Tzu: Basic Writings*, trans. Burton Watson [New York: Columbia University Press, 1964], 46–48).

**15** Laozi, *Daodejing*, 61.

**16** *Mencius*, trans. D.C. Lau (New York: Penguin, 1970), 83.

**17** Csikszentmihalyi, *Flow*, 225. Philosophy in the West has often subordinated the active life to the contemplative life. However, for a few more nuanced accounts—quite different from each other—see Hannah Arendt, *The Human Condition* (Chicago: The University of Chicago Press, 1998), Matthew B. Crawford, *Shopcraft as Soulcraft* (New York: Penguin, 2010), and Henry David Thoreau, *Walden* (Princeton, NJ: Princeton University Press, 1971).

**18** See Richard Shusterman, *Thinking Through the Body: Essays in Somaesthetics* (Cambridge: Cambridge University Press, 2012), especially 47–67.

**19** See Csikszentmihalyi, *Flow*, 113.

**20** Michel Serres, *The Five Senses: A Philosophy of Mingled Bodies*, trans. Margaret Sankey and Peter Cowley (London: Continuum, 2008), see especially the last chapter, "Joy"; *Variations on the Body*, trans. Randolph Burks (London: Continuum, 2008); *Angels: A Modern Myth*, trans. Francis Cowper (Paris and New York: Flammarion, 1995), and *The Natural Contract*, trans. Elizabeth MacArthur and William Paulson (Ann Arbor, MI: The University of Michigan Press, 2008)—particularly the final section on "casting off."

**21** Serres, *Variations on the Body*, 33. See here the echo of Confucius and Mencius, treated above.

**22** Ibid., 15–16.

**23** Ibid., 16.

**24** See below for the example of Cook Ting. Additionally, our hypothetical butcher may have a rich intellectual life that is separate from his or her means of paying the mortgage: Spinoza was a lens-grinder; William Carlos Williams was a doctor; Wallace Stevens was an insurance company executive; Dennis O'Driscoll worked in the Irish Office of the Revenue Commissioners. There is no *prima facie* justification for dismissing the possibility that our butcher might be a talented poet, a passionate amateur botanist, or lover of maths.

**25** Françoise Dastur, *How Are We to Confront Death?: An Introduction to Philosophy*, trans. Robert Vallier (New York: Fordham University Press, 2012), 29.

**26** Ibid., 28.

**27** Ibid., 25 ff. She identifies "the cult of the body," "risky behavior," and "celebrity" as three examples.

**28** Ibid., 28.

**29** Ibid., 29. As Norman Maclean observed: "It is very important to a lot of people to make unmistakably clear to themselves and to the universe that they love the universe but are not intimidated by it and will not be shaken by it, no matter what it has in store. Moreover, they demand something from themselves early in life that can be taken ever after as a demonstration of this abiding feeling" (Norman Maclean, *Young Men and Fire* [Chicago: University of Chicago Press, 1992], 28).

**30** The issue of control parallels a point Dastur herself makes when she characterizes the "cult of the body," the fetishization and pursuit of youthful appearance, as another manifestation of "illusory immortality." Just as we can deny our mortality by pretending to be ageless, we can deny our mortality by pretending we can cheat death by "following the rules" or acting "safely," as if doing so would allow us to avoid death indefinitely. Dastur thinks the "feeling of plenitude" that so captivates adventurers leads to feelings of omnipotence (Dastur, *How Are We to Confront Death?*, 28), that they are seeking an "escape from death" rather than a true assumption of finitude. But as I've suggested, there is another possible explanation here: that seeking these feelings of plenitude is a celebration of life-in-light-of-inevitable-death, something that is predicated on recognizing our finitude and creatureliness rather than fleeing from them. Thus, properly undertaken, vitality accomplishes precisely what Dastur thinks philosophy should: "*both* the overcoming *and* the acceptance of finitude *at the same time*" (Ibid., 36). As Leopardi writes, "it is commonly thought that men of the sea, and of war, being very often in danger of death, hold their lives in less esteem than others do. I for the very same reason believe that life is by very few persons so loved and prized as it is by soldiers and sailors. . . . Who ever numbered among human blessings just having a little dry land under his feet? No one, except for sailors" (Giacomo Leopardi, *Moral Essays* [New York: Columbia University Press, 1983], 161).

**31** Sigmund Freud, "Thoughts for the Times on War and Death" in *The Standard Edition of the Complete Works of Sigmund Freud*, trans. James Strachey (The Hogarth Press, 1975), 290–291. Goethe wrote that "the [sacred] shudder" experienced in the face of the sublimity of nature is "the best part of man. However dearly the world makes him pay for it. . ." (Goethe, *Faust*, Part 2, 1. 6272 in *Théâtre complet* [Paris, 1958], 1127; cited in Pierre Hadot, *The Veil of Isis* [Belknap Press, 2006], 280). And, similarly, Michel Serres: "What we learn in the middle of the night is that the world makes us flinch, and that we would do anything not to hear it, to keep it far from us, *were it not for that tiny pinch of bitter-but-magnificent joy that draws us to it*" (Serres, *The Five Senses*, 134. Emphasis mine).

**32** Leopardi, *Moral Essays*, 89–90. Tennyson concurs in his "Ulysses": "Life piled upon life were all too little" (Alfred, Lord Tennyson, "Ulysses" in *The Norton Introduction to Poetry* [New York: W.W. Norton and Co., 1981], 358–360).

**33** Csikszentmihalyi, *Flow*, 90.

**34** Vitality should not be equated solely with a kind of *Strum und Drang*; and lest one be put off by the tendency to illustrate the consequences of hard reality with stereotypically "rugged" examples, Serres suggests that other endeavors conform to a similar rule: "higher mathematics, fine arts, high virtuosity, high-level mysticism, all correspond in every way to high mountains or the high seas, worlds where the cords [binding us to hard reality, to others, or both] remain taut" (Serres, *The Natural Contract*, 113). This seems to indicate that "risk" is a consequence of either the fact that such endeavors require the agent to conform to or otherwise defer to hard reality, or that there are existential consequences for failure. Nor should we equate vitality with various corruptions with which it may at times be found. Serres, for example, takes pains to insist that his emphasis on sport, climbing, sailing, and similar instances of bodily engagement with the world must be understood in terms of a distinction between "noble" and "ignoble" sport. The former "makes bodies blossom and teaches the physical and moral virtues," while the latter, corrupted by money or other non-intrinsic goals, cultivates vices and "spreads fascism" (Serres, *Variations on the Body*, 35–6). Noble sport should make us humble. After all, most people are not top athletes and therefore "lose" a great deal of the time; and even champions "lose" eventually. No climber will ever be able to climb every route; no boxer will reign indefinitely as champion; no runner is capable of running perpetually. Noble sport is antithetical to triumphalism, Social Darwinism, and "Nazi victory hymns" (Ibid., 36): "this is what [the] ascesis [of noble sport] teaches: losing, to be sure, against the others, but winning in the things themselves and for oneself. . ." (Ibid., 36). This is a sentiment congenial to the Taoist account of *wu-wei*: "The way of sages acts and does not compete" (Laozi, *Daodejing*, 167). Although Serres offers moving accounts of time spent at sea or in the mountains, he does give other examples of engagement with hard reality. We find one of his most beautiful accounts in a story about sharing a bottle of 1947 Chateau d'Yquem with two friends, a description of exquisite detail that concludes, "it took us so long to finish this bottle that we are still talking about it" (Serres, *The Five Senses*, 152). That is, he is still talking about it and writing about it these many decades later. The language (soft) with which we are compelled to communicate has remained—or has striven to remain—faithful to the actual, carnal experience (hard) of the wine. Insofar as it has done so, that experience of joy, in which eternity broke into the everyday experience of wine and fellowship, never came to an end for him.

**35** Again, Tennyson: "all times I have enjoy'd / Greatly, have suffer'd greatly" (Tennyson, "Ulysses," 358–60).

**36** The principle here is not unlike that posited by William James in "The Moral Equivalent of War" (William James, "The Moral Equivalent of War" in *William James: Writings 1902–10* [New York: The Library of America, 1987], 1281–93). James argues that we would do well to separate the virtues associated with conflict—endurance, tenacity, inventiveness, fidelity, self-sacrifice, and the like—from the moral catastrophe that characterizes war. Challenging circumstances help people to develop essential human virtues that can only be, or are best, cultivated *in extremis*.

**37** Richard Kearney and Brian Treanor, *Carnal Hermeneutics* (New York: Fordham University Press, 2015). Also see Richard Kearney, *Touch* (New York: Columbia University Press, 2021).

**38** Serres, *The Five Senses*, 129.

**39** See Jacques Derrida, *Applying: To Derrida* (London: Palgrave Macmillan, 1996) and John D. Caputo, *The Insistence of God* (Bloomington, IN: Indiana University Press, 2013), 189–96.

**40** Serres, *The Five Senses*, 41. There is, on my reading, no dualism at work or implied here. See my "Vitality: Carnal, Seraphic Bodies," *The Journal of French and Francophone Philosophy*, Vol.XXV, No.1 [2017], 207): "the purely hard and the purely soft are nowhere to be found; we have, rather, degrees on a spectrum of hardness and softness. Nevertheless, we should not abandon the language of the hard and the soft because it is rhetorically, didactically, and philosophically useful"; we "recognize aspects, parts, or experiences of that reality as either harder (reality imposed on us, reality to which we must conform, reality "as if we were dead," and so on) or softer (meaningful reality, experienced reality, reality 'while we are here' and 'with which we are involved'), all the while recognizing that there is only one reality." Also see my "Mind the Gap: The Challenge of Matter" in Kearney and Treanor, *Carnal Hermeneutics*, 69–70.

**41** Ibid., 58–9 and 152–4.

**42** See *Carnal Hermeneutics*, eds. Richard Kearney and Brian Treanor (New York: Fordham University Press, 2015), as well as my "Lateralization and Leaning" in *Somatic Desire*, eds. Sarah Horton and Richard Kearney (Lanham, MD: Lexington, 2019) and "Earthy Hermeneutics: Beyond the Metaphor of the Text" in *Continental Philosophy and the Environment*, ed. Jonathan Maskit (Lanham, MA: Rowman and Littlefield International, forthcoming). Here it is worth noting an interesting implication of hermeneutics "beyond the text": the significance of embodiment vis-à-vis emplotment. Hermeneutics has rightly made much of differences in the ways that cultures, traditions, and narratives shape one's horizons. But those differences, while significant, seem minor compared to the differences by which different *bodies*, human and non-human, perceive the world. If the foundation of hermeneutics is perspective rather than language, what presents us with a greater hermeneutic difference: the distinction between Protestant and Catholic, or the distinction between human and, say, dolphin?

**43** Annie Dillard, *Pilgrim at Tinker Creek* (New York: Harper Perennial, 2007), 31.

**44** Ibid., 244.

**45** Ibid., 36.

**46** Ibid., 245. As Thoreau writes of a similar light in a riparian valley: "There needs no stronger proof of immortality. All things must live in such a light. O Death, where was thy sting? O Grave, where was thy victory, then? (Thoreau, *Walden*, 317). Clearly, neither Dillard nor Thoreau steps out of the hermeneutic circle when encountering the tree; their language is heavy with accreted tropes of "flame," "praise," and "immortality." The "new eyes" that see the "glory" reveal a truth, not The Truth.

**47** Serres, *The Natural Contract*, 97 ff. "If the mountain finally turns out to be difficult, appallingly tough, then the contract itself takes on a different function: it no longer binds just the mountaineers among themselves, but in addition anchors itself to the rock face at specific strong points" (Ibid., 104). Here the *corde* connects us not only to our ropemates, a social contract among people, but also to the rock, the hard reality of the world. A natural contract joins the social contract.

**48** Maurice Merleau-Ponty, *The Phenomenology of Perception*, trans. Colin Smith (London: Routledge, 1989), and Richard Shusterman, *Thinking Through the Body* (Cambridge: Cambridge University Press, 2012).

**49** The full import of this example was brought out to me by Elizabeth Sikes.

**50** Marcel Proust, *In Search of Lost Time*, *Volume I*, *Swan's Way*, trans. C.K. Scott Moncrieff and Terence Kilmartin (New York: The Modern Library, 2003), 60–4, and *In Search of Lost Time*, *Volume VI*, *Time Regained*, trans. Andreas Mayor and Terence Kilmartin (New York: The Modern Library, 2003), 255–7. With respect to the later instance, on the cobblestones of the Guermantes Way, Proust states explicitly the power of involuntary memory to restore an entire world: "Almost at once I recognized the vision: it was Venice, of which my effort to describe it and the supposed snapshots taken by my memory had never told me anything, but which the sensation which I had once experienced as I stood on two uneven stones in the baptistery of St. Mark's had, recurring a moment ago [stumbling outside the Guermantes's mansion], *restored to me complete* with all the other sensations linked on that day to that particular sensation, all of which had been waiting in their place—from which with imperious suddenness a chance happening had caused them to emerge—in the series of forgotten days" (Proust, *Time Regained*, 256. Emphasis mine). This account cannot help but bring to mind the discussion of "unstable equilibrium" in Serres's *Variations on the Body* (45–7, 137–8, etc.). Note that Proust also says the happiness of this experience/memory gave him a "certainty. . . which sufficed, without any other proof, to make death a matter of indifference to me" (Ibid., 257). This latter point, that of the sufficiency of the present moment, links the world-engaging and world-delivering aspects of vitality to a wider conception of joy-in-finitude addressed in chapter two.

**51** Proust, *Swan's Way*, 61. On indisputability or ineluctability, see chapter six below.

**52** Cf. Ed Casey, *The World at a Glance* (Bloomington, IN: Indiana University Press, 2007). On the nature of these "epiphanies" in Proust, see Richard Kearney, "Sacramental Imagination: Eucharists of the Ordinary Universe in the Works of Joyce, Proust, and Woolf," in *Through a Glass Darkly: Suffering, The Sacred, and The Sublime in Literature and Theory*, eds. Jens Zimmerman, Lynn Szabo and Holly Nelson (Waterloo, ON: Wilfred Laurier University Press, 2010).

**53** Henry David Thoreau, *The Maine Woods* (Princeton, NJ: Princeton University Press, 2004), 71.

**54** Thoreau, *Walden*, 350. Also see Gary Snyder, *Practice of the Wild* (Berkeley, CA: Counterpoint Press, 1990), 25: "Practically speaking, a life that is vowed to simplicity, appropriate boldness, good humor, gratitude, unstinting work and play, and lots of walking brings us close to the actual existing world and its wholeness."

**55** Henry Rollins, "The Iron" in *Details Magazine*, January 1993. Insight from a punk-rock, spoken-word icon that is reflected directly in Serres's account of the "iron law" of hard reality.

**56** ". . .the researcher who cheats or lies neither finds nor invents, just as the high jumper neither cheats nor lies with gravity. . . this iron law turns its back on every practice on the part of the collectives whether professional, political, media, or academic. . . that crown mobsters and puts the mediocre in power. Respect the thing itself that, alone, commands and not opinion, this above all else teaches the world-producing life" (Serres, *Variations on the Body*, 34).

**57** William Shakespeare, *As You Like It*, Act II, Scene 1. On the degree to which we find in nature "tongues in trees, books in the running brooks / Sermons in stones, and good in every thing" (as Duke Senior continues in the passage cited), and regarding the claim that one of the things nature "says" to us is to be ourselves ("persuade us what we are"), see chapter five below.

**58** On anamorphosis, see Jean-Luc Marion, *Being Given*, trans. Jeff Kosky (Stanford, CA: Stanford University Press, 2002), §13.

**59** Serres, *The Natural Contract*, 111.

**60** Ibid., 112. It is, perhaps, for this reason that Nietzsche tells us "our most sacred convictions, the unchanging elements in our supreme values, are judgments of our muscles" (Friedrich Nietzsche, *The Will to Power*, trans. Walter Kaufmann and R.J. Hollingdale, ed. Walter Kaufmann [New York: Random House, 1967], 173 [§314]).

**61** Serres, *The Natural Contract*, 112.

**62** See C.S. Lewis, *The Screwtape Letters* (New York: Harper Collins, 2001) 165–9.

**63** And so, Nikos Kazantzakis writes, "Within me, even the most metaphysical problem takes on a warm physical body which smells of sea, soil, and human sweat. The Word, in order to touch me, must become warm flesh. Only then do I understand—when I can smell, see, and touch" (Nikos Kazantzakis, *Report to Greco*, trans. P.A. Bein [New York: Simon and Schuster, 1965], 43).

**64** Plato, "Phaedo," 98, (Bekker 62b) and 101 (Bekker 65b) respectively. René Descartes, *Meditations on First Philosophy*, trans. John Cottingham (Cambridge: Cambridge University Press, 1986).

**65** This is certainly evident in cases of habit and training, as in Serres's examples; but it is also the case in situations in which hard reality surprises us. Anyone who has had the experience of being a few rungs down on the food chain in the presence of apex predators can attest that the experience is, especially at the outset, as close to prelinguistic (i.e., hard) as we are capable of having. The hermeneutics of *nous* withdraws and the hermeneutics of the *soma* emerges; the hermeneutics of the Axial Age, Renaissance, and Enlightenment give way to the hermeneutics of the early Pleistocene.

**66** Serres, *Variations on the Body*, 78.

**67** Ibid., 42. A provocative critique of flow can be found in Gail Montero's *Thought in Action: Expertise and the Conscious Mind* (Oxford: Oxford University Press, 2016). Montero, herself a former professional ballet dancer, argues that most elite performers are, in fact, always thinking, always adjusting, and that this thinking is required for success at the highest level. A full engagement with Montero's work is not possible here; but among the relevant considerations that would need to be unpacked (some of which are treated by Montero, others not) are the difference between improvisation and rote execution, the goal of the action in terms of harmonization with the environment versus imposition on the environment, and the difference between actions that result in happiness and those that result in success.

**68** Serres, *Variations on the Body*, 77.

**69** *The Book of Chuang Tzu*, 23.

**70** Ibid., 23. "This remark signals to us that we should be taking the story of the ox as a metaphor: we are Butcher Ding's blade, and the bones and ligaments of the ox are the barriers and obstacles that we face in life. Just as Butcher Ding's blade remains razor-sharp because it never touches bone or ligament—moving only through the gaps in between—so does the *wu-wei* person move only through the open spaces in life, avoiding the difficulties that damage one's spirit and wear out one's body" (Slingerland, *Trying Not to Try*, 21). Consider, as another example, the Japanese Zen Buddhist practice of drawing the *ensō* (circle). This, perhaps, is one indication of the way in which flow has a wider significance than the focused, technical expertise and skill that is Montero's focus.

**71** As William James notes: "There are two ways of looking at our duty in the matter of opinion, —ways entirely different, and yet ways about whose difference the theory of knowledge seems hitherto to have shown very little concern. *We must have the truth*; and *we must avoid error*. —these are our first and great commandments as would-be knowers; but they are not two ways of stating an identical commandment, they are two separable laws. Although it may indeed happen that when we believe the truth *A*, we escape as an incidental consequence from believing the falsehood *B*, it hardly ever happens that by merely disbelieving *B* we necessarily believe *A*" (William James, *The Will to Believe* [New York: Dover Publications, 1956], 18).

**72** See Jonathan Haidt, *The Righteous Mind: Why Good People are Divided by Politics and Religion* (New York: Pantheon, 2012).

**73** Dillard, *Pilgrim at Tinker Creek*, 36.

**74** Rather than Heideggerian *unheimlichkeit* (uncanniness), this experience is one of *heimelige* (hominess)—a form of authenticity tied to our embodiment, our worldliness, and our creatureliness, an acceptance of what we are and an appreciation for where we are. This fittedness for the world is not the average everydayness of Heideggerian *heimelige*, which is characterized by the banal, quotidian odor that accompanies idle talk (*Gerede*), distracting curiosity (*Neugier*), and ambiguity (*Zweideutigkeit*), and which for Heidegger serves primarily as the backdrop against which the insight of *unheimlichkeit*, so captivating to continental philosophers, might manifest itself. It is, rather, a deeper form of hominess that is more an experience of communion than, as in Heidegger, practical handiness or fascination (*benommen*). See Martin Heidegger, *Being and Time*, trans. John Macquarrie and Edward Robinson (San Francisco, CA: Harper San Francisco, 1962).

**75** On being and having, see Gabriel Marcel, *Being and Having* (New York: Harper Torchbooks, 1965). In a similar vein, Erazim Kohák distinguishes between the having of possessions and the mutual relationship of belonging: "The bond of belonging that grows up over years of life, love, and labor is the most basic truth of being human in a world" (Kohák, *The Embers and the Stars*, 107). The relationships of being and having apply to environments, places, and worlds as well: "the land will belong to those who belong to it" (Ibid.).

**76** Anxiety is a *Grundstimmung*; it is not the only *Grundstimmung*. Vitality and joy, like anxiety (*Angst*), are just capable of pulling us out of ordinary everydayness; they, just as much as *Angst*, break us from the bonds of routine, comfort, and domestication that occlude authentic thinking. Jean-Yves Lacoste makes this point, although in a quite different context and chord, in *Experience and the Absolute: Disputed Questions on the Humanity of Man,* trans. Mark Raferty-Skehan (New York: Fordham University Press, 2004), 194.

**77** Kazantzakis, *Report to Greco*, 153.

**78** "The virtue of vitality," claims Serres, "imparts life, plus love" (Serres, *Variations on the Body*, 50). See below, chapter five.

**79** Proust, *Time Regained*, 257.

**80** Heidegger, *Being and Time*, 83.

**81** Thoreau, *Walden*, 282.

**82** Thus, Csikszentmihalyi advises: "When we are unhappy, depressed, or bored we have an easy remedy at hand: to use the body for all it is worth" (Csikszentmihalyi, *Flow*, 94). This does not, however, mean that we can use the body for any ends whatsoever. My colleague James Taylor asked me what, if anything, could distinguish between the "flow" experienced by a skilled surfer and that experienced by a skilled sniper. A partial answer and promissory note would be that this account of flow—building, as it does, on Taoist accounts of *wu-wei*—would insist that genuine flow is an experience of being in harmony with the universe, which requires both an inner or subjective condition (joy, stillness, inner peace) and an external or objective condition (the state of flow, successful application of skill in a given endeavor). Each of these conditions is necessary; but neither is sufficient. Thus, one might argue that "flow" in the service of murder, disorder, and so forth is not flow at all, or at least that it is not flow in the sense in which I am using that category to shed light on vitality. My thanks to another colleague, Fr. Tom Sherman, S.J., for helping me to see the potential for this response in Laozi. See, for example, chapter 31 of the *Daodejing*:

> As weapons are instruments of evil,
> They are not properly a wise man's instruments;
> Only on necessity will he resort to them.
> For peace and quiet are dearest to his heart,
> And to him even a victory is no cause for rejoicing.

# Chapter 4 A Twilight Hope

**1** An assertion by Julian of Norwich in her *Revelations of Divine Love*, XXXII, which was made more famous by reuse in T.S. Eliot's "Little Gidding" (*Four Quartets* [New York: Harvest Books, 1943], 57). The claim, and the question of its validity, plays a major role in Annie Dillard's *Holy the Firm* (New York: HarperPerennial, 1998), which reflects on the presence of inexplicable evil in a world that, in its other aspects, is so clearly majestic and good. Dillard tells the story of "Julie Norwich," a young child who, though she survived, had her face burnt off in a plane accident near Dillard's retreat on the San Juan Islands. See chapter six, note 30.

**2** Cf. Seamus Heaney, *The Cure at Troy: A Version of Sophocles' Philoctetes* (New York: Farrar, Straus and Giroux, 1991), 77.

**3** Roger Scruton, *The Uses of Pessimism* (Oxford: Oxford University Press, 2013), 2.

**4** Ibid., 1.

**5** The title of this chapter is meant to evoke *Ragnarök/Ragnarøkkr*, the "doom" or "twilight" of the gods, and the question of what it would mean to hope in the face of an inescapable doom that forecloses all possibility of hope in the quotidian sense (i.e., hope as desire, wish, or expectation). "The sun turns black, earth sinks into sea, / the bright stars vanish from the sky; / steam rises up in the conflagration, / a high flame plays against heaven itself" (*The Poetic Edda*, trans. Carolyne Larrington [Oxford: Oxford World Classics, 1996], 11). True, the *Voluspa* and *Edda* do foretell the birth of another world after *Ragnarök*; but the doom is utterly inescapable for Odin, the one who hears the *Voluspa*, and for most of the rest of the universe. The "twilight of hope" might also be taken to allude to Nietzsche's *Twilight of the Idols*, in particular its criticism of life-denying tendencies in philosophy (Fredrich Nietzsche, *Twilight of the Idols*, trans. Duncan Large [Oxford: Oxford University Press, 1998]). Finally, the question of whether and how to "hope in the dark," cannot but evoke both Rebecca Solnit, *Hope in the Dark* (Chicago, IL: Haymarket Books, 2004) and John D. Caputo, *Hoping Against Hope* (Minneapolis: Fortress Press, 2015).

**6** My account of hope here is deeply indebted to the work of Gabriel Marcel. See, for example: Gabriel Marcel, "On the Ontological Mystery" in *The Philosophy of Existentialism*, trans. Manya Harari (New York: Citadel Press, 1995); *The Mystery of Being*, vol. 1 and 2 (London: The Harvill Press, 1950 and 1951); *Being and Having* (New York: Harper Torchbooks, 1949); *Creative Fidelity*, trans. Robert Rosthal (New York: Farrar, Straus, and Co., 1964); and *Homo Viator*, trans. Emma Crawford (New York: Harper Torchbooks, 1962). However, my own account differs from Marcel's in important respects, and so this should not be taken to be a strictly Marcelian description of hope.

**7** W.H. Auden, "Twelve Songs, Autumn Song, IX" in *W.H. Auden: Collected Poems*, ed. Edward Mendelson (New York: Vintage International, 1976), 141.

**8** "Sense" here taken in the way it is used by Erazim Kohák, as a kind of foundational, global impression based on experience (and, later, reflection). "Philosophy can claim to be the *scientia generalis* because it seeks to see and articulate the *sense* of being as it presents itself primordially, prior to the imposition of any special perspective or purpose" (Erazim Kohák, *The Embers and the Stars* [Chicago: The University of Chicago Press, 1984], 49, emphasis mine).

**9** Gabriel Marcel, "On the Ontological Mystery," 26.

**10** William James, *The Will to Believe* (New York: Dover Publications, 1956), 34.

**11** Marcel, "On the Ontological Mystery," 29.

**12** Marcel, *Being and Having*, 117.

**13** See Marcel, "On the Ontological Mystery" and *Homo Viator: Introduction to a Metaphysic of Hope*. This parallels a similar distinction in Marcel between "faith that . . ." and "faith in. . . ." In practice, deep hope and quotidian hope can be, and perhaps often are, in conflict. Insofar as deep hope expresses *faith in* the goodness of being in the present and quotidian hope resembles a *desire for* a future, the former is grounded in the sufficiency of the present moment, while the latter seems to focus on an insufficiency in the present. However, in principle these two forms of hope can coexist in a single person, precisely because we can reject the unqualified endorsement of a situation—as expressed, for example, in Nietzsche's "eternal return of the same"—while preserving a commitment to and a full-throated affirmation of *this* world. Thus, it is possible to both hope (be faithful to the present) and 'hope' (desire improvement in the future) at the same time.

**14** Marcel, "On the Ontological Mystery," 28. See also Gabriel Marcel, *Position et approches concrètes du mystère ontologique* (Paris: Vrin, 1949), 68. While neither Marcel's account of hope nor my description of "deep hope" is compatible with a desire for a particular object or event, Marcel's account is more congenial to a future oriented aspect of hope than is deep hope. Marcel calls hope a "memory of the future" (Gabriel Marcel, *Homo Viator*, trans. Emma Crawford [Chicago, IL; Henry Regnery, 1952]). He also emphasizes the "active" nature of hope as committed to bringing something about; and while that activity and that desire for something-better-to-come is not incompatible with deep hope—both can exist in one person—the latter is more deeply committed to a present-focused temporality.

**15** William James, *Pragmatism* (New York: Dover, 1995), 20.

**16** Marcel, "On the Ontological Mystery," 18.

**17** "Philosophy has, to a large degree, ignored the problem of faith. Faith means belief in something concerning which doubt is still theoretically *possible*; and as *the test of belief is willingness to act*, one may say that faith is the readiness to act in a cause the prosperous issue of which is not known to us in advance" (James, *The Will to Believe*, 90).

**18** James, *The Will to Believe*, 59. The "enormous class" of cases certainly includes both faith in the religious sense and faith in the sense of faith in other persons (the latter being the very example James uses to illustrate his point).

**19** Ibid., 62. James's position is, famously, one that rejects both simple materialism and simple idealism.

**20** The idea of a "broken world," a characterization made by Marcel, does not imply some prelapsarian Eden, or that our world is not good. The "brokenness" of the world is an effect of our alienation from it and from each other. It also suggests that the world is in a sense "incomplete," still being made, and that we have a hand in making it. On our contribution to the ongoing unfolding of being, see chapter five below.

**21** These examples are instructive because they make clear that the "response" of the world is not a matter of the world giving us what we desire. Surely Boethius and Bonhoeffer would have preferred not to be executed; Mandelstam and Havel would have preferred not to be imprisoned. To say that the world responds to our deep hope is, rather, to say that we become sensitive to the goodness that was already there, amidst the wreckage. In this sense, the "response" precedes our hope; it is, in fact, a call.

**22** James, *The Will to Believe*, 60. The similarities between a certain reading of pragmatism and a certain conception of hermeneutics are well worth exploring: the role of the wager; the emphasis on perspective and epistemic fallibility; a conception of truth that we only know partially; and more.

**23** Robinson Jeffers, "The Answer" in *The Collected Poems of Robinson Jeffers*, vol.2 (Stanford, CA: Stanford University Press, 1989), 536. But, in line with the reflections throughout the current work, Czesław Miłosz reminds us that "the earth teaches more" than inhumanism, which is the spirit animating Jeffers's work (Czesław Miłosz, "To Robinson Jeffers" in *New and Collected Poems* [New York: HarperCollins, 2003], 252–53). It is not, I think, that inhumanism is false, but rather that it is incomplete.

**24** Horace, *Odes and Epodes* (Cambridge, MA: Loeb, 2004), 44.

**25** Marcus Aurelius, *Meditations*, trans. C.R. Haines (Cambridge, MA: Harvard University Press, 1999), 195.

**26** *Japanese Philosophy: A Sourcebook*, eds. James W. Heisig, Thomas P. Kasulis, and John C. Maraldo (Honolulu: University of Hawai'i Press, 2011), 149.

**27** Matthew 6:28.

**28** See Henry David Thoreau, "Life Without Principle" in *The Higher Law* (Princeton, NJ: Princeton University Press, 2004), 160.

**29** Václav Havel, "The Politics of Hope" in *Disturbing the Peace: A Conversation with Karel Hvížala*, trans. Paul Wilson (New York: Vintage Books, 1990), 181.

**30** Cf. "The heart has its reasons, which reason does not know. We know this in a thousand things" (Blaise Pascal, *Pensées*, ed. and trans. Roger Ariew (Indianapolis, IN: Hackett, 2004), 216.

**31** Gabriel Marcel, "On the Ontological Mystery," 28.

**32** Erazim Kohák, *The Embers and the Stars* (Chicago, IL: University of Chicago Press, 1987).

**33** Henry Bugbee, *The Inward Morning* (Athens, GA: The University of Georgia Press, 1999). Also see Sean McGrath, *Thinking Nature: An Essay in Negative Ecology* (Edinburgh University Press, 2019).

**34** Hadot, *The Present Alone is Our Happiness* (Stanford, CA: Stanford University Press, 2011), 8. Note that here Hadot is citing Michel Hulin's *La Mystique sauvage* (Paris: PUF, 2008).

**35** Havel, "The Politics of Hope," 181.

**36** Ibid. Both Havel, an agnostic, and Marcel, a Catholic, agree that hope must rely on something beyond the self. Compare Havel, "The Politics of Hope," 181 and Marcel, "On the Ontological Mystery," 32.

**37** James, *The Will to Believe*, 32.

**38** Marcel, "On the Ontological Mystery," 14. Emphasis mine.

**39** Marcel concedes that it may be the case that ontological exigence is never fully satisfied, and cannot be fully satisfied. See Gabriel Marcel, *Tragic Wisdom and Beyond*, trans. Stephen Jolin and Peter McCormick (Evanston, IL: Northwestern University Press, 1973), 50.

**40** Sam Keen, "The Development of the Idea of Being" in *The Philosophy of Gabriel Marcel*, eds. Paul Arthur Schilpp and Lewis Edwin Hahn, The Library of Living Philosophers vol. 17 (La Salle, IL: Open Court, 1984), 105. See also my *Aspects of Alterity* (New York: Fordham University Press, 2006).

**41** Evoking, respectively, Tennyson's "In Memoriam A.H.H.," Matthew Arnold's "Dover Beach" (in *The Poetical Works of Matthew Arnold* [New York: Thomas Y. Crowell and Co., 1897], 214), and the treatment in chapter two of Dillard's *Pilgrim at Tinker Creek*, Gilbert's "A Brief for the Defense," and the films of Terrence Malick. Malick's *The Thin Red Line* notes that two people observing the same thing can have very different experiences; one might see nothing but meaningless suffering and the other, confronted with that same suffering, might nevertheless feel something "smiling" behind it or on the fringes of it. Henry Miller captures this ambiguity well in his *Big Sur and the Oranges of Hieronymus Bosch* (New York: New Directions, 1957), 23: "The enchanting, and sometimes terrifying, thing is that the world can be so many things to different souls. That it can be, and is, all these at one and the same time." The notion of a "smile" is evocative of Caputo's characterization of hope as "returning the smile of the universe" (John D. Caputo, *Hoping Against Hope*, 7, 42, 166, etc.).

**42** Martin Heidegger, *The Principle of Reason*, trans. Reginald Lilly (Bloomington, IN: Indiana University Press, 1996), 36. See also Angelus Silesius, *The Cherubic Wanderer*, trans. Maria Shrady (New York: Paulist Press, 1986), 54. Note that Shrady translates the second line as "forgetful of itself, oblivious to our vision," which more forcefully suggests the "inhuman" aspects of "without why" compared to the common rendering by continental philosophers as "it cares not for itself, asks not if it's seen." The rose without why is not merely a beautiful eruption of eternity in time (*à la* Kohák or Woolf), or the unconditional in the conditional (with Caputo); its "without why-ness" also reminds us, precisely, that we too are without firm *arche* or clear *telos*, unmoored, adrift in the cosmos, and only temporarily.

**43** John D. Caputo, *The Mystical Element in Heidegger's Thought* (New York: Fordham University Press, 1986), 100. *Gelassenheit* admits of both religious and secular readings; but this means it will likely be viewed with suspicion from all corners. It seems a bit too religious to atheists: it's a term coined by Meister Eckhart, the most well-known of the Rhineland Mystics, and a Dominican priest to boot; it has the odor not only of Christianity, but Taoism and Zen as well. And, perhaps precisely because of its resonances with Taoism and Zen, it seems insufficiently orthodox to many theists—after all, Eckhart was duly examined by the Inquisition and a number of his propositions deemed heretical.

**44** Martin Heidegger, *Country Path Conversations*, trans. Bret W. Davis (Bloomington, IN: Indiana University Press, 2010) and Bret Davis, "Will and *Gelassenheit*" in *Martin Heidegger: Key Concepts* (Durham, UK: Acumen Publishing, 2010).

**45** Heidegger, *Country Path Conversations*, 134. It is not lost on me that the man who wrote this is also a man who involved himself in National Socialism, a moral failure made all-the-more stark by his utter unwillingness to address it after the fact. He seems, for this reason, a poor authority to opine on what is evil. Nevertheless, the criticism of the will and its desire for mastery seems relevant for a present-oriented hope; indeed, one can read it as a critique of Heidegger's own earlier, problematic valorization of the will (see Bret Davis, "Will and *Gelassenheit,*" 170–75). And, equally important, it also brings to mind the work of Heidegger's critic, Emmanuel Levinas (*Totality and Infinity*, *Otherwise than Being*, etc.).

**46** For other engagements with this ambiguity, see Davis, "Will and *Gelassenheit*," 175–80 and Caputo, *The Mystical Element in Heidegger's Thought*, 178 ff. Marcel suggests this letting go—"relaxation and abandon[ing]"—is central to the process of recollection, "the act whereby I re-collect myself as a unity" and am able to take up a position with respect to my life (see Marcel, "On the Ontological Mystery," 23–4).

**47** See Silesius, *The Cherubinic Wanderer*, 54 and Heidegger, *The Principle of Reason*, 32–40.

**48** Caputo, *The Mystical Element in Heidegger's Thought*, 248-49. And while Heidegger's account of the "there is" of being also implies the "giving" of Being (*es gibt*, it gives), in certain passages that seems hardly more comforting than the "lurking menace" of the "there is" (*il y a*) of Being in Levinas (Emmanuel Levinas, *Existence and Existents*, trans. Alphonso Lingis [Pittsburgh, PA: Duquesne University Press, 2001]). This slippage is perhaps exacerbated by the fact that *il y a* is the French rendering of *es gibt*.

**49** Caputo, *The Mystical Element in Heidegger's Thought*, 251.

**50** Ralph Waldo Emerson, *Self-Reliance* in *Essays and Lectures* (New York: Library of America, 1983), 270.

**51** W.S. Merwin, *The Essential W.S. Merwin*, ed. Michael Weigers (Port Townsend, WA: Copper Canyon Press, 2017), 325

**52** Antoine de St. Exupéry, *Wind, Sand, and Stars*, trans. Lewis Galantière (New York: Harcourt Brace, 1967), 11.

**53** Caputo, *Hoping Against Hope*, 29.

**54** Hadot, *Philosophy as a Way of Life*, 223. Emphasis mine. Simone Weil wrote, "All the tragedies which we can imagine return in the end to the one and only tragedy: the passage of time" (Simone Weil, *Lectures on Philosophy*, trans. Hugh Price [Cambridge: Cambridge University Press, 1978], 197). This remark was brought to my attention by reading Joshua Foa Dienstag, *Pessimism: Philosophy, Ethic, Spirit* (Princeton: Princeton University Press, 2009). And, on a related note, also cited by Dienstag (Ibid., 168), we might observe that Nietzsche felt that the root of pessimism was "time-sickness" [*Zeit-Krankheit*].

**55** Pascal, *Pensées*, 16. According to the *Dictonnaire des synonymes* (René Bailly ed. [Paris: Larousse, 1946]), *espérer* carries the meaning of "*suppose le desir de quelque chose d'heureux, de favorable, que l'on souhaite de voir arriver*"; and so, given the distinctions made in this chapter, here we might amend Pascal to read: "So, we never live, but *desire* to live. . . ." And that, if my analysis of hope and desire is correct, is precisely the problem.

**56** Kohák, *The Embers and the Stars*, 217–218. Love for the present can take many forms, and not all are dreamy or quixotic. Consider Thoreau's fable about the "artist of Kauroo," who becomes so engaged and occupied with perfecting his work that time itself ceases to affect him (Thoreau, *Walden*, [Princeton: Princeton University Press, 2004], 326).

**57** Derek Parfit argues in a series of well-known articles, as well as in his *Reasons and Persons* (Oxford: Oxford University Press, 1984), that the use of the social discount rate—the process by which we devalue, economically or otherwise, the future and the persons who may exist there—is untenable. His various arguments hinge on the ways in which some justifications for discounting are flawed, and the ways in which the things for which we might be justified in discounting (e.g., probability or uncertainty) only partially overlap the thing for which we do discount (i.e., distance in time). Such distinctions, it seems to me, are important; but they do not undermine the legitimacy of what I might call an "existential discount rate" with respect to the value of the future, which is ultimately based on something like probability. We do not have, and may not have, a future to experience. Any happiness or value or meaning we experience is *in the present*, which is why Marcel emphasizes so strongly the role of *presence* in hoping. The future is uncertain; experiencing the meaningfulness of life is now or never.

**58** Plato, *Timeaus* in *Collected Dialogues*, ed. Edith Hamilton and Huntington Cairns (Princeton, NJ: Princeton University Press, 1989), 1167 (37d).

**59** "An Grafen Paar" in *Goethes Sämtliche Werke*, vol. 3 (Cottasche Jubliäumsausgabe: Stuttgart, 1902), 13. Cited in Pierre Hadot, *Philosophy as a Way of Life*, 231. In a similar vein, C.S. Lewis writes that "the Present is the point at which time touches eternity" and "the Future is, of all things, the thing least like eternity" (C.S. Lewis, *The Screwtape Letters* [San Francisco: Harper San Francisco, 2001], 76 and 77).

**60** Henry David Thoreau, *Journal*, April 24, 1859, ed. Bradford Torrey (Boston, MA: Houghton Mifflin, 1906), 159. Elsewhere he reminds us: "In eternity there is indeed something true and sublime. But all these times and places and occasions are now and here. God himself culminates in the present moment, and will never be more divine in the lapse of all the ages" (Thoreau, *Walden*, 97).

**61** Kohák, *The Embers and the Stars*, 85.

**62** Caputo, *Hoping Against Hope*, 34–7. Conditional time is calculating, utilitarian, pragmatic; experiencing time conditionally, we do one thing in order to get, or avoid, something else. Unconditional time, in contrast, is intrinsically valuable, filled with things we do or experience or value for themselves, not for the relationship to some other end. Thus, for Caputo, unconditional time does not signal another world but, rather, embodies another way of living in this world; and it is not an intimation of immortality but, rather, a forcible reminder of mortality (Ibid., 33.). Nevertheless, deconstruction does appear to be in tension with both Caputo's account of hope and the account offered here. Deconstruction seems to stress a kind of dissatisfaction with the present—hankering for the justice-to-come, the democracy-to-come, and so on. Moreover, there is an emphasis on a certain type of futurity, even if that future—*l'avenir*, the undecidable, always-to-come but never-arrived, something-I-know-not-what—is structurally deferred and, never arriving, leaves us to live in the present.

**63** And, certainly, if we widen our gaze a bit to look beyond Western philosophy and theology, we find additional examples. Rika Dunlap makes a fascinating argument for a form of hope rooted in an alternative temporality in her "Hope Without the Future: Zen Buddhist Hope in Dōgen's *Shōbōgenzō*" in the *Journal of Japanese Philosophy*, vol. 4, 2016.

**64** Pierre Hadot, *Philosophy as a Way of Life*, 225; and *The Present Alone is Our Happiness*, 166, 173.

**65** Dennis O'Driscoll, "Admissions" from *Dear Life* (Port Townsend, WA: Copper Canyon Press, 2013). Emphasis in original.

**66** Thoreau, *Walden*, 91.

**67** Mary Oliver, "The Summer Day" in *House of Light* (Boston, MA: Beacon Press, 1990), 60, and Nikos Kazantzakis, *Report to Greco*, trans. P.A. Bein (New York: Touchstone, 1965), 18. Or, as Oliver suggests in her "When Death Comes," we want to *live* in the world, not simply visit it (Mary Oliver "When Death Comes" in *Devotions: The Selected Poems of Mary Oliver* [New York: Penguin, 2017], 285).

**68** Hadot, *The Present Alone is Our Happiness*, 173. See also Hadot, *Philosophy as a Way of Life*, 225. Thus, Gabriel Marcel says that it is an "atrophied sense of wonder" that puts a person on the road to despair (Marcel, "On the Ontological Mystery," 13).

**69** Hadot, *The Present Alone is Our Happiness*, 162.

**70** Ibid., 165. This is especially important, and difficult, when the moment in question seems wanting in some way.

**71** Caputo, *Hoping Against Hope*, 32.

**72** See Hadot, *Philosophy as a Way of Life*, 227, as well as his *The Present Alone is Our Happiness*. This echoing Ms. Ramsey's exclamation "It is enough!" (Virginia Woolf, *To the Lighthouse* [Dublin: Roads, 2013], 73).

# Chapter 5 Amor Mundi

**1** Plato, *Symposium* in *The Collected Dialogues of Plato*, trans. Michael Joyce (Princeton, NJ: Princeton University Press, 1989), 526–74.

**2** Aristotle, *Nicomachean Ethics*, trans. David Ross (Oxford: Oxford University Press, 1980), 192.

**3** The language here is striking, and suggests that even omniscience (understanding "all mysteries and all knowledge") and omnipotence (faith that can "move mountains") are without worth absent love. Of God's supposed attributes—omniscience, omnipotence, and omnibenevolence—it is the last that is of greatest significance. This, perhaps, is why various forms of "weak theology" are willing to equivocate on omnipotence in order to preserve omnibenevolence. See above, chapter two.

**4** George E. Vaillant, "Happiness is Love: Full Stop." Accessed March 13, 2019. http://www.yuruuniverse.com/wp-content/uploads/2014/12/

happiness-is-love.pdf. Also see George E. Vaillant, "Yes, I Stand by my Words: 'Happiness Equals Love—Full Stop'." Accessed March 13, 2019. https://positivepsychologynews.com/news/george-vaillant/200907163163. The reduction of love to "warm, personal attachments" would seem to reduce love to affection (*storge*), ignoring a more nuanced discussion of friendship (*philia*), romantic or erotic love (*eros*), and love-qua-charity (*agape*, *caritas*). While there may well be grounds on which to criticize any of the latter accounts, "warm, personal attachments" is a very loose catch-all for something as complex as love. The two essays cited are brief summaries of Vaillant's work on the Grant Study. Also see George E. Vaillant, *The Triumph of Experience* (Cambridge, MA: Harvard University Press, 2015).

**5** Virgil, *Bucolics*, Book X, at the *Internet Classics Archive*. Accessed November 17, 2019. http://classics.mit.edu/Virgil/eclogue.10.x.html. It is worth noting, however, that in the context of the poem it is apparent that Gallus, who utters these words, is portrayed as mad, dying with love for a woman who has left him for another. The line itself is in response to Apollo's question: "*Galle, quid insanis*?" Why this madness? It's far from clear that love "conquers all" in the *Bucolics* in the manner it might be said to "conquer all" in, for example, Dante. In retrieving and ruminating on ancient sources regarding love, we ought to be careful to distinguish original sources from Hallmark or Bartlett's Familiar appropriations thereof. Note as well that this poem is from Virgil's *Bucolics*, also known as the *Eclogues*, the natural setting of which foreshadows our concern with love of the nature below.

**6** Novalis, *Die Liebe ist der Endzweck der Weltgeschichte, das Amen des Universums*, Fragments I, Chapter 22. Project Guttenberg. Accessed 24 April, 2019. https://gutenberg.spiegel.de/buch/fragmente-i-6618/22.

**7** I confess I have never been persuaded by the implications of Wittgenstein's "whereof we cannot speak, thereof we must remain silent" (Ludwig Wittgenstein, *Tractatus Logico-Philosophicus*, trans. Bertrand Russell [London: Routledge, 2001]). The ineffable things are, in the end, the things most worth talking about, most worth trying to understand, articulate, and communicate. Love, death, hope, God, meaning—these topics are not, I think, ones to which our language will ever really be adequate. Nevertheless, we are compelled by our very nature to attempt, inevitably inadequately, to "eff the ineffable" (cf. Samuel Beckett, *Watt* [New York: Grove, 2009], 50). The things we cannot say are, in the end, the only things worth trying to say; and the inadequacy of our saying is why we must attempt again and again to resay, to say for the first time, that which we are forever incapable of saying adequately. We are all poets, trying to express the inexpressible. Here, philosophy's demand for clarity and completeness works against it, and poetry's tolerance for ambiguity and openness is an asset. As Michel Serres observes, "only philosophy can go deep enough to show that literature goes still deeper than philosophy" (Michel Serres, *The Troubadour of Knowledge*, trans. Sheila Faria Glaser and William Paulson [Ann Arbor, MI: University of Michigan Press, 1997], 65). And so we find ourselves, again, with Beckett: "I can't go on, I'll go on" (Samuel Beckett, *The Unnameable* [New York: Grove, 1958], 407, although similar expressions are found in *Waiting for Godot*, for example: Estragon: "I can't go on like this." Vladimir: "That's what you think."). "Going on," however, can be undertaken either as a sorrowful passage inflicted upon us (as in Cormac McCarthy's *The Road* or, in a different chord, Camus's *The Myth of Sisyphus*) or, as Thoreau experienced it, an adventure in life. See below, chapter six.

**8** While the main focus of this chapter will be love of the world, in particular love of wildness, that in no way diminishes the significance of various forms of loving other people, which are probably the most widely experienced expressions of love. Love of wildness is significant, first, because it draws our attention to an under-appreciated manifestation of love, and therefore adds something useful to the conversation, and second because love of wildness highlights a specific manifestation of love: appreciative-love.

**9** Thoreau had an early infatuation with Ellen Sewall, and he actually proposed marriage, although only after his brother, who also loved Ellen, was rejected. However, after that incident, Thoreau seems to have had remarkably little interest in romance, leading to no shortage of speculation about his sexuality among contemporary scholars. But while it may seem odd to many people, the root of this disposition appears to have been nothing stranger than genuine disinterest, a lack of that particular need. A number of his closest friends commented on his seeming freedom from particular passions or appetites. In this respect he seems to have been not too different from the fictional Larry Darrell of Somerset Maugham's *The Razor's Edge* who, on being questioned about chastity, comments: "I am in the fortunate position that sexual indulgence with me has been a pleasure rather than a need" (Somerset Maugham, *The Razor's Edge* [New York: Penguin, 1992], 280). A similar observation might be made about Augustine's close friend Alypius, who was able to give up sex easily while Augustine struggled mightily with his desire. Not surprisingly, it turns out that people with different constitutions and temperaments experience love in different ways.

**10** C.S. Lewis, *The Four Loves* (New York: Harvest, 1988).

**11** This is a historical observation, not an evaluative or normative one. While it is certainly true that there are other "voices" informing the intellectual and cultural traditions coming out of western Europe and, to an even greater degree, the United States—one thinks, for example, of the increasing influence of cultural and intellectual traditions rooted in China or South Asia—it is also the case that Greek philosophy, Christian religion, and the cultural and intellectual impacts of the Enlightenment loom particularly large.

**12** Lewis's Christian commitments are front-and-center in his treatment of love, and his account includes—sometimes centrally and sometimes peripherally—biases that will no doubt strike many contemporary readers as problematic, perhaps disqualifying. One thinks particularly of comments about homosexual love and about friendship between men and women. To these problems we should add, I will suggest later in this chapter, the charge that Lewis is insufficiently sensitive to the depth and significance of love of the natural world. Nevertheless, Lewis is well worth reading on love. First, he offers an eminently common-sensical account of many manifestations of love, one that will ring true in many respects even for those who differ from him radically in terms of their first principles or metaphysical commitments. Moreover, and importantly for reading him well, Lewis does moderate or qualify many of the positions contemporary readers might feel to be biased, even in the context of *The Four Loves*. For example, while it is no doubt problematic, or at least anachronistic, that Lewis thinks genuine friendship between men and women is so exceptional, he makes it clear that this is a culturally-constructed difficultly, and that there are many counterexamples ready to hand even in his own experience (e.g., authentic friendships between men and women in academia). The rarity of heterosexual friendship in his experience is not rooted in some ontological difference between men and women; it is a consequence of insufficient shared interests among them in his culture.

Likewise, his view of homosexuality as sinful does not exhibit either the obsessive fixation or the poisonous vitriol one sometimes sees among Christians. While Lewis does think homosexuality is sinful, he does not attach particular importance to it as a sin, wondering why people obsess over it to the exclusion of other sins (e.g., fornication, masturbation, and the like). Moreover, he insists that sins related to cruelty are worse than those associated with lust, and he is dismayed that his countrymen seem so fixated on the latter while quite often minimizing or even excusing former. In his autobiography, *Surprised by Joy*, he speaks of the common and fairly open homosexual relationships at his boarding school (C.S. Lewis, *Surprised by Joy* [New York: Harvest, 1955], 83–117, esp. 107–10). The account suggests that these relationships, though they were problematic to Lewis's mind, were also ones he viewed as an expression of *eros*. These relationships were "the only foothold . . . for certain good things" (e.g., *eros*) at his school, and perhaps the only respite from what were significantly worse sins to Lewis's mind: abuses of power by the strong over the weak, cruel social struggle, violent competitiveness, bald and selfish ambition (Ibid., 109). Thus, even if one does not share Lewis's views on homosexuality—and I do not—one can, I think, read his account of erotic love with those views bracketed. Just as Aristotle's distorted treatment of women in his work does not, for most people, invalidate the wisdom and insight of the *Nicomachean Ethics*, so too Lewis's own biases ought not preclude us from admiring the wisdom that is in his work. And there is much wisdom there, expressed with a healthy dose of intellectual humility, ordinariness, and authorial *bonhomie*.

**13** Lewis, *The Four Loves*, 1.

**14** Ibid., 4. On a Christian account, a person needs—is dependent on, not merely psychologically but ontologically—God. Similarly, I'll suggest below that we should acknowledge that people need, are dependent on, the presence and the good graces of the more-than-human world—and not just materially, but spiritually as well.

**15** Augustine, *Confessions*, trans. John K. Ryan (New York: Image Books, 1960), 98. The quasi-Stoic implication is that we should only love perishable things as perishable. "When giving your wife or child a kiss, repeat to yourself, 'I am kissing a mortal.' Then you won't be so distraught if they are taken from you" (Epictetus, *Enchiridion*, trans. Robert Dobbin [New York: Penguin, 2008], 222). But one cannot help wondering if apathetic love is really love at all. "Apathy" from *apathie*, *apathia*, *apatheia*: "without suffering," but also "without feeling" or "without undergoing." My suspicion is rather that, however wisely we love, however often we remind ourselves that love of mortal things is subject to decay, to love more is to suffer more.

**16** W.H. Auden, "Twelve Songs IX" in *W.H. Auden: Collected Poems* (New York: Vintage, 1991), 141. In chapter two, we noted that true despair entails a "loss or orientation" in the world. So it is noteworthy that, in the same poem, Auden compares his lost love to the cardinal points: north, south, east, and west.

**17** Lewis, *The Four Loves*, 11.

**18** Ibid., 13. Emphases mine.

**19** Pearl Buck, *The Goddess Abides* (New York: John Day Company, 1972), 77.

**20** "If the doors of perception were cleansed every thing would appear to man as it is: Infinite." William Blake, *The Marriage of Heaven and Hell*, (Compass Circle, 2019).

**21** Lewis, *The Four Loves*, 14.

**22** Ibid., 16.

**23** As Horace notes, such joys are eternal; our appreciation of them can never be unmade. See John Dryden's free translation of Horace's "Happy the Man": "not Heaven itself upon the past has power; / But what has been, has been, and I have had my hour" (John Dryden, *The Poetical Works of John Dryden* [Boston, MA: Little, Brown, and Company, 1854], 176).

**24** The use of "sub-human" here reveals some of the prejudices that color Lewis's ability to fully appreciate what nature might teach us. Compare this to the contemporary idiom, after David Abram (*The Spell of the Sensuous*, [New York: Vintage, 2012]) of "more-than-human" nature.

**25** Lewis, *The Four Loves*, 20.

**26** This perhaps a consequence of Lewis's famously combative nature as an intellectual, a disposition that seems primed to "interrogate" rather than simply "experience." See chapter four, note 53.

**27** Lewis, *The Four Loves*, 19.

**28** Ibid. As Lewis says, in nature we find "worms in the belly as well as primroses in the wood." If we try to reconcile them or to suggest that one is more essentially natural, we move beyond love of nature into the realm of metaphysics or theodicy (ibid., 21)—that is, beyond love of nature and into philosophy, which is where we ought to be taught of such things. "The only imperative that nature utters is, 'Look. Listen. Attend'" (ibid., 19). Of course, that's not nothing. Would that I could get my own students to do as much and to do it well! Looking, listening, and attending can teach us a great deal, as Thoreau, Dillard, Leopold, Shepherd, Macfarlane, and others make abundantly clear.

**29** Daivd Hume, *A Treatise of Human Nature* (Oxford: Clarendon Press, 1978), 469 (Book III, Part I, Section I).

**30** A point lost on a large number of climate change skeptics. When dealing with tax policy, I might suggest one number and you might suggest another, and we might compromise in the middle and get some, but not all, of what each of us hopes to accomplish. Not so with hard reality. If, for example, good science suggests that 350 parts per million carbon dioxide equivalent is the upper limit of what the atmosphere can absorb without triggering potentially dangerous feedback loops, and human activity is currently pushing that level to 415ppm en route to something closer to 500ppm, we cannot turn to nature and say, well, how about splitting the difference? What do you think about 425ppm? Will that work for you? Physics and chemistry do not negotiate.

**31** Although even in a country garden the attentive gardener will no doubt find that nature often stubbornly resists domestication. For an excellent account of this experience, read Michael Pollan's *Second Nature: A Gardener's Education* (New York: Grove Press, 1991). Chapter two, "Nature Abhors a Garden," offers some fine observations regarding nature's "intransigence." The garden does connect us to nature, but on a more compact, easier, "humbler" scale (as Thoreau says of Walden Pond).

**32** Serres, *The Natural Contract*, trans. Elizabeth MacArthur and William Paulson (Ann Arbor, MI: Michigan University Press, 1995), 42 and Serres, *The Troubadour of Knowledge*, 115–25.

**33** For one attempt at applying these traditional categories to nature, see Bryan Bannon, "Being a Friend to Nature: Environmental Virtues and Ethical Ideals" in *Ethics, Policy, and Environment*, 20:1, 44–58. It is not surprising, then, that personalist philosophers like Erazim Kohák and Henry Bugbee figure prominently among the rare birds who do speak extensively about love and nature: "Shall we conceive of the world around us and of ourselves in it as *personal*, a meaningful whole . . . or shall we conceive and treat it, together with ourselves, as *impersonal* . . . That answered, all else follows" (Erazim Kohák, *The Embers and the Stars* [Chicago, IL: University of Chicago Press, 1987], 124–5).

**34** As an environmental philosopher, I am well aware of the debates around whether or not we can, or ought to, maintain a distinction between nature and culture. However, nature and culture remain useful didactic categories whether or not one thinks they are legitimate metaphysical or ontological ones; and the options above do not commit us to any particular position in terms of human naturalness or a nature-culture dualism or anything of the sort.

**35** Jack Turner, *The Abstract Wild* (Tuscon, AZ: University of Arizona Press, 1996) 19–37 and Henry Bugbee, *The Inward Morning* (Athens and London: University of Georgia Press, 1999), 51–4.

**36** See, among the many other expressions, Erazim Kohák, *The Embers and the Stars*, 3–13.

**37** Robert Macfarlane, *The Wild Places* (London: Penguin, 2007), 236.

**38** Ibid., 202.

**39** Henry David Thoreau, *Walden* (Princeton, NJ: Princeton University Press, 1971), 28. And, again, "Here is this vast, savage, howling mother of ours, Nature, lying all around, with such beauty, and such affection for her children, as the leopard; and yet we are so early weaned from her breast to society, to that culture which is exclusively an interaction of man on man" (Henry David Thoreau, *Walking* in *The Portable Thoreau* [New York: Penguin, 1975], 621).

**40** Also see Michel Serres, *Biogea*, trans. Randolph Burks (Minneapolis, MI: Univocal, 2012).

**41** Richard Louv, *Last Child in the Woods* (Chapel Hill, NC: Algonquin Books, 2006).

**42** Thoreau, *Walking*, 610. Nicolas Bouvier makes an important observation with respect to travel: "When I went home, there were many people who had never left who told me that with a bit of imagination and concentration they travelled just as well, without lifting their backsides off their chairs. I quite believed them. They were strong people: I'm not. I need that physical displacement, which for me is pure bliss" (Nicolas Bouvier, *The Way of the World*, trans. Robyn Marsack [New York: New York Review Books, 1992], 47). We might make a similar observation with respect to what type of, and how much interaction with, "wildness" is necessary to counteract the effects of alienation from nature. On the one hand, it is no doubt true that we can train our powers of observation and appreciation so that we can find wildness even in the midst of urban blight—the plants pushing through cracks in the sidewalks, and the animals (racoons, coyotes, and more) who adapt to urban environments. Perhaps certain "strong natures" are better at this. However, on the other hand, it is all-too-easy to underestimate the seriousness of our alienation and illness. It may be that many of the folks who find wilderness in the garden are able to do so precisely because they have not encountered bigger, wilder places. Some people, as Bouvier suggests, will need "stronger medicine," and this could be the case either because they are more gravely ill (i.e., alienated), or because weaker medicine no longer has the desired effect (i.e., they are experienced), or simply because of their nature.

**43** Robert Macfarlane, *Landmarks* (New York: Penguin, 2016), 220. For a philosophical account of the significance of material places, see my "Earthy Hermeneutics: Beyond the Metaphor of the Text" in *Continental Philosophy and the Environment*, ed. Jonathan Maskit (Lanham, MA: Rowman and Littlefield International, forthcoming).

**44** "I believe there is a subtle magnetism in Nature, which, if we unconsciously yield to it, will direct us aright. It is not indifferent to us which way we walk" (Thoreau, *Walking*, 602). And nature does more than influence our preferences for space. Thoreau, one of nature's great students, wrote the following about leaves in his posthumous *Autumnal Tints*:

> How beautifully they go to their graves! how gently lay themselves down and turn to mould! . . . They that soared so loftily, how contentedly they return to dust again, and are laid low, resigned to lie and decay at the foot of the tree, and afford nourishment to new generations of their kind, as well as to flutter on high! *They teach us how to die*. One wonders if the time will ever come when men, with their boasted faith in immortality, will lie down as gracefully and as ripe,—with such an Indian-summer serenity will shed their bodies, as they do their hair and nails (Henry David Thoreau, *Autumnal Tints* [Bedford, MA: Applewood Books, 1996], 35, emphasis mine).

Dylan Thomas's "rage, rage against the dying of the light"—whether read as hatred of death or a love of life—could learn something from Thoreau's leaves. Here nature's teaching can help us to approach the harshest of her conditions, death, with some measure of equanimity.

**45** Serres, *Biogea*, 48. Here one cannot help but hear echoes of Lynn White Jr. and his oft-referenced—with either admiration or frustration—"The Historical Roots of Our Ecological Crisis," in *Science*, vol.155, no.3767 (March 10, 1967), 1203-7. On the sacred and profane experience of nature see Mircea Eliade, *The Sacred and the Profane*, trans. Willard R. Trask (New York: Harcourt Brace and Company, 1959).

**46** Serres himself has a significantly different view of monotheism in other works. See, for example, *The Troubadour of Knowledge*, where he writes approvingly of God's "holding back" from overwhelming Creation: "I discover that God is good and maybe even infinitely weak. He holds back with modesty and shame . . . I laugh at the old gigantomachy of small local gods, forever on the brink of war, like us. Already, I find myself less pagan" (Serres, *Troubadour*, 117). On the weakness of God, see chapter two. Thomas Merton—poet, mystic, and Trappist monk—insists that "It is not Christianity . . . but post-Cartesian technologism that separates man from the world" (Thomas Merton, *When the Trees Say Nothing* [Notre Dame, IN: Sorin Books, 2003], 47). Clearly the relationship between "pagan" sensibilities and "monotheistic" sensibilities is more complicated than simple dichotomies of good/bad, world-loving/world-hating, sacred nature/profane nature would have us believe. Catholic dogma, for instance, is so far from its anti-somatic caricature that it actually insists on the resurrection of person's particular, material body. Celtic Christianity, Provençal Christianity, Chinese Christianity, and many other expressions all retain something of a fidelity to the supposedly "pagan" spirituality of nature, place, and materiality. Tellingly, while there are certainly exceptions (e.g., Eriugena, Bruno, Teilhard de Chardin, and others—all accused of pantheism in some form), among Christians it was often the "elite"—philosophers and theologians, working in cities and well-removed from the land—who lost contact with the local and 'pagan' spirituality that valued the sacredness of the world. It was the ordinary believers who acknowledged and valued the sacredness of place as part of their everyday expression of faith (see, for example, Mircea Eliade, *The Sacred and the Profane*, 107, 152). On this point, my thanks to Dan Bradley, who held me to account for the ambiguity and complexity of this point after reading an early version of the manuscript.

**47** Macfarlane, *Landmarks*, 220.

**48** In addition to helping us hear nature and pay attention to the more-than-human world, silence can help us to interact more harmoniously with it. In chapter three we noted how vitality—the active body engaged in the world—can help us to see the world differently. And in many cases, achieving vitality or flow is assisted by breaking away from conscious, willful, linguistic engagement with things, by ceasing our chatter, whether external or internal. "Have you noticed how badly people dance when they are talking?" (Michel Serres, *The Five Senses: A Philosophy of Mingled Bodies*, trans. Margaret Sankey and Peter Cowley [London: Continuum, 2008], 113).

**49** Critiquing the frustration that God—or, here, Nature—does not speak to us in the natural languages in which we speak to each other (e.g., French, English, Chinese), Denise Levertov reminds us that we are spoken to "in myriad musics, in signs and portents"; it is our failure to attune our hearing that makes the world seem silent (Denise Levertov, "Immersion" in *This Great Unknowing: Last Poems* [New York: New Directions, 1999], 53).

**50** Gretel Erlich, *The Solace of Open Spaces* (New York: Penguin, 1985), 127. Erlich makes this observation with respect to the autumn, which speaks in a "double voice: one says everything is ripe; the other says everything is dying" (ibid.).

**51** Gary Snyder, *The Practice of the Wild* (Berkeley, CA: Counterpoint, 1990), 31. Thus, as Thoreau wrote, "there can be no very black melancholy to him who lives in the midst of nature and has his senses still" (Thoreau, *Walden*, 131).

**52** Lewis, *The Four Loves*, 22. But one cannot help but observe that this no different than going to Church, or to another meeting of the Communist Party, or to recreate with friends. Can we plan or schedule a mystical experience in Church with any more accuracy and control than a mystical experience in nature? Beauty, glory, and meaning are there; but they are not on offer like coffee at a café, which we can order and purchase at will. We can—should, must—keep ourselves open to the glory; but when and how it comes is always, as Dillard notes, something of a surprise.

**53** Annie Dillard, *Pilgrim at Tinker Creek* (New York: HarperPerennial, 2007), 10. Or, as Thoreau reflects in one of his journal entries, "Wood, earth, mould, etc. exist for joy . . ." (Henry David Thoreau, *The Journals of Henry David Thoreau*, vol.9, eds. Bradford Torrey and Francis Allen [Boston: Houghton Mifflin, 1906], 207).

**54** Philip Zaleski and Carol Zaleski, *The Fellowship: The Literary Lives of the Inklings* (New York: Farrar, Strauss and Giroux, 2015), 250.

**55** Nan Shepherd, *The Living Mountain* (Edinburgh: Cannongate, 2011), 23. Robert Macfarlane's admiration of Shepherd's work brought this truly remarkable and under-appreciated book to the attention of myself and many other people.

**56** Erlich, *The Solace of Open Spaces*, 84. This is not, I think, some poetic expression of the naturalistic fallacy, a claim that we ought to simply "act naturally," even if we are inclined to selfishness, rapaciousness, or and other vicious traits. It is, rather, an invitation to accept ourselves and live as good creatures in a shared world with other creatures. Different from them in certain respects to be sure, but kin with them in many others, not separated from the world or our fellow creatures by some metaphysical watermark.

**57** Lewis, *The Four Loves,* 120.

**58** Julian Barnes, *The Only Story* (New York: Knopf, 2018), 3. Perhaps then the time-boundedness of our love—that fact that we are mortal, and that the objects of our loves are mortal—should induce a very different response. Not Stoic *apatheia* that purchases less suffering at the price of tepid love, but rather immoderate, passionate, wild loving, precisely because we are mortal and our time is limited.

**59** Nikos Kazantzakis, *Report to Greco*, trans. P.A. Bien (New York: Simon and Schuster, 1965), 423. In this passage, Kazantzakis names the Buddha as the "great prestidigitator" in what seems to be an oversimplification of and reaction to Buddhism's stated goal of eliminating desire to escape suffering. This must be read in the context of Kazantzakis's own understanding of Buddhism (likely influenced by Schopenhauer) and his spiritual journey from Orthodox Christianity to his final, quasi-Zorbian testament in *Report to Greco*, with stops along the way in Nietzschean atheism, (his version of) Buddhism, Communism, and more. In any case, the charge of "blowing out the candle of the world" is not particular to Kazantzakis's understanding of Buddhism; it would certainly apply to Stoicism and Epicureanism, various manifestations of Christian Neoplatonism, and Schopenhauer's pessimism as well. Kazantzakis does not want to escape the world. Somerset Maugham's Larry Darrell, himself a student of Advaita Vedanta, expresses a similar sentiment on receiving enlightenment: "If in those moments of ecstasy I had indeed been one with the Absolute, then, if what they said was true, nothing could touch me and when I had worked out the karma of my present life I should return no more. The thought filled me with dismay. I wanted to live again and again. I was willing to accept every sort of life, no matter what its pain and sorrow; I felt that only life after life, life after life could satisfy my eagerness, my vigour, and my curiosity" (Maugham, *The Razor's Edge*, 278–9).

**60** Marilynne Robinson, *Gilead* (New York: Farrar, Straus and Giroux, 2004), 245.

**61** Nan Shepherd, *The Living Mountain*, 102. Emphasis mine. Annie Dillard makes a similar point. "We are here to witness," she writes, "that is why I take walks: to keep an eye on things," that is, to keep an eye out for the extraordinariness in the ordinary (Annie Dillard, *Teaching a Stone to Talk* [New York: HarperCollins, 1982], 90 and 91).

# Chapter 6 Melancholic Joy

**1** The question is, as Paul Roberts, the protagonist of Julian Barnes's *The Only Story* puts it: "Which [is] the correct—or the more correct—formulation: 'Life is beautiful but sad' or 'Life is sad but beautiful'? One or the other was obviously true; but he could never decide which" (Julian Barnes, *The Only Story* [New York: Knopf, 2018], 245–6).

**2** See Philip Larkin's "Aubade" in *Collected Poems* (New York: Farrar, Straus and Giroux, 1984), 190.

**3** "Every now and then a man's mind is stretched by a new idea or sensation, and never shrinks back to its former dimensions." Although this observation is often attributed to Oliver Wendell Holmes, Jr., they are in fact the words of his erudite but less-well-remembered father (Oliver Wendell Holmes, Sr. "The Autocrat of the Breakfast Table" in *The Atlantic Monthly*, vol. II [September 1858], 502).

**4** Paul Ricoeur, *The Symbolism of Evil*, trans. Emerson Buchanan (Boston, MA: Beacon Press, 1967), 347–57.

**5** Thus, Terence tells us, "while there is life, there is hope," with the unspoken implication (not to affirm the consequent) that "where there is no hope, there is no life" (Terence, *Heauton Timorumenos*, trans. E.S. Schuckburgh [Cambridge, 1869], 120).

**6** Cormac McCarthy, *The Road* (New York: Vintage, 2006), 110.

**7** Ellen Bass, "The Thing Is" in *Mules of Love* (Rochester, NY: BOA Editions, 2002). Bass's poem captures well the complexity of melancholic joy, as well as the movement from first naiveté, through doubt, to second naiveté. After facing up to evil—entropy, death, loss, suffering, injustice—any joy we win back will inevitably be tinged by melancholy.

**8** See C.S. Lewis, *The Screwtape Letters* (New York: HarperCollins, 2001), 167–9.

**9** Ibid., 168.

**10** Ibid.

**11** Ibid., 169.

**12** Antoine de Saint-Exupéry, *Wind, Sand and Stars*, trans. Lewis Galantière (New York: Harcourt Brace and Co., 1992), 218. Thus, Proust says that his insights—perhaps epiphanies would be a more apt term—were not the result of a "new train of reasoning," nor the result of a compelling or "decisive argument" (Marcel Proust, *In Search of Lost Time*, vol. VI, *Time Regained*, trans. C.K. Scott Moncrieff and Terence Kilmartin [New York: The Modern Library, 2003], 255). Rather—evoking our discussion of vitality—the physical experience of stumbling on cobblestone delivered a truth in the face of which all his previous difficulties (in finding that truth) dropped away.

**13** Annie Dillard, *Pilgrim at Tinker Creek* (New York: HarperPerennial, 2007), 271. We must realize that there is a danger in forgetting either the beauty for the horror or the horror for the beauty.

**14** Proust, *Time Regained*, 260.

**15** Nikos Kazantzakis, here quoting one of his "favorite Byzantine mystics" (Nikos Kazantzakis, *Report to Greco* [New York: Touchstone, 1975], 45). Or, as Proust puts it: "The only true voyage, the only bath in the Fountain of Youth, would be not to visit strange lands but to possess other eyes, to see the universe through the eyes of another, of a hundred others, to see the hundred universes that each of them sees, that each of them is; and this we can do with an Elstir, with a Vinteuil; with men like these we do really fly from star to star" (Marcel Proust, *In Search of Lost Time*, vol. V,

*The Captive and The Fugitive*, trans. C.K. Scott Moncrieff and Terence Kilmartin [New York: The Modern Library, 2003], 343). Here Proust suggests that art, music, poetry, literature—that is imagination—can give us "new eyes" with which to see the same reality, and that such new eyes give us a new lease on life.

**16** J.A. Baker, *The Peregrine* (New York: New York Review of Books, 2005), 19.

**17** Wallace Stegner, "Haunted by Waters: Norman Maclean" in *Where the Bluebird Sings to the Lemonade Springs* (New York: The Modern Library, 2002), 192. Stegner continues, observing, "perhaps the time of youth always has dew on it."

**18** Nan Shepherd, *The Living Mountain* (Edinburgh: Cannongate, 2011), 106. "These moments come unpredictably, yet governed, it would seem, by a law whose working is dimly understood . . .the flesh transparent . . . Flesh is not annihilated but fulfilled. One is not bodiless, but essential body . . .I discover most nearly what it is *to be*. I have walked out of the body and into the mountain" (ibid.). Shepherd's assertion that in these moments "one can read at last the word that has been from the beginning" is wonderfully evocative of the conclusion of Norman Maclean's *A River Runs Through It*: "Eventually, all things merge into one, and a river runs through it. The river was cut by the world's great flood and runs over rocks from the basement of time. On some of the rocks are timeless raindrops. Under the rocks are the words, and some of the words are theirs. I am haunted by waters" (Norman Maclean, *A River Runs Through It* [Chicago: The University of Chicago Press, 2001], 104).

**19** Henry David Thoreau, *Autumnal Tints* (Bedford, MA: Applewood Books, 1996), 58. In this vein, Thoreau also wrote, in his journal, that "the perception of beauty is a moral test" (Henry David Thoreau, *The Journal of Henry David Thoreau*, vol.5 [Princeton, NJ: Princeton University Press, 1997], 120). On the tropes of "morning" and "awakening," see Henry David Thoreau, *Walden* (Princeton, NJ: Princeton University Press, 1971). Like Thoreau, Nikos Kazantzakis comments on the perpetual freshness of the world for those who are sensitive enough to perceive it: "Each morning the world rediscovers its virginity; it seems to have issued fresh from God's hands at that very instant . . . It neither recalls what it did the day before nor frets about what it will do the day after. It experiences the present moment as an eternity" (Kazantzakis, *Report to Greco*, 478).

**20** Flannery O'Connor, *The Habit of Being: Letters of Flannery O'Connor* (New York: Farrar, Straus and Giroux, 1988), 57. The letter is to Elizabeth and Robert Lowell, dated 17 March 1953. O'Connor's own experience of Catholicism could give this account the flavor of a decidedly stronger theology (and theodicy) than I endorsed in chapter two; however, I choose to hear in her words a reminder, not that the suffering itself is a blessing, but rather something in the spirit of Louis Aragon's "*Je dirai malgré tout que cette vie fut belle*." Despite everything, life, the world, and reality are beautiful and even worth it.

**21** Consider *Sentenced to Life*, a collection of poems written by Clive James after being diagnosed with terminal leukemia. Gratitude for the gift of life and the opportunity to experience the wonder of it all fairly drips from the pages of the volume. See, in particular, "Japanese Maple," in which James testifies to an expanded perception and appreciation of beauty as he experiences his decline (Clive James, "Japanese Maple" in *The New Yorker*, September 8, 2014 and reprinted in *Sentenced to Life* [New York: Liveright, 2016], 53). Humorously, but happily, thanks to an unexpectedly successful experimental treatment, James lived to express "embarrassment" at still being alive after announcing, in 2015, that he was "near to death, but thankful for life." He died in 2019.

**22** Laura Dassow Walls, *Henry David Thoreau: A Life* (Chicago: University of Chicago Press, 2018), 495. Regarding Thoreau dying well, he maintained, during his illness, "I am enjoying existence as much as ever, and regret nothing" (ibid., 497). Sam Staples, the very person who famously imprisoned Henry over his failure to pay taxes—an episode immortalized in *Civil Disobedience*—visited Thoreau on his death bed and reported: "Never saw a man dying with so much pleasure & peace" (ibid.).

**23** Hannah Arendt, *Love and Saint Augustine* (Chicago: University of Chicago Press, 1996), 52. Harkening back to chapter five, Arendt had intended to call the work that became *The Human Condition*, "Amor Mundi," which expressed her conviction that we should love the world even with presence of the evil and suffering in it. Arendt is one of the great thinkers of love in the 20th century, though in a somewhat different key than that sounded in the present work.

**24** Proust, *Time Regained*, 264–5.

**25** Michel Serres, *The Five Senses: A Philosophy of Mingled Bodies*, trans. Margaret Sankey and Peter Cowley (London: Continuum, 2008), 166. Consider accounts of time being distended and stretched out for those close to death—the man smoking his last cigarette before the firing squad, not out of cowardice but because there is an entire lifetime in such a cigarette, or Kazantzakis's Christ, who experiences an entire alternative life in the pause between two words while suffering on the cross (Nikos Kazantzakis, *The Last Temptation of Christ*, trans. Peter Bien [New York: Simon and Schuster, 1998]). For a classic account of such time-distention, see Ambrose Bierce, "An Occurrence at Owl Creek Bridge" in *The Collected Works of Ambrose Bierce*, vol.2 (New York: Gordian Press, 1966).

**26** Nikos Kazantzakis, *Zorba the Greek*, trans. Peter Bien (New York: Simon and Schuster, 2014), 342. For myself, I find Zorba's enthusiasm both indiscriminate and self-centered—a bit too hedonistic, a bit too Nietzschean. Kazantzakis's own story, as reported in his autobiography, *Report to Greco,* strikes me as more both more palatable and admirable.

**27** Coming from a good Irish-American family, I'm well aware that, strictly speaking, alcoholism is a disease, not a choice. Nevertheless, the bottle has traditionally been one of the ways in which people cope or self-medicate in the wake of speculative melancholy.

**28** Somerset Maugham, *The Razor's Edge* (New York: Penguin, 1992), 72. Isabel's exasperation is rooted in her own desire for a very different idle life, one rooted in material rather than spiritual wealth. But her argument with Larry also reveals her frustration with mystery: "But Larry," she smiled, "People have been asking those questions for thousands of years. If they could be answered, surely they'd have been answered by now." Larry, at this point years into his studies, responds, "on the other hand you might say that if men have been asking them for thousands of years it proves that they can't help asking them and have to go on asking them. Besides, it's not true that no one has found answers. There are lots more answers than questions, and lots of people have found answers that were perfectly satisfactory for them" (ibid.).

**29** On the ambiguity of melancholy, see Richard Kearney, *Strangers, Gods, and Monsters* (London: Routledge, 2003), 163–77.

**30** This expression is from Julian of Norwich, *Revelations of Divine Love*, trans. Elizabeth Spearing (New York: Penguin, 1999), 22. However, variations on the expression pop up in other places. It featured in T.S. Eliot's celebrated *Four Quartets* (London: Harcourt and Brace, 1943) and, as mentioned in chapter two, figured in Annie Dillard's *Holy the Firm* (New York: HarperPerennial, 1998). Camus cites a similar phrase—though with a decidedly different implication—from Dostoevsky's *The Possessed*: the last words of Kirilov before his suicide, "all is well" (see Albert Camus, *The Myth of Sisyphus*, trans. Justin O'Brien [New York: Vintage Books, 2018], 109). Nietzsche sees the spirit of this claim hidden in many places: the belief in progress or perfectibility, forms of meliorism, and other ways in which we "trust in the course of things" (Fredrich Nietzsche, *The Will to Power*, trans. Walter Kaufmann and R.J. Hollingdale [New York: Vintage, 1968], 140).

**31** This is because in our lived experience it is difficult to fully separate appreciative love from desire, gift, need, and so forth; so practically speaking it is impossible to love without being hurt to some degree, even if only by the melancholic or bittersweet realization that what one appreciates will come to an end, and all-too-soon. When a person dies, those who loved her most are *both* most deeply wounded (by the loss of a loved one) *and* most profoundly consoled (by the appreciation they have for having experienced the relationship).

**32** Epictetus, a Stoic, enjoins us to whisper "tomorrow you'll die" as we kiss our children (See Epictetus, *Discourses* [Oxford: Oxford University Press, 2014], 207). Although, presumably, the whisper is meant to remind the parent that he or she is kissing a mortal (as in the *Enchiridion*, chapter 3), it is hard to get past the effect such a gesture—*tomorrow*?—would have on the affection of the parent, to say nothing of the child.

**33** Albert Camus, *The Myth of Sisyphus*, trans. Justin O'Brien (New York: Vintage Books, 2018), 123.

**34** Ibid., 27.

**35** Ibid., 17.

**36** Ibid., 35. He criticizes phenomenology, specifically Husserl, for suggesting we can look at ordinary objects and find them enriched and enriching, for suggesting that thinking is, or includes, "learning all over again to see," so that ordinary things are experienced in a "privileged moment," all of which sound quite like seeing through "new eyes" (see Camus, *The Myth of Sisyphus*, 26). Here Camus seems to echo Cioran, though the former is much less a miserabilist. Compare this to Nieman, who writes, "What binds the real [what is] and the rational [what ought to be] together must be so fragile that it will seem miraculous—and on occasion the miracle occurs. As with any other miracle, it takes something like faith to perceive it" (Susan Neiman, *Evil in Modern Thought: An Alternative History of Philosophy* [Princeton, NJ: Princeton University Press, 2015], 327.

**37** Ibid., 27. Emphasis mine.

**38** See Martha Nussbaum "Form and Content" in *Love's Knowledge* (Oxford: Oxford University Press, 1990), 19.

**39** Camus, *The Myth of Sisyphus*, 121.

**40** Ibid., 64.

**41** Samuel Beckett, *The Unnameable* (New York: Grove, 1958), 407, William James, *The Will to Believe* (New York: Dover Publications, 1956), and Simon Critchley, *Very Little . . . Almost Nothing* (London: Routledge, 1997). Critchley argues—drawing on Wallace Stevens, Stanley Cavell, and others—for an "atheist transcendence" through the "achievement of the ordinary or the everyday without the rose-tinted spectacles of any narrative of redemption" (ibid., 27). There is certainly a kinship between the "achievement of the everyday" in which the "queer poverty" and "eerie plainness" of things is seen anew and what I have described as the "new eyes" of melancholic joy, which see the world otherwise. However, Critchley strays close to the Sisyphean conclusion that the best we can do is simply "carry on" (ibid., 83); although, it does seem to me that there is room for a version of Critchley's "atheist transcendence" in melancholic joy.

**42** Cormac McCarthy, *The Road* (New York: Vintage, 2006). Although I have mentioned McCarthy in passing above, I was reminded that the theme of "going on" is so central to *The Road* by Prof. Amanda Parris, whose paper at the 2018 meeting of the Pacific Association for the Continental Tradition took up McCarthy's apocalyptic vision. An expanded version of that paper is forthcoming in the edited collection, *Philosophy in the American West* (London: Routledge, 2020). In it, Parris references a number of the occasions in which McCarthy makes clear that the man and boy's lives have been stripped of meaning or sense (and the implication, perhaps, that it was never there to begin with). This theme appears in other works by McCarthy as well. "They rode on" is an oft-repeated phrase in *Blood Meridian* (New York: Vintage, 1985).

**43** Ibid., 152.

**44** A claim made by Oedipus at the outset of *Oedipus at Colonus*, not, as is sometimes said, *Oedipus Rex*. The French is: "*Qui accueillera aujourd'hui, avec de maigres dons, Oedipe errant, demandant peu et recevant moins encore ? Ce qui me suffit cependant, car mes misères, le long temps et ma grandeur d'âme me font trouver que tout est bien*" (*Œdipe à colone*, trans. Charles Marie René Leconte de Lisle [Paris : A. Lamerre, 1877]). Depending on the translation from the Greek, one might hear resonances with Julian of Norwich and T.S. Eliot, who I've mentioned above. However, the claim "*tout est bien*" would be surprising in the mouth of Camus's Sisyphus because, for Camus, all is *not* well. Things are absurd, a product of the non-correspondence between our knowledge and the world. We *want* to know and to understand everything, but this is not possible. See Camus, *The Myth of Sisyphus*, 122–3. Note, however, that other English translations render the Greek as "I am content," which seems perhaps closer to Camus's Sisyphus than "*tout est bien*."

**45** McCarthy, *The Road*, 230 and 46.

**46** Camus, *The Myth of Sisyphus*, 61.

**47** Ibid., 63.

**48** Camus would no doubt be quick to mock, or at least retort, that "the absurd man does nothing for the eternal" (Camus, *The Myth of Sisyphus*, 66) because, for Camus, the eternal is an otherworldly myth. But we know by this point in our analysis that Thoreau was right to remind us that "heaven is under our feet as well as above our heads" (Thoreau, *Walden*, 283). Camus's objection is still rooted in the strong theology he denies. The eternity of melancholic joy is not an escape from this world to another, but rather living fully within this life and this world.

**49** Friedrich Nietzsche, *Werke: Kritische Gesamtausgabe* (Berlin: De Gruyter, 1996), volume 8, book 2, 121. Cited in Joshua Foa Dienstag, *Pessimism:*

*Philosophy, Ethic, Sprit* (Princeton, NJ: Princeton University Press, 2006), 188. Dienstag offers an exciting and compelling reading of Nietzsche, despite the differences that I take to remain between "Dionysian pessimism" and "melancholic joy." Perhaps the most tempting reading of Nietzsche vis-à-vis melancholic joy is found in chapter five of Dienstag's work—see especially pages 186–7.

**50** Nietzsche's attack on religion is not the problem; indeed, it is—and many religious philosophers agree—salutary in many respects. For some representative work see: John D. Caputo, *The Insistence of God* (Bloomington, IN: Indiana University Press, 2013), Richard Kearney, *Anatheism* (New York: Columbia University Press, 2010); Merold Westphal, *Overcoming Onto-theology* (New York: Fordham University Press, 2001); Jean-Luc Marion, *God Without Being*, trans. Thomas A. Carlson (Chicago: The University of Chicago Press, 1991). These philosophers, and others, seek to philosophize about God having accepted in one way or another Nietzsche's "death of God." I've already noted that Nietzsche is a famously "flexible" philosopher, and open to quite diverse interpretations. Readers interested in a more detailed account of the "death of God" as the death of an onto-theological idol should pursue some of the works referenced above.

**51** Lou Salomé, *Nietzsche*, trans. Siegfried Mandel (Champaign, IL: University of Illinois Press, 2001), 24.

**52** Ibid.

**53** Siegfried Mandel, "Introduction" to Lou Salomé, *Nietzsche*, trans. Siegfried Mandel (Champaign, IL: University of Illinois Press, 2001), lxii. Of course, everything hinges on just what one means by "mysticism," because we have already seen that there are different ways in which we can experience the transcendent. For his part, the famous translator and interpreter Walter Kaufmann describes the *Übermensch* as privy to a kind of rupture of the eternal within the flow of time in his *Nietzsche: Philosopher, Psychologist, Antichrist* (Princeton, NJ: Princeton University Press, 2013), which sounds quite similar to the "eternity" of joy I've described.

**54** See John D. Caputo, *On Religion* (London: Routledge, 2001) and *The Prayers and Tears of Jacques Derrida: Religion without Religion* (Bloomington, IN: Indiana University Press, 1997).

**55** Graham Parkes's "Introduction" to Fredrich Nietzsche, *Thus Spoke Zarathustra*, trans. Graham Parkes (Oxford: Oxford World's Classics, 2005), xx. Here citing his own "Nature and the Human 'Redivinized': Mahāyāna Buddhist Themes in Thus Spoke Zarathustra" in *Nietzsche and the Divine*, eds. John Lippitt and James Urpeth (Manchester, UK: Clinamen Press, 2000), 181–99.

**56** Bruce Benson, *Pious Nietzsche: Decadence and Dionysian Faith* (Bloomington, IN: Indiana University Press, 2008).

**57** Friedrich Nietzsche, *Ecce Homo*, trans. Walter Kaufmann (New York: Vintage, 1989), 295. Nietzsche links this inflection point in his thinking to a change in his taste for music, lending credence to Benson's theory that Nietzsche's mature "piety" was related to music. See Bruce Benson, *Pious Nietzsche* (Bloomington, IN: Indiana University Press, 2008).

**58** Nietzsche, *Ecce Homo*, 306, which, in a footnote, also refers the reader to *Thus Spoke Zarathustra*, 200–3.

**59** Friedrich Nietzsche, *The Gay Science*, trans. Walter Kaufmann (New York: Vintage, 1974). There are many philosophical and literary engagements with Nietzsche's doctrine of eternal return. For example, Milan Kundera's brilliant *The Unbearable Lightness of Being* (New York: Harper Perennial Modern Classics, 1999), which struggles with the question of which fate is really the more difficult burden: the "weight" of eternal return or the "lightness" of a world in which things—events, actions, relationships—are unique and unrepeatable (*Einmal ist keinmal*, "one instance is not significant").

**60** One might wonder whether eternal return undermines the idea of free will in the universe, insofar as we are repeating choices we have already made. Here is not the place for an extended discussion of free will and determinism; however, suffice it to say that such a vision is still compatible with free choice in the first iteration of things, which is then repeated indefinitely. Such a possibility raises the "existential" question of eternal return addressed above. For a nice cinematic depiction of such a situation, consider the Japanese film *Wandafuru Raifu* (1998), in which recently deceased people are deposited in a kind of waystation where they are tasked with choosing a single memory from their lives that they will then live out unceasingly for the rest of eternity. See chapter four, note 57 for comments about an existential discount rate for the future.

**61** Although Nietzsche was powerfully influenced by Ralph Waldo Emerson, a better model for joy would be Emerson's most famous friend: Henry David Thoreau, who also extols us to "awakening" and "saying Yes to the world." Thoreau loves the world as exuberantly as anyone. He exhorts us to embrace it, whatever our circumstances:

> However mean your life is, meet it and live it; do not shun it and call it hard names. It is not so bad as you are. It looks poorest when you are richest. The fault-finder will find faults even in paradise. Love your life, poor as it is. You may perhaps have some pleasant, thrilling, glorious hours, even in a poorhouse. The setting sun is reflected from the windows of the almshouse as brightly as from the rich man's abode; the snow melts before its door as early in the spring (Thoreau, *Walden*, 328).

The entirety of Walden is structured around the theme of "awakening," which exhibits parallels with Nietzsche, as well as a sense of the eternal becoming of nature. However, Thoreau could not endorse the "normative" account of eternal return I've critiqued above. One can think of a number of things to which Thoreau would certainly not say an eternal "yes": the existence of slavery, the destruction of wilderness, the elimination of Native Americans and their cultures, and the drawn-out and painful death of his brother John at just twenty-seven years old.

**62** Nietzsche, *The Gay Science*, 223.

**63** Nietzsche, *Ecce Homo*, 258.

**64** See Joshua Foa Dienstag, *Pessimism: Philosophy, Ethic, Sprit* (Princeton, NJ: Princeton University Press, 2006). Dienstag points out that Nietzsche's pessimism is characterized by (at least) two conditions: (1) the recognition that the becoming of the world "aims at *nothing* and achieves *nothing*," and (2) the refusal to "*sit in judgment of this condition*" (Ibid., 178, here citing Nietzsche, *The Will to Power*, 12–3). Dienstag's own definition of pessimism is that "(a) there is no *formula* for producing freedom and happiness in this world, (b) that there is no other world in which there is such a formula, [and] (c) that time it linear . . . [and, further, that] a Dionysian pessimist believes (c) is only provisionally true" (ibid., 264). This version of "pessimism" is all well and good, and its emphasis on the importance of an alternative temporality is congenial to a number of the things I've said above; however, it seems rather remote from the standard understanding of "pessimism." Who, we might ask, is distorting the definition of pessimism—the critics of pessimism or its defenders?

**65** Here recalling our engagement with Virginia Woolf in chapter two. However, as Woolf's painful example illustrates, different circumstances are more or less conducive to joy, deep hope, appreciative love, vital activity, and the like. No circumstances guarantee them; and very few circumstances preclude them. Nevertheless, we cannot avoid the fact that there are limit situations, circumstances that are beyond joy, beyond hope, impossible to love appreciatively. Marcus Aurelius says of pain "what we cannot bear removes us from life. What lasts can be borne" (Marcus Aurelius, *Meditations*, trans. C.R. Haines [Cambridge, MA: Harvard University Press, 1999], 179). Well, perhaps; in general. But there is such a thing as pain that is so intense, so unrelenting, so meaningless that a person cannot bear it. Not pain so extreme that she dies, but pain so extreme that life is no longer worth living (although that is not the same as saying pain so intense that life is not worth having lived). No philosophy of life that is honest can fail to recognize the reality of such situations.

**66** And because melancholic joy is sensitive to the suffering of the world, and recognizes that in certain cases something can be done to alleviate that suffering, it will also reject Epicurean *ataraxia* or other forms of quietism.

**67** *The Epic of Gilgamesh*, trans. N.K. Sandars (New York: Penguin, 1960), 102.

**68** See T.S. Eliot, "Burnt Norton" in *Four Quartets* (London: Harcourt and Brace, 1943), 14.

**69** "Surely joy is the condition of life!" (Henry David Thoreau, *The Natural History Essays* [Layton, UT: Gibbs Smith, 2011], 4).

**70** This image brings to mind Annie Dillard, as she struggles with whether or not her experience of the goodness of the "illuminated cedar tree" required, in the spirit of theodicy, that she affirm the corruption or galls that were in all likelihood afflicting the tree to be part of that goodness: "Can I say then that corruption [the galls in the cedar tree] is one of beauty's deep-blue speckles, that the frayed and nibbled fringe of the world is a tallith, a prayer shawl, the intricate garment of beauty? It is very tempting, but I honestly cannot" (Dillard, *Pilgrim at Tinker Creek*, 245). Dillard rejects the idea that the corruption would itself be beautiful, part of some hidden perfection; she seems to suggest, rather, something closer to the description of mystery in chapter two, that the beauty is there, mysteriously, amid the corruption, or that the corruption (and the finitude, the transience) is there, mysteriously, in the beauty.

**71** Paul Ricoeur, *Fallible Man*, trans. Charles A. Kelbley (New York: Fordham University Press, 1986), 140.

**72** "*Je dirai malgré tout que cette vie fut belle*" (I would say that, despite it all, life was beautiful). This is the final line of Louis Aragon's "*Que la vie en vaut la peine*" in *Les Yeux et la mémorie* (Paris: Gallimard, 1954).

**73** The first phrase came to be used in the coronation ceremonies of various Popes and antipopes, and a variant was made famous in Thomas á Kempis's *De Imitatione Christi*: "*O quam cito transit gloria mundi*" (Oh, how quickly the glory of the world passes away). See Thomas á Kempis, *The Imitation of Christ* (New York: Image Books, 1955), 36. *Transit*, from *transeo*, means "to cross," "to pass," or, of time, "to pass away." However, I would suggest that, hermeneutically, we can read "thus 'passes' the glory of the world" in at least two ways: the glory of the world passing in terms of "slipping away" or passing in terms of "happening, unfolding, or proceeding." The origin of the later phrase—*dum vivimus vivamus*—is unclear; but it is generally accepted to express an Epicurean sentiment. These two independent historical phrases are used together in a playful Valentine poem written by Emily Dickinson (*The Poems of Emily Dickinson* [Cambridge, MA: Harvard University Press, 1998], 53), in which context it is worth noting that Dickinson herself wrestled with the topics of despair—illness and death being major themes in her work—and joy.

# Index

absurdity 14, 16–17, 70, 130–3
"all things shining" 39, 42, 83, 102, 115 119, 122–3, 132, 142
*amor fati* 139, 142
anatheism 31, 45, 156 n.23
*Angst* 10, 12–13, 15, 71
anthropocentrism 32–3, 84
anxiety 6, 13, 71, 82, 93, 125, 140, 172 n.76
appreciation *see* love, appreciative
Arendt, Hannah 125, 194 n.23
Aristotle 25, 51–2, 95
atheism 19, 20, 25, 28–33, 42, 85, 152 n.58, 196 n.41
Auden, W.H. 12, 75
Augustine 29, 99, 183 n.9

Barnes, Julian 191 n.1
Bass, Ellen 142
beauty 67, 69, 112–15, 117, 121, 124
  and corruption 201 n.70
  and entropy 127, 138
  as a moral test 193 n.19
Beckett, Samuel, 132, 153 n.1, 182 n.7
being
  affinity for 37, 50, 102, 108, 111, 114–15
  goodness of 19, 37, 39, 42, 72, 81, 84, 86, 92, 111, 135, 142
  moments of 42–3, 71
  mystery of 34–5, 129, 140
  and non-being 19
  toward death 10, 14, 38, 57, 71, 125
  versus having 34, 102
  in the world 77, 79, 111, 122–4
belief *see* faith
Benatar, David 11
Benson, Bruce 135
black box 61, 63
Boethius 29, 81
Bouvier, Nicolas 161 n.55, 187 n.42
Brassier, Ray 10, 12–13, 158 n.43
*Brothers Karamazov*, *The*
  and gratitude 40
  and theodicy 26–7, 29, 35–6, 38, 117, 120, 128, 139, 153 n.7
Buck, Pearl 102
Buddhism 10, 82, 95, 147 n.28, 171 n.70, 191 n.59
Bugbee, Henry 84, 108
Butcher Ding *see* Cook Ting

Camus, Albert 13, 16, 25, 130–3, 140, 154 n.9, 195 n.30, 197 n.44
Caputo, John D. 28, 30–1, 91, 180 n.62
Christianity 25, 98–9, 106, 113, 115
  and evil 25–6
  and Nietzsche 134–5
  and the world 110–11, 188 n.46
  *see also* Judeo-Christian
Cioran, E.M. 10–13, 25, 28, 144 n.12, 147 n.28, 148 n.29

climate change 3, 6, 17, 31–2, 81, 146 n.20, 186 n.30
Confucius 52–3
continental philosophy 9–10, 13–16, 20, 29, 87
  and *Gelassenheit*, 147 n.26
  origins of, 172 n.74
Cook Ting 69, 171 n.70
creatureliness 38, 57, 99, 113, 127–8
Critchley, Simon 13, 132, 147 n.26, 196 n.41
Csikszentmihalyi, Mihaly 50–3, 57–9

Dante, Alighieri 5, 118, 132
dark 7, 15–19, 29, 42, 44, 74, 76, 115, 118–20
Dastur, Françoise 56–9
death 2, 5–6, 10, 17, 27, 45, 50, 112, 125
  cheating 56–9
  being-toward 14, 38, 57, 125
  of God 4, 10–11
  indifference to 71
  not-yet 57, 125
  of the universe *see* second law of thermodynamics
Descartes 68
desire 20, 32, 34, 38, 86
  and absurdity 130
  and Chinese philosophies 52
  and death 125
  contrasted with hope 72–9, 81–2
  and motivated reasoning 106
  and need 100–3
  and suffering 114
despair 2–3, 6, 67, 73–4, 118–19, 122
  contrasted with hope 75–8, 83, 85
  and evasion 127
  and faith 20
  and love 97–9, 103–4, 107, 110
  and melancholic joy 140–1
  as a mood 14–15, 17, 25, 126
  and poetry 89
  and resignation 129
  and suicide 13, 119
  and theodicy 128–9
Dienstag, Joshua Foa 148 n.40, 179 n.54, 197 n.49, 200 n.64
Dillard, Annie 62, 70, 101, 120, 145 n.16
Dionysian pessimism *see* pessimism, Dionysian
disappointment 13, 88, 126, 130
disenchantment 3, 20, 88, 121
Donne, John 47
Dostoevsky, Fyodor 26, 40, 103, 153 n.7, 195 n.30

Eliade, Mircea 188 n.46
Eliot, Thomas Sterns 160 n.50, 173 n.1, 195 n.30, 197 n.44
Emerson, Ralph Waldo 9, 44, 89
embodiment 53–7, 61, 68, 70, 83
entropy 8
  alternative views of 160 n.54
  as implacable 28, 35, 96, 118, 127–8, 142
  *see also* second law of thermodynamics
Epicurean 49, 92, 129–30, 201 n.73
Erlich, Gretel 190 n.50
eternal recurrence 29–30, 45, 136–8, 140, 142, 175 n.13, 199 n.59
eternity *see* time, and eternity
evil
  compensation for 24, 39, 162 n.67
  and the goodness of being 37
  and hope 78
  and mystery 33–6, 118
  persistence of 133, 138
  problem of 20, 23–37
  and resignation 129
  and second naiveté 119–21, 139–40

and theodicy 26–30, 32, 35, 76, 128
and willing 87

fact *see* reality, and fact
faith 17, 19–20, 25, 134
and action 79–81
anatheistic 31
and despair 75–8, 96, 126
haunted by 28
leap of 19, 81, 83, 120
and Nietzsche 134–6
in reality 70, 76
and reason 131
and the transcendent 85
fear 75–6, 78, 114, 125, 151 n.57
fidelity 81, 113, 125
finitude 36, 43, 99–100, 127, 137
and hope 88
and joy 45
of perspective 29, 70
*see also* death
first principles 20, 106, 134, 161 n.56
flow 51–4, 57–9, 63–4, 171 n.67, 173 n.82
freedom 4, 26–8
Freud, Sigmund 10, 58, 69
Frost, Robert 158 n.39
future *see* time

*Gelassenheit* 87–8
Gilbert, Jack 44–5, 142
Gilgamesh 9, 141
God 18, 100
attributes of (omnipotence, etc.) 24, 28–30
death of 4, 10–11, 16
and evil 26–9, 32–3, 39
and love 95, 98
and nature 104–7
non-traditional characterizations of 31, 84
silence of 14, 24–5, 92
gods, Greek 24, 25, 28
grace
as a gift 36, 113–14
and nature 40, 111
way of 39–41
grand narrative 3, 31
Griffiths, Bede 113

Hadot, Pierre 85, 89–92
hard *see* reality, soft and hard
Havel, Václav 81–2, 85
having *see* being, versus having
Heaney, Seamus 174 n.2
hedonism 4, 27–8, 105
Heidegger, Martin 10, 14, 71, 87–8, 172 n.74
Henry, Michel 10
hermeneutics 10, 15, 49, 60–3, 69–70, 77, 106, 120, 171 n.65
*see also* wager
Holocaust 16, 24, 31, 139
hope 10, 12, 45, 73–94, 98
and calculation 81–3
compensation of 86
and death 125
deep 13, 74–8, 80–1, 88–9, 134
"hope in. . ." contrasted with "hope that. . ." 78–9
and the transcendent 83–6
Hopkins, Gerard Manley 2
Hume, David 106
Huxley, Aldous 4, 49, 59

innocence 11, 18, 26, 39, 62, 118, 120, 127–8
innocent eye 61, 120, 124–5
innocent joy 141–2

James, Clive 194 n.21
James, William 20–1, 76, 79, 80–2, 83, 132, 172 n.71
Jeffers, Robinson 81, 176 n.23
Job 9, 29, 39, 107, 128, 156 n.28

Joyce, James 151 n.57, 161 n.62
Judeo-Christian 20, 24, 29, 84, 95, 97, 108

Kazantzakis, Nikos 71, 93, 122, 126, 129, 171 n.63, 191 n.59, 193 n.19, 194 n.25, 195 n.26
Kearney, Richard 31, 156 n.23
Kempis, Thomas 39–40, 201 n.73
Kierkegaard, Søren 10–11
Kohák, Erazim 21, 37–9, 42, 45, 84, 91, 107, 113, 142, 157 n.33
Kristeva, Julia 10
Kundera, Milan 144 n.12, 199 n.59

*lacrimae rerum* 43, 92
language 61–2, 106, 108, 111–12, 163 n.3
Laozi 52–3, 71, 167 n.34, 173 n.82
Leopardi, Giacomo 9–11, 13, 25, 28, 58, 166 n.30
Levertov, Denise 161 n.55, 189 n.49
Levinas, Emmanuel 10, 26
Lewis, C.S. 67, 98–100, 103–7, 109, 112–13, 120–1, 184 n.12
love 2, 39–42, 74, 95–115
  appreciative-love 102–4, 114–15
  classical types (*eros*, *agape*, *storge*, *philia*) 97–8
  gift-love 98–100, 104
  and hope 88
  as the human vocation 114–15
  and mystery 34
  and nature 107–15
  need-love 98–100, 103
  and the world 19, 76
Lyotard, Jean-François 10

McCarthy, Cormac 132, 140
Macfarlane, Robert 108–9
Maclean, Norman 165 n.29
Malick, Terrence 39–42, 45, 103
Manichean 156 n.28
Marcel, Gabriel 2, 10, 33–4, 74–6, 78–9, 83–6, 88
Marx, Karl 69
Maslow, Abraham 50, 157–8
Maugham, Somerset 127, 183 n.9, 191 n.59, 195 n.28
Meister Eckhart 87–8
Mencius 52
Merleau-Ponty, Maurice 53, 63
Merwin, W.S. 89
Miller, Henry 164 n.5
Miłosz, Czesław 176 n.23
miserabilism 9, 15, 126–7, 139
*mono no aware* 43, 92
monotheism 25, 28, 110–11, 188 n.46
Montero, Gail 171 n.67
mood 16, 71, 76, 135, 149 n.47
Moore, Jim 2
Moreau, David 150 n.53
mortality *see* death
Muir, John 103
mystery 60, 83, 85, 104, 107, 122, 127
  and Camus 129–31
  contrasted with the problematic 33–5
  and evil 37, 117, 201 n.70
  and deep hope 74–9, 83
  and love of the world 107, 138, 140
  and reductionism 121

naiveté
  and innocence 17–18, 117, 127
  and optimism 74
  and perception of the world 62, 70, 93
  second naiveté 19, 117–19, 124–6, 131
nature
  alienation from 109
  and grace 40, 89, 113
  and hard reality 65, 106–7
  as honest 113

listening to 111–12
love of 107–10
as personal 84
red of tooth and claw 5, 39, 87, 142
as teacher 104–7
the way of 40–1
Neiman, Susan 25, 153 n.4, 156 n.29, 196 n.36
new eyes 62, 89, 112, 115, 122–6, 135, 192 n.15
*see also* innocent eye
Nietzsche, Friedrich 4, 10–11, 60, 69, 87, 105, 179 n.54
and eternal return 29, 142
and pessimism 133–40
and religion 134–6
and theodicy 32
nihilism 11
as conditioned by tradition 15, 17, 87
and continental philosophy 9, 147 n.26
weak 27–8, 33, 86
Novalis 96

O'Conner, Flannery 124
O'Driscoll, Dennis 25, 92, 165 n.24
Oliver, Mary 92, 181 n.67
ontological exigence 86
optimism 3, 8, 14, 21, 74, 139, 140, 142, 148 n.29, 152 n.58, 162 n.72

paganism 110–11, 188 n.46
parasitism 5, 27, 99, 120, 142
Parfit, Derek 179 n.57
Parkes, Graham 135
Pascal, Blaise 13, 24, 88, 90
past *see* time
Peirce, Charles Sanders 131
personalism 84
pessimism 10–18
Dionysian 11, 133–9, 200 n.64
as distortion of reality 140, 172 n.72
meaning of 19, 139
as a religious disease 20, 152 n.58
and suicide 81
as a temperament 21, 172 n.72
Plato 4, 13, 49, 68, 91, 95, 97
Platonism 29, 134, 191 n.59
predation *see* parasitism
presence 84, 88, 104
present *see* time
problem
as contrasted with mystery 33–6, 75–8, 131
and technology 16
*see also* evil: problem of
progress 5, 12, 33, 128
Proust, Marcel 64, 71, 122, 169 n.50, 192 n.12
Proustian 12, 102

reality
cooperation with 83–5, 103
and existential moods 15
and fact 80
full scope of 120–6, 140–1
soft and hard 55, 61–2, 65–8, 70, 106–7, 110, 167 n.34, 168 n.40, 186 n.30
reason
and absurdity 130–2
disembodied 49, 70, 83
motivated 106
and mystery 131
religion
and nature 105
Nietzsche's rejection of 134–6
and the problem of evil 25–6; *see also* evil, problem of)
without religion 26, 33, 135
*see also* faith
responsibility 31, 36–7, 85
revolt 130–3

Ricoeur, Paul 45, 69, 77, 119, 142
Rousseau, Jean-Jacques 9

St. Exupéry, Antoine de 90, 121
Salomé, Lou 135
Sartre, Jean-Paul 10–11
Schopenhauer, Arthur 10
Scruton, Roger 74
second law of thermodynamics 8, 146 n.23, 158 n.43
  as example of hard reality 45
  and the future of the universe 8, 13, 39, 76, 140
  *see also* entropy
second naiveté *see* naiveté, second
sensation
  as reliable 69–70, 163 n.3
  and the unity of experience 63–4
Serres, Michel 54–5, 61, 65–8, 110, 120–1
Shakespeare, William 29, 86, 146 n.19, 148 n.41, 154 n.11, 162 n.67, 170 n.57
Shepherd, Nan 113, 115, 193 n.18
Shusterman, Richard 63
silence 111–12, 123
Silesius, Angelus 87
Sisyphus 13, 130–2, 197 n.44
Snyder, Gary 59, 105, 112
soft *see* reality, soft and hard
Stegner, Wallace 124
*Stimmung* *see* mood
Stoicism 82, 92, 129, 185 n.15
suicide 13, 40, 76, 81, 126, 132–3, 141

Taoism 50–6, 69, 173 n.82
technics 33–5, 77, 93
Tennyson, Lord Alfred 145 n.17, 166 n.32, 167 n.35
text, metaphor of 60, 62
  *see also* hermeneutics
Thacker, Eugene 10–13, 20
theodicy 26, 29–33, 36, 45, 67, 128–9
  and eternal return 138
Thoreau, Henry David
  and desperation 144 n.12, 149 n.47
  and "heaven" 72
  and immortality 169 n.46, 179 n.56
  on living and dying 124–5, 127, 142, 188 n.44, 194 n.22, 199 n.61
  and love 91, 97
  and optimism 15
  and reality/contact 65
  and wildness 109–10, 187 n.39
time 37, 44, 71, 88–91, 93
  circular 144 n.12
  deep time 7, 13, 19, 120
  and eternal return 136–8
  and eternity 37–8, 42–3, 45, 71, 91–3, 126, 133, 139
  and pleasure 101–2
topography 110
tragedy 20, 24, 39, 40, 129, 139
  of birth 10, 12
  characteristic of human condition 81, 117
  and continental philosophy 14–15, 150 n.49
  of death 2, 122
  Greek 25, 150 n.49
  and hope 76
  and time 179 n.54
transcendence 19, 43, 76, 138
  and atheism 196 n.41
  and hope 83, 85–6
  horizontal versus vertical 85, 134
  self 55
truth
  goal of 69
  as ineffable 182 n.7
  as ineluctable 36, 121
  as troth 161 n.57
Turner, Jack 108

*Unheimlichkeit* 10, 172 n.74

Van Gogh, Vincent 90, 143 n.1
vocation 90, 114–15, 126, 128, 140

wager 19, 20, 62, 76–8, 81–3, 88, 120
  *see also* faith, leap of
Whitman, Walt 55, 92
wild 31, 65, 97, 107–10, 113, 183 n.8, 187 n.42
Wilde, Oscar 5, 151 n.57
Woolf, Virginia 1, 42–4, 71, 149 n.43, 154 n.9, 160 n.50, 200 n.65
wu-wei 51–4, 62, 88, 167 n.34, 171 n.70, 173 n.82

Zapffe, Peter Wessel 10, 28
Zhuangzi 52
  *see also* Taoism

CPSIA information can be obtained
at www.ICGtesting.com
Printed in the USA
FSHW020807070421
80227FS